WILL YOU STILL
LOVE ME TOMORROW?

To
Martin
(who – hopefully! – will)
and to
Sarah, Joanna and Juliet
(who all need to know)

will you still
love me
tomorrow?

ADRIENNE BURGESS

Vermilion
LONDON

1 2 3 4 5 6 7 8 9 10

First published in
the United Kingdom in 2002 by Vermilion,
an imprint of Ebury Press
Random House Group
Random House
20 Vauxhall Bridge Road
London SW1V 2SA

Random House Australia (Pty) Limited
20 Alfred Street, Milsons Point, Sydney,
New South Wales 2061, Australia

Random House New Zealand Limited
18 Poland Road, Glenfield,
Auckland 10, New Zealand

Random House (Pty) Limited
Endulini, 5A Jubilee Road, Parktown 2193, South Africa

Random House UK Limited Reg. No. 954009
www.randomhouse.co.uk
A CIP catalogue record is available for this book from the British Library.

ISBN: 009185615-9
Designed and typset by seagulls
Printed and bound in Great Britain by Bookmarque, Croydon, Surrey

contents

ACKNOWLEDGEMENTS

Thanks are due to Gail Rebuck and Fiona MacIntyre, who commissioned this book, and to my agent, Carole Blake, my publicist, Niccy Cowen, and my editor Jacqueline Burns whose taste, commitment and patience have been crucial to its development. To my partner Martin Cochrane, who gave me the title, and provides love and support every day of my life. To the couples who allowed me to pry into their lives, and to the many academics cited in my bibliography, whose meticulous, patient study has brought such breakthroughs in our understanding of love and sex. In particular, I thank Jack Dominian, Frank Fincham, Christopher Clulow, John Simons and Adrian Stringer, who also allowed me some of that priceless commodity, their time. Thanks are due to the One Plus One and Pimlico libraries, to the British Library, which offers such an amazing service to independent researchers, and to my wonderfully well-organized assistant and friend, Carole Hobson.

Adrienne Burgess
January 2002

how to use
this book

Although this book contains many answers, none of them is simple. Reading it should be like painting by numbers: as you piece together the facts and figures, the whole should gradually become clear.

Even then you should be cautious. You need not run a mile from a partner who doesn't fit the bill (unless they're about to kill you) nor throw in the towel because you realize your love-affair started badly, or one or other of you has a fatal flaw. Small adjustments can pay off big time, and relationships can prove surprising: the most inauspicious may flourish, while the most promising may not survive the night. You may even choose your mate for the worst of reasons (out of a sense of failure and deep despair) only to discover later that, in them, you have found your perfect partner.

As the experts repeatedly caution, you must take a 'holistic' view: all the studies cited here chart averages (and to every average there are many exceptions); positives can cancel out negatives, just as negatives can wipe out positives; and no risk factor (or even cluster of risk factors) dooms a love affair. It's what you do with them that counts.

introduction

DREAMS OF LEAVING

Every few years, some busy-body researcher, somewhere in the world, sets out to discover whether what people want from love is changing. And every time, the answer comes back loud and clear: it is. Increasingly (as you might have guessed) what men and women are looking for is *romantic love* – 'passion and joy' – and this even in places where a match has traditionally been made with half an eye (or a whole eye) on what the extended family or society might get out of it.

While there's no single recipe for human happiness, one necessary ingredient (for almost everyone) is some kind of satisfying, close relationship. For most grown-ups, this takes the form of a sexually based partnership. And it's *quality* that counts. The research shows that people in *bad* relationships do worse than people who live alone: bad relationships produce hateful demons out of perfectly nice folk, and then add to the nation's health-care bills by making them ill. Meanwhile, men and women in *loving* relationships do better (on average) than those who live alone: not only do they look after each other, they also have more success in looking after themselves and way above average success in raising healthy, happy children.

Forty years ago, hanging on grimly in unhappy, soul-destroying relationships was routine; now it's rare. The rocketing divorce rate of the late 1960s and early 1970s was largely in reaction to that human misery; and, today, only 7% of couples live together wretchedly without seeing a way out through separation or divorce. We are no longer in the business of making heroic sacrifices in order to present a united front, which is why this book is called 'will you still *love* me tomorrow' (not 'will you *stay with* me tomorrow').

A truly positive spin-off from our 'divorce culture' is that we are setting much higher standards for love than we used to. One reason the divorce rate in places such as the US and Northern Europe is high is that people in these countries are no longer so willing to tolerate bad behaviour from their mates. As the old certainties dissolve, so we must make new rules. Suddenly there's a lot to argue about: who's the boss? who'll look after the children? who'll earn the money? how will it be spent? As families become smaller and more spread out, and as people live on for thirty and forty years after their children have left home, they are brought face-to-face with their partner at every turn. Early death no longer liberates the miserably enchained, and the satisfaction people get from their closest relationship begins to matter very much indeed.

At the same time, there are many more, tempting, alternatives. One thing that makes a country's divorce-rate spiral is a continuing supply of alternative partners entering and re-entering the Mate Market. And as many more people can support themselves financially, going it alone becomes another option. Laid out before us, like dishes at a feast, is an exciting range of possibilities: no longer just marriage, but cohabitation (living together unmarried), multiple partners, semi-detached love (being a couple yet living apart), out-of-the-closet homosexuality, single parenting, gay parenting, no parenting, divorce, living alone, serial monogamy ... And because sex no longer leads inexorably to babies, much of the morality it was dressed up in is melting away. Never before in the history of the world have both women and men been able to take love so lightly, and this can be enriching. Some of the most compelling, passionate and revealing encounters that resonate in our bodies and minds until we die, occur in love that barely lasted yesterday.

Nevertheless, when the time comes to have children, or as middle age looms, most men and women hope for a love that will last tomorrow. To achieve this, they need to be on their toes, but not necessarily in the way their leaders tell them. Politicians and family-fundamentalists would batten down the hatches. Whenever there's a surge in the divorce rate or in the number of single mums, they reach for the moral outrage. Relationship breakdown (they tell us) is occurring because people are *bad*. Schools are ordered to teach the value of marriage, churches the value of chastity. Adults are told to shun selfish individualism, to work grimly at their relationships and to marry instead of living together. Whether such strategies would be effective, let alone enforceable, is never explored. Why? Because this moral outrage is a diversion: the real reasons, the *sad* (not *bad*) reasons that relationships fall apart need subtle, well-informed and creative thinking (and often a lot of money) to put right.

Yet there is much we can do as individuals, to help ourselves. One in three British couples (and one in four American couples) who've been together since the 1970s declare themselves happy, while many others have found joy second time around. These people find happiness not by being grimly determined, but by being smart – and by being lucky. Even the world's leading love scientists nod to luck: Professor John Gottman, whose famous 'love lab' has produced some of the most serious, scientific research, has remarked that he and his (second) wife were *lucky* to find each other. Another top US love researcher, Richard Rapson, says of his long marriage to the equally famous Elaine Hatfield: 'of course I may have been *lucky*'. Nor does Ms Hatfield underestimate luck. Everyone, she points out, comes to love with such specific likes and dislikes, and so individual a life-history, that it's nothing less than a small miracle when they link up with a suitable life-partner.

Yet as these love gurus know, there's more to it than luck. Elaine Hatfield, remembering how she blundered through her first marriage comments that, 20 years on, 'I am much *smarter* about love'. The happy love lives of so many of the top researchers result in great part from accumulated wisdom. In developing their own research and reading other people's, they've learned a thing or two.

Today neither women nor men mate for better or worse. They mate for better or else, and this is a very good thing. The fact that they can entertain dreams of leaving causes them to monitor and judge their closest relationship as their parents and grandparents never did. This book has a simple purpose: to provide some of the tools and information you need to do this effectively, so that you too can be smarter about love and, like the love gurus, can learn to make your own luck.

1
meeting

getting together

When and where an affair begins can supply important clues as to whether it's likely to last. We all sense that certain beginnings are suspect: only the truly desperate or the stunningly naive would feel confident about a relationship conceived on holiday, on the rebound, or at the office Christmas party. But why this is (and which other love launches should also be eyed with mistrust) isn't usually understood.

As everyone knows, a dry mouth, pounding heart or sweaty palms can mean we fancy someone. But these symptoms can also be caused by other things: physical exertion, certain drugs, loud music, fear of discovery, an exciting or competitive atmosphere, even laughter. Simply standing near a person of the sex and type we personally label as attractive can set our pulse racing (especially if we're drinking a strong cup of coffee at the same time). From there it's but a short step to labelling our physical agitation as attraction – even 'love'.

And it seems that even the happily married can be fooled. Sometimes, when you're straining and sweating at the gym (for example), your mind can play tricks on you, creating an 'excitement link' between your pulse rate and a nearby body (very possibly, as Madonna and others can testify, that of your personal trainer). Instead of muttering 'what a great workout!' you murmur 'what a great person!' and another marriage bites the dust.

Other, more ancient, motivations (which some believe date from our evolutionary past) may also be lying in wait to trick us. Researchers were intrigued to discover that the women who were dressed most sexily and behaving most flirtatiously at a disco tended to be at the most fertile point in their monthly cycle. It's as though the likelihood that they might conceive was, without their being aware of it, driving them to advertise their wares.

What is perhaps most interesting, is that passionate love is much less likely to strike when our lives are on an even keel and we're in a good state to make decisions about our future. It's much more likely to crop up when we're feeling anxious or miserable. One reason love and distress so

LOVE-TALK ...

I do not like my state of mind:
I'm bitter, querulous, unkind.
I find no peace in paint or type.
My world is but a lot of tripe.
My soul is crushed, my spirit sore;
I do not like me any more ...
I shudder at the thought of men ...
I'm due to fall in love again.

DOROTHY PARKER

WORRIED LOVE

● when preschoolers fall intensely in love (which they can do) they are often already anxious or fearful

● teenage passion, too, may be fuelled by anxiety working on hormones: teenagers' anxiety-levels *before* they fall in love are the best predictors of *whether* they'll fall in love

● the poorest and least self-confident girls and women are the most likely to become pregnant, stay pregnant, and believe in the power of romantic love

● love and anxiety are also linked in adults: one college student in three falls in love in the first semester

often go together, is that (like physical exertion or an exciting atmosphere) emotions such as anxiety, jealousy, loneliness, horror, grief and embarrassment can physically agitate. And here, again, it's but a short step to anchoring that agitation in another human being, and labelling it attraction or love. One reason actors (for example) so often fall for each other is that they spend much of their working lives in a state of high anxiety.

You wouldn't be surprised if you found yourself in bed with someone you'd met at a wedding, but you might be shocked and surprised if the same thing happened after a funeral, which it often does. But the most sinister mislabelling of fear and distress occurs in war. While most soldiers recognize their own sweaty palms, prickling neckhairs or swelling groins as indicating fear, a few don't. These men, on sight of a suitable sex object, label their physical sensations as lust and act on them, raping indiscriminately. Not for nothing did the Greeks name their goddess Aphrodite, goddess of love – and of war.

Research shows that people who are anxious types experience romantic highs more often and more intensely than emotionally secure people, but also that their relationships tend to be very off and on. And relationships are unlikely to last (or to last happily) when they began when one partner has had problems at work, has been doing too much, has been involved with the law or has been seriously ill or recently lost someone close to them (a parent, partner or child). Love on the rebound is also every bit as risky as you might suspect. Only 10% of people who leave an established relationship for a new lover go on to marry that person. One reason is that they can end up associating the upset they experienced as they left the old relationship with the person who helped them leave it.

TEST 1:
READY FOR LOVE?

Rate each statement below as it applies to you. Enter the total in the box on page 54. You may want your partner to do the same.

6	5	4	3	2	1
True		Neutral		Not true	

1 I prefer operating as an individual, rather than being 'one half' of a couple

2 A serious relationship is not a priority for me at the moment

3 Romantic love is a bit of a 'con'

4 Being in love can get in the way of the rest of your life

5 My sex life is better and more satisfying when I'm not with just one person

6 I rarely feel lonely

Physical or emotional trickery isn't always a bad thing, however. Sometimes it can kick-start a relationship that wouldn't have begun otherwise and which then goes on to greater things. But it's always risky, because when our agitation subsides or we stop labelling it as attraction or love, somebody, somewhere, often gets hurt.

Crisis affairs often go well when the pressure's on. It's when life returns to normal that love withers. Why? People can behave untypically during a crisis, and the power balance can shift dramatically once it is over. Or behaviour that suited us when we were feeling low can seem much less appealing when we're back on form; for example, a nurturing partner can suddenly seem smothering. As we feel more capable, we may be able to admit to and face real incompatibilities to which, in our hour of need, we've been turning a blind eye.

There's also a feel-good factor achieved via romantic love which can, under some circumstances, prove its undoing. When you're in love and believe you could conquer the world you aren't far wrong. Being in love not only

LOVE-TALK ...

Falling in love tends to occur at points of transition in people's lives, and can serve to distract them from having to change and adapt to new circumstances or a new stage of development.

FRANK PITTMAN

makes you feel competent; it can actually make you behave more effectively. College students measured before and after they have fallen in love
show higher self-esteem scores and more effective behaviour while they
are in love. This can make some people feel so good about themselves
that they feel capable of coping with life on their own, and no longer need
the person whose love helped them feel so positive.

satisficing

Given that, in the West today, being in love is widely accepted as the best
possible reason for making a life commitment, the number of people who
partner for other reasons is nothing less than astounding. *Recent* research
shows that in the US only 65% of people who enter a life commitment do
so because they really want to be with that particular partner. Most of the
rest (30%) partner *in reaction to* life stresses: they have lost another lover,
a friend, a relative, hope of promotion, or they feel under other pressures.
The final 5% partner because they have *quite coldly decided* to make a
particular commitment: 'it seemed the thing to do'. Many people even settle
for a partner with whom they *know* they're incompatible, because at the
time and place where they felt impelled to make a 'forever' choice, they saw
no alternative. Couple researchers have created the word *satisficing* (a
combination of sacrificing and satisfying) to describe the act of seriously
settling for less. Satisficing is reckoned to be a major *divorce predictor*.

People who study divorce statistics have long noticed that women are
more likely to seek divorce than men, and have wondered why. One
reason may be that women satisfice more often. Women are more likely
than men to report having been more intensely in love with someone else
at some time in their lives, and to have been disappointed in love *just*

LOVE NOTES

FALLING IN LOVE
- only 2% of men and women have never been in love
- men fall in love as frequently and as intensely as women
- 68% of men and women fall seriously in love between 2 and 5
times; 20% between 6 and 15 times; 1% *more* than fifteen times
- people who settle down with a partner they describe as 'the love
of my life' are the most likely to stay happy and contented

before their current relationship. Both of these are risk factors for later unhappiness.

Why are women more likely to satisfice than men? Women's thirty-something panic is usually put down to fears that Mr Right won't turn up until after the last fertile ovum has signalled over and out. But back in the 1960s, singleton twenty-somethings were panicking just as profoundly, even though they were decades away from Final Ovulation. A major reason that women feel under mating pressure is that catching a man is seen as proof of status (studies of US High School Year Books have found pretty girls marrying quite a lot younger than their less attractive class-mates). Also, finding a mate makes good financial sense for a woman, whose disposable income almost invariably rises when she hitches up with a man. A man's disposable income, by contrast, usually drops when he creates a household with a woman. What's more, a man's status remains higher the longer he stays *un*attached (up to a certain point, somewhere in his forties, after which he starts to look like a bit of a loser). The research shows that the men who partner youngest are not, usually, the most desirable males. In contrast to women, they tend to be the *least* desirable: less healthy, less handsome and of lower status than the men

THE LOVE QUIZ

TEST 2: PASSIONATE LOVE

How passionate is your partnership? Rate each statement below as it applies to you and enter your total on page 54. Your partner may want to do the same.

6	5	4	3	2	1
True		Neutral		Not true	

1 The attraction between my partner and myself was immediate
2 We became physically or emotionally involved rather quickly
3 Our sexual relationship is very intense and satisfying
4 Physically s/he is my ideal type
5 Our relationship feels as if it were meant to be
6 We understand each other very well
7 I would feel despair if my lover left me
8 When I'm doing something to make my lover happy I feel very pleased
9 I would rather be with my lover than with anyone else

WOMEN WHO
WAIT TO BE ASKED

Women

- 35% would never even hint they want a man to ask them out
- 62% would indicate they'd like to be asked out
- only 3% would ask a man out

Men

- 30% would like to be asked out by a woman they fancy
- 67% would like a woman to indicate if she'd like to be asked out
- only 3% want a woman to wait to be asked

who marry for the first time when they're older. The suburban Lotharios we call 'commitment phobes' are nothing so exciting. They're ordinary men who have grasped that settling down isn't (yet) to their advantage.

Two other things make women less likely than men to start out with a partner they really want. First, women's self-esteem is usually lower than men's, and low self-esteem can make people stick with unsatisfactory partners. It can also make them continually sacrifice themselves, since they have a deep belief that their partner has made a huge sacrifice in choosing them. What's more, since women expect to be asked, rather than to do the asking, they may see their field of eligible men as quite small. Unlike men, women do not feel *entitled* to fancy anybody and everybody. When a man looks around he sees a world full of attractive women, any one of whom he is (theoretically) entitled to approach. When a woman looks around she sees two kinds of men: those who have shown interest in her and those who haven't. Despite 150 years of organized feminism, she is highly unlikely to approach a man in that second group. Indeed, one woman in three actually goes out of her way to make sure that a man she fancies (but who has not yet made a move towards her) doesn't know she is interested.

Even women who are fiercely proactive in other areas of their lives may approach the business of finding a mate with deep passivity, adopting what is sometimes called a Sleeping Beauty approach: instead of taking positive steps to find a mate, they wait (like Newfoundland) to be discovered. Even women who actually come into contact with a lot of potential mates may operate as if they hardly meet any, settling on Partner A not because they have decided 'he's the one' but because 'at least he's better than Partner B', and Partner B is the only other man currently making it clear that he's interested in them. This kind of negative choice-making might not matter, were it not that while passionate love cannot predict a happy future, *without* a period of intense, passionate feelings the outlook isn't great. A major American study found that women who were still married after 15 years were more likely than divorced or separated women to have reported strong romantic feelings for their

LOVE-TALK ...
Starting a relationship with a romance may be a good beginning: when the romance is recalled years later, the true love is strengthened somehow.
PITTMAN AND WAGER

young husbands early on. Other long-term studies have also come up with the finding that a majority of long and satisfying partnerships began with considerable passion on both sides. When passion is not equal, it's better (from the point of view of long-term love) if it's the man who loves more. A man's strong 'in love' feelings (meaning fondness and admiration) are quite a good predictor that the relationship will continue.

Some writers have been scathing about 'in love' feelings, declaring that deep disappointment is certain if a relationship starts on a high. In fact, disappointment is not only less *probable* when a relationship begins in high satisfaction, but also dawns less *quickly*. Nor is disappointment inevitable: while most relationships do become less satisfying to both partners over the first few years, one in ten becomes steadily *more* satisfying. And many of those were especially satisfying *to start with*.

unpacking passion

How relevant is love *at first sight*? Thirty-three per cent of us have experienced it; and 75% believe it can last. As soon as Anne Heche met *Ellen* star Ellen DeGeneres she was almost blinded with love. 'I just knew bliss in that moment.' Michael Caine was also allegedly smitten 'at first sight' by his wife-to-be, Shakira, and among more ordinary people, every survey of smug marrieds turns up a percentage who vow they 'knew right away'.

In fact, turning love at first sight into a long-term relationship is really rare, which is something romantics choose to forget. Only 7% of love-at-first-sight events even develop into dates. Looking back, people simply do not remember the strangers across crowded rooms who remained strangers. Or the 'meant for each other' rapture that became 'meant for anyone *but* each other' disappointment: only 4% of women (7% of men) report marrying an 'at first sight' lover (even Anne Heche has now run off with a man).

INSTANT WHIPS

- 13% of established couples say they recognized within moments that their relationship could be important
- 25%–30% knew within 24 hours that they were seriously interested
- after just four meetings 15% of women (27% of men) report thinking that this could be 'it'
- after eight weeks 70% felt deeply emotionally engaged, and many commented that they knew this wasn't just strong attraction: they had 'fallen in love'

Nevertheless, love at first sight should not be dismissed as irrelevant: when a relationship develops from it, this is just as likely to last as a relationship which started out more gradually and apparently sensibly.

It is interesting to learn that when a relationship is going to be important, both partners usually sense this early on. In fact, it seems that only 25% of men (34% of women) need more than two months to fall in love. This means that in most cases where men (in particular) are going to commit themselves they're likely to show clear interest within a very short while. This doesn't mean that leaping into deep commitment is to be encouraged. Short courtships bode very badly for long-term love: in fact, one study found that long-married couples had courted for an average of 44 months before marrying, compared with an average 29-month courtship among couples who later split up. Even the second group hadn't exactly sprinted to the altar.

When asked how it is possible to distinguish a crush from real passion, researchers often shrug and say that only time can tell. This is not useful, nor is it true. Clues to the reliability of passion are many, if you know what you're looking for. You can gauge a lot about your relationship by asking yourself *why* you are in it. If the first things that spring to mind are to do with your partner's appearance, then lust is probably driving it. If you give *external* reasons (your families get on well or s/he makes a good living) then your future together isn't as bright as if your reasons are *internal* (you just love being with him/her). External reasons aren't necessarily bad in themselves, but a relationship built *mainly* on them is likely to be at risk.

Feelings of friendship are important. Until recently, experts didn't think that lovers in the first flush of passion experienced much in the way of friendship. Companionate love (as they call it) was supposed to emerge in the second stage, as a rather grim consolation prize once passion had cooled. Now, however, they've found that long-lasting love generally has a strong friendship element *from the start*. And while passionate sexual feelings do decline over time, their decline (as you'll see in Chapter 3) is

THE LOVE QUIZ

TEST 3:
LOVE OR LUST?

Rate each statement below as it applies to you. Your partner may want to do the same. Now turn to page 54

6	5	4	3	2	1
True		Neutral		Not true	

1 My partner is physically attractive in many ways
2 A major reason I'm with my partner is the way s/he looks
3 My partner is noticeably better-looking than I am
4 My partner has habits which, in someone else, I'd find irritating
5 When I'm with my partner I'm sometimes stuck for anything to say
6 My partner is not the type of person I usually go for

THE LOVE QUIZ

TEST 4:
REAL LOVE?

Rate each statement below as it describes your situation. Enter your score on page 54. Your partner may wish to do the same.

6	5	4	3	2	1
True		Neutral		Not true	

1 My lover has some really irritating habits
2 My lover often criticizes me over little things
3 I won't do better than my partner: no one more desirable would look at me
4 I catch myself thinking '*anyway*' thoughts, such as 'let's get married *anyway*' '*anyway*, couples don't always have to agree' '*anyway*, marriage is hard work'
5 I catch myself thinking '*when*' thoughts, such as '*when* we have our own place s/he'll be tidier' '*when* s/he feels more settled s/he'll be less depressed'
6 In this relationship I don't feel good about myself

not as great as is often believed. Many couples together for more than 30 years describe themselves as still experiencing some, or a great deal, of emotional and sexual passion. This is probably what Sir Paul McCartney has tried to express when saying of his late wife Linda that 'she was always my girlfriend'.

love hurts

Although intense sexual and emotional absorption in our partner can be rather a good sign the other classic in-love symptoms of emotional and physical *distress* aren't. Contrary to romantic myth, painful love isn't the best love. When we are truly interested in someone, we are immediately vulnerable to their approval or disapproval; and while we aren't sure how sincerely they return our passion, we'll feel anxious. It's this anxiety that causes the pain element in romantic love but, as the relationship becomes better established, anxiety should subside, along with painful longing, obsessive thoughts and so on. If these persist, they should be regarded with suspicion. They indicate *either* that the relationship isn't moving on to a secure footing; *or* that you are innately anxious people who need a lot of reassuring. What they *don't* indicate is that this love is particularly special and worth fighting for.

Painful longing as a dominant way of loving actually seems to run in families, to such an extent that some researchers have even wondered if it's an inherited tendency. And although examples of such love are found in all known cultures, many people who are confident they have been very much in love have never experienced painful passion.

Unrequited love tends to be most intense *either* when there's a perceived huge status gap between lover and beloved (so that the idea of

STUPID CUPID
UNREQUITED LOVE
- 93% of men and women have been romantically rejected
- 75% of men and women report that unrequited love has provided their most intense love experience
- in 50% of these cases, the love-object wasn't even aware of how the lover felt
- when passion is painful and intense, the outcome is usually unsuccessful

a relationship with the admired person seems incredibly wonderful and amazing) or when the would-be lover has a reverential attitude towards romantic love itself. In both cases it says more about lov-er than lov-ee, and bears no relation to the two people's compatibility.

Why can unrequited or unstable love be more gripping than success-ful love? The experts believe this is because the love experience is inten-sified by a *mix* of emotions. Passionate love actually feels stronger when it's fuelled by ecstasy *and* jealousy, closeness *and* insecurity, joy *and* grief. This helps explain why otherwise perfectly sane people will put up with being stood up; and why girls are so often attracted to dare-devil boys. *Variations* in a lover's behaviour can also strengthen passion, trick-ing us into thinking we're deeply in love, when in reality we're deeply in doubt. The scenario goes something like this: someone you could find attractive acts distant or hostile at first. After a bit they *change* their approach and begin behaving in a friendly manner. And what happens? You feel more attracted to them than if they'd been straightforwardly pleasant right from the beginning.

This feeling occurs because the switchover in attitude from negative to positive has the effect of strongly *reducing anxiety*. Amazingly, we tend to feel grateful to someone who reduces our anxiety – even if that person actually caused our anxiety in the first place. Through their surprise approval, we may also feel more competent, as though some-thing we have done has caused them to change their mind.

We may also stick with someone who makes us miserable because of a phenomenon researchers call *attachment*. *Attachment* relationships have two qualities that distinguish them from other relationships: they provide security and a sense of belonging; and, without them, there is loneliness and restlessness. *Attachment* can be different from love. When you say you're 'in love' that phrase implies that you are interested in another person because you think they are wonderful. By contrast, the term *attachment* acknowledges an emotional dependence that may have little or nothing to do with how highly you rate the other person, or how

LOVE-TALK ...

For seven long years his fancies were tormented
By one he often wheedled, but in vain.
At last, oh Christ in heaven, she consented
And the next day he journeyed on again.

KINGSLEY AMIS

TEST 5:
PAINFUL LOVE?

Rate each statement below as it applies to you and enter your total on page 55

6	5	4	3	2	I
Not True		**Neutral**			**True**

1 Being apart from my lover is very painful to me

2 Although we've been together a while now, I still feel butterflies in my stomach when I think about him/her

3 I worry about whether my partner really loves me

4 There are things I want to say, but when we're together I find it difficult

5 I write my lover letters I never send

6 I spend a lot of time planning my next step

7 As my lover has cooled towards me I've become more passionate

satisfactorily they meet your needs. Children and parents are usually 'attached' to each other, and children are as often as deeply attached to parents who treat them badly as to parents who treat them well.

As adults, people can be in love without (yet) being deeply attached. They can also fall out of love yet remain attached: couples who continue to fight after divorce are often still profoundly attached, although both may be absolutely clear that they never want to live together again.

An *attachment* relationship often develops without your really noticing it, creeping up on you over time. Unlike love, attachment is often unconscious: you may not realize you are attached to someone, until they make a move to leave. Attachment can also click in quite suddenly, even within the first few moments. This phenomenon that has been observed in the animal kingdom, when newborn ducklings attach to (and follow) the first moving object they see. Feelings of attachment for a lover have a lot in common with (and often echo) important attachments we experienced during our childhood. One woman we interviewed who had been surprised by the strength of her feelings for a man she'd only been out with once, recognized the attachment element when, in a vivid dream, she saw him as her mother. No-one knows exactly how attachment is activated. Maybe something about a particular person (the way they look, sound, move or behave) activates early memories of being loved and

STUPID CUPID
LOVE AND SELF-ESTEEM

- people with low self-esteem often report the strongest experiences of romantic love
- they don't necessarily enjoy it, describing their feelings as hard to predict or control
- they tend to be very committed to their relationships, because they aren't confident they'll find an alternative
- they tend to stay loyal longer to a partner who thinks badly of them than to a partner who thinks better of them
- they often choose lovers who are very different from themselves (storing up trouble for later)

cared for by parents. Whatever the reason, attachment bonds can be so powerful, that once they're in place a lover's expressions of anger or discontent may not drive us away but may actually encourage us to cling closer as we try to fix the relationship.

Another reason people may stick with a lover who makes them miserable has to do with *self-esteem.* If your ideas about yourself are negative (that is, you have low self-esteem) you may choose partners who confirm that view. In one very striking piece of research, experimenters raised people's self-esteem artificially. (It's quite easy to do this. You simply give them an IQ test and tell them they've done well, even if they haven't). The researchers were then intrigued to discover that men whose self-esteem had been artificially raised started chatting up attractive women. Those whose self-esteem had been lowered went for less attractive females even if, in fact, they were quite attractive themselves. People with low self-esteem often choose lovers who treat them badly because they confirm the low level of esteem *in which they already hold themselve*s.

It is worth noting that people with low self-esteem are unlikely to leave a destructive partner if that person is criticized or attacked by outsiders. They already know their partner is treating them badly, but think this is just what they deserve. They are most likely to leave when their own self-esteem improves, possibly through getting a job or going to college. Self-esteem is a really big issue for lesbian couples: low self-esteem in even one partner can be really bad for the relationship. Among gay males, low self-esteem doesn't seem to be such a problem.

Although a person's self-esteem usually stays fairly constant through their teens, research now suggests that it can gradually improve as they get older. And taking self-esteem courses can help. Self-esteem is built partly out of feeling *worthy* and partly out of feeling *competent*, so developing skills, seeing projects through and building on successes are all useful. It makes sense that people who, for whatever reason, come to feel more worthy and more competent, may make better love choices.

sexual bargaining

Whether a relationship gets past first base depends not only on how it began but on each partner's respective *mate value*. This term has been coined by researchers keen to put a label on the qualities that make people sought after by the opposite sex (or by the same sex, if that's their inclination). *Mate value* refers to our status in what might be called the Mate Market.

When official matchmaking was routine, mate value differences could be spoken of without embarrassment. 'I'm sorry your majesty' a seventeenth-century envoy may have said 'but if you want a princess to link the crowns of England and Spain, then she won't be pretty. The daughters of King Charles are notoriously ugly.' Today, when true love is supposed to be the reason we wed, this *sexual bargaining* process has

TEST 7:
MATE VALUE – PART 6

Rate each statement below as it reflects your situation and enter your score on page 55. Now ask your partner to do the same.

6	5	4	3	2	1
True		Neutral		Not true	

1 My partner's family background is superior to mine

2 My partner is better educated than I am

3 My partner is cleverer than I am

4 My partner is more creative than I am

5 My partner has a more positive outlook than I have

6 My partner has travelled more widely than I have

7 More people envy my partner's job than mine

8 My partner is doing better at work than I am

9 My partner earns more or has more money from other sources

gone underground. But it hasn't gone. In fact, it underpins the most passionate and apparently romantic of love affairs.

In the search for a partner, as in other things, people are keen to better themselves. And so they seek a mate with the highest possible mate value, mentally ticking off their pluses and minuses and measuring them against their own. Much of the misery people experience during the dating-process comes from our pursuit of partners whose mate value is (or seems to them to be) higher than their own. This behaviour is so common that researchers call it the Groucho Marx effect (after the great comic's famous comment about not wanting to belong to any club that would have him as a member).

Although it might at first appear clever to bid for a partner with much higher mate value, in fact it isn't. Why not? Because, in being with a lower-value partner, a higher-value partner feels under-benefited: that is, they know that they are missing out on better deals. One result of this is that they won't stand much nonsense: if their lower-value partner flirts with someone else, they are likely to call the whole thing off.

Meanwhile, a lower-value partner does not, for very long, feel triumph at having snared someone above their station. On the contrary, this makes them very worried. Research shows that lower-value partners say they are quite likely to tolerate their mate's flirting, or even sleeping with, another person. So, if a friend's partner is cheating and you are wondering whether to blow the whistle, you should first estimate the pair's relative mate value. If it's the lower-value partner who is being cheated on, don't say anything: they almost certainly won't want to know.

Most people are acutely aware of mate value difference, men particularly so. An air hostess whose pilot-boyfriend had left her, told us rather wistfully that she thought his current relationship was working out because his new partner was also a pilot – 'she's more on his level'. She was very possibly right. In the past, even though men have frequently married lower-status women (pilot/air hostess, boss/secretary) this has been mostly due to a poor supply of attractive equals. As far back as the early 1970s, college-educated men were saying they wanted college-educated mates.

Of course a couple's relative mate value can change over time. When this happens an insecure partner is often seen trying to redress the mate value balance. *Weight Watchers* magazine publishes many letters from women who report that their husbands are sabotaging their diet; or are withdrawing from them sexually as they grow thinner (a clear 'I'll leave you before you leave me' strategy). In the 1960s and 70s in the US, many middle-class girls married at a young age and worked to put their husbands through graduate school as an investment in a joint future. Sadly (and predictably, the experts say) when their husbands qualified (and their mate value soared) they often left, usually pairing up with better-educated women. Where a couple's education levels are different, it is the better-educated partner (male or female) who is likely to file for divorce.

Youth is an important mate value ingredient, as are light-coloured hair and skin, and these may all be related. Some researchers think that since, in most races, skin and hair darken with age, fairness may be read by our pre-civilization instincts as indicating youth. This would explain

---

HOW LOWER-VALUE PARTNERS COPE

- they 'put up and shut up' when badly treated (often poisoning the relationship with silent resentment)
- they have affairs ('I'll leave you before you leave me')
- they try to restrict their partner's freedom (often, as a result, driving them away)
- they put their partner down (in an awkward attempt to create a more level playing field)

why light hair and skin are particularly valued in women (for 'youth' read 'fertility') and indeed the saying goes that while women like men who are 'tall dark and handsome, gentlemen prefer blondes'.

Other researchers put forward a different explanation. They point out that in agricultural communities richer people (particularly richer women) tend to spend less time labouring out of doors. Fair skin and hair may suggest higher caste. In an interesting reversal in the West today, *artificially* tanned skin represents high mate value, because it indicates expensive holidays.

A fashionable wardrobe increases your mate value because it implies both wealth and taste. Class, wealth, income, occupation, intelligence, artistic talent, education and a calm, optimistic nature all contribute to a person's mate value, and a foreigner ranks lower than a national, especially if they don't speak the language. However, an incomer's mate value may be greater than a national's if the country they come from has high world-status, a position long held by US military all over the world. In the United Arab Emirates, the government is considering bringing in laws to stop its men marrying Westerners: 28% of the country's one million people are married to foreigners and 79% of UAE men who divorce local wives go on to marry a foreign one.

LOVE CONNECTIONS
HOW MONEY FITS IN

● the idea of romantic love as a basis for marriage was developed in the Middle Ages by penniless young lower-caste men (troubadours) who sought to persuade rich girls to marry out of their social class and bring their fortunes with them

● in later centuries, poor men were forbidden by law to call on rich women, a clear indication that many tried to

● since the 1920s, women's popularity as dating partners has largely rested on their ability to buy fashionable clothes and belong to the 'right' clubs

● older men and women who are in receipt of a pension are the most likely to attract a second glance from prospective mates

● older men with younger partners are very rarely poor men

looking good

Although we all tacitly admit the significance good looks have on mate value by taking special care with our appearance when we're on the hunt, few of us are willing to admit how much we care about a partner's looks. When questioned about their ideal mate few people (men or women) put physical attractiveness at the top of their list. Instead, they insist they value qualities like sincerity and kindness. They are lying. At the point of initial attraction looks are *the* most important thing – to both sexes. The hard truth is, that if you plan to attract a mate whose value is as high as or higher than your own, you are quite right to pay serious attention to your looks. Yes, Michael Douglas *needed* that face-lift; and 'Barbie Make-over' girls aren't wrong when they claim that plastic surgery puts them in a different league in the mating game.

Why should good looks matter so much? It may be that a person's appearance is the most obvious (initial) information that is received. Or perhaps people want to believe that the world around them is consistent, that an outside reflects an inside. Some researchers have suggested that hankering after particular beauty standards stops men and women from mating only with people like themselves (which, as shown in Chapter 2, is a strong tendency) and therefore encourages them to spread their genes around.

LOVE CONNECTIONS
HERE'S LOOKING AT YOU

● when blind-date couples are told they've been computer-matched for compatibility (but have actually been paired at random) and are then asked how they liked their partner, only one factor consistently predicts liking for *both* sexes: looks

● when asked to name the person from their social group with whom they'd most like to have a relationship, *both* women and men nominate the good-looking trend-setters

● good-looking students of *both* sexes are most likely to have an interesting and socially successful first college year

● when three-year-old boys *and* girls are shown pictures of faces and asked to press a button to select their favourite, they are twice as likely to choose a beautiful face

In fact there may be less of a contradiction than at first appears between people's claims to value sincerity and kindness and everyone's clear preference for stylish good looks. For the research shows that human beings are convinced that what is beautiful is good: experiment after experiment has shown that good-looking people are regarded by others as kinder, cleverer, friendlier and more successful, although it's not just the physical arrangement of their features that counts.

Do men care more about their partner's looks than women do? Certainly, men are more willing to admit to wanting good-looking partners. And where a woman is much older than her male partner she's often rather attractive, while older men with younger partners need not be. Physically attractive women also have higher dating averages than plainer women, and this difference isn't found so clearly among men. However, this may not be because women care less about having a cute partner, but because (as pointed out earlier) it's mainly men who ask women out.

Do relationships develop more smoothly if the partners are gorgeous? Clearly some of the most beautiful folk on the planet are what Woody Allen calls 'Kamikaze people', that is, emotional and sexual disaster zones. However, if you look at *averages*, there is modest evidence that good-looking people find love more easily than plainer people and are also more satisfied with their relationships over time. This is probably because they tend to feel better about themselves (remember, high self-esteem is good for love) and because some of the other goodies their looks provide tend to help love along: for example, good looking people earn (on average) 12% more than the norm. Their communication skills are often

---

CLEVER CUPID

BEAUTY BOOSTERS

- Voice: a human face seen on film with different voices dubbed onto it, is rated better looking when the voice is appealing
- Selectivity: men rate moderately selective women (i.e. those who are neither stand-offish nor eager) as better looking and more intelligent than they 'really' are
- Humour, a sunny personality and intelligence also cause both men and women to be rated physically better looking
- Dominance is a clear beauty booster for men, and comes out neutral for women: men are not turned off by dominant women
- Warning: when a man or woman is seen as domineering, they are also seen as physically less good-looking

better, too: attractive male students spend more time in conversations and less on other activities than average-looking students.

Beautiful people do face some disadvantages in the search for long-term love. Competitiveness between partners is a big negative in relationships and when both partners are very attractive competitiveness over looks is not uncommon. This is probably because attractive people become used to the power their looks give them, and fearful of losing it. Competitiveness over looks can be a big problem among gay couples, who tend to be judged on the same scale, so gay couples who hope for long-term love should seriously aim for similar levels of good looks. Twelve per cent of straight men (25% of straight women) also become anxious when their partner is rated better-looking.

The study of couples that had paired up young in the 1970s found that men who had rated themselves physically attractive and a 'good catch' were, on average, highly satisfied with their relationships 15 years on. However, the attractive women in this group were significantly *less* satisfied with their relationships after 15 years than were plainer women. Why this should be was not clear. Was it a sign of the times? Had women's expectations changed so much over that period that high-value women

WHEN LOOKS AREN'T EVERYTHING

● a woman who is plainer than her partner is likely to have a sunnier disposition and a better sense of humour

● face and figure matter more in attracting a mate than in keeping them, even over a couple of months, let alone 20 years

● where partners continue to focus on appearance this is an indicator that their relationship may break up

● high clothes-consciousness in a couple can also mean trouble ahead

were particularly likely to think they had undersold themselves by becoming early homemakers?

Perhaps another piece of research, carried out at around the same period, provides a clue. This showed that while young attractive men tended to be more assertive than more average males, young attractive females in the 1970s were actually *less* assertive than plainer girls. Possibly they'd had less need to assert themselves in order to get what they wanted, because they'd been able to rely on their looks. This seems to suggest that to have a higher-than-average chance of remaining happy with a life partner, it's not enough to be good looking. Both sexes need to be assertive, too.

Interestingly, the handsome and the beautiful do not actually date very many more people than those who are rated average in terms of looks. The women and men who really struggle in the dating game are those who are seriously physically *un*attractive. However, even they need not despair. 'I'm not attractive but I keep myself well,' one woman told us, with penetrating truthfulness. To do well in the dating game, seriously unattractive people don't need to struggle to be super-models: they need only bring their appearance up to average.

mating by numbers

Mate market ratings are affected by scarcity. Women of all ages complain that there are no men around, but in fact at younger ages more women are likely to be in sexual relationships than men. This only changes after the age of 40 when men start to be in short supply. This is partly because more have died, and partly because 22.6% of women (compared with 1% of men) are looking for older partners. At this point, provided he is willing to hunt within his own age group, the mate value of a healthy, sane, solvent male increases and many a nerd comes into his own.

Is the plight of the older woman made worse, as is sometimes suggested, by more men than women being gay? Not really. For a start, men aren't more likely to become gay as they grow older, and while there are about twice as many gay men as gay women at any life stage, the figures are too small to have much effect on the 'straight' mate market. As adults, 7% of men (4% of women) have had at least one same-sex experience; but only 2% men (1% women) consider themselves exclusively homosexual and only half of these have had a same-sex connection in the past 12 months.

Although until recently a big man/woman imbalance has been seen after the age of 50 (with 20% of women and only 9% of men on their own) this is likely to change. A major reason for twentieth-century man shortages in Europe was two world wars, and today very few Western males will be killed in battle. Men have also started living longer: recent UK research has charted a 50% drop in the number of widows over 50, since fewer of their husbands have died from work-related illnesses like emphysema.

Women are also beginning to be less rigid about the kind of mate they'll accept. Because they've been expected to raise children and have usually earned far less than men, many have had to look to men as 'meal tickets'. However, new research is showing that as women earn more, they are less concerned about a partner's wealth or prospects. This

---

SEX SURPRISES
THE 'MAN SHORTAGE' MYTH

- up to the age of 34, women are *more* likely than men to have a current or recent sexual partner
- only after the age of 34 does the balance shift, and then the difference is small
- even in their late 30s while 11% of women are without a sexual partner, so are 8% of men
- in their early 40s 8% of men and 15% women are without a sexual partner
- between the ages of 45 and 49 the gap narrows again: 12% of men (17% of women) do not have sexual partners

CLEVER CUPID
HERE'S LOOKING AT YOU

● mate value is more looks-based in some countries (e.g. America) than in others (e.g. Russia and Japan)

● British women rate 'small sexy buttocks' as men's most desirable feature, with 'muscular chest and shoulders' tenth out of a list of 11

● a woman with firm, rounded buttocks has higher mate value in Rio de Janeiro than in New York, where breasts are the feature of choice

● breast-value, too, varies by location: Baywatch Busts are favoured in Europe and the US but in Africa, the Hottentots and the Mpongwe prefer long, pendulous bosoms

● in Japan, 40% of men pluck their eyebrows and 1% of girls are anorexic

means that women are beginning (again like the trail-blazing Madonna) to consider younger partners.

Many older people who do not have partners have chosen to live that way. Living alone suits some people very well, though they may be quite long in the tooth before they will easily admit it to themselves, let alone to others. Neither women nor men who remain alone after divorcing show up, in surveys, as being less happy or contented than people who have found new partners. And when women don't have a regular sexual partner, only 1 in 20 says this is because she can't find one. This is just as true among older as among younger women. Researchers investigating African American communities, where women over 50 are very unlikely indeed to re-partner, found that they were *six* times less likely to be in a new relationship as African American men, and the ratio of women to men in this age group is certainly *not* 6:1. Most of the women were staying single because they *wanted* to. Their definition of 'being with a man' involved feeling obliged to wait on him and, in light of this, they preferred to remain unattached.

Do many people buy younger partners through having a lot of money? Some (particularly male) celebrities have very public liaisons with young and strikingly beautiful women. But 'the rich' (as F. Scott Fitgerald wrote in *The Great Gatsby*) may be 'different': in the population at large, researchers have *not* often found women trading looks for wealth and influence. When women are physically more attractive than their mates, the men do not tend to be richer (or more highly educated).

playing it cool

Both men and women give high mate value ratings to partners they believe to be independent and self-confident. Also highly rated (particularly by women) are people who are 'popular', that is, who are sought after by other potential mates. In fact, if a woman knows that another woman is interested in a man, she's often inspired to try to date him herself and there's evidence that being married can make a man more, not less, sought after by other females. This doesn't work the other way around. Men do not find married women especially attractive and are not likely to go after one because a friend fancies her.

If you bear in mind that independence, self-confidence and popularity improve your mate value, then advice given in self-help books to play things cool at the beginning of a relationship starts to make sense. When you appear *too* eager, you are signalling 'your mate value is higher than mine'. And if you are *always* available, the message you send out is 'my time is free because my mate value is low'.

Since in the earliest stages of a relationship actually *being* popular or self-confident may not be as important as just *appearing* popular or self-confident, does a woman who asks a man out (when men are supposed to be the ones to take the initiative) blow her chances? Not at all. A woman's mate value is not dented if she's the one who picks up the phone.

While appearing too interested too early is rarely a good idea, this doesn't mean that anyone (man or woman) needs to wait weeks before

WHEN WOMEN ASK MEN OUT

● first dates instigated by men generally lead to slightly longer dating

● female-instigated dates also do well: they lead to an average of 13 dates

● when a woman asks a man out, he often expects the date to end in sex

● in fact, woman-instigated dates are *less* likely to result in sex than dates instigated by men

returning a lover's call. The best tack is to be neither too aloof nor too enthusiastic. Researchers have found that too much cool can be as much of a turn-off as trying too hard. In one fascinating experiment, they had males invite out, by telephone, women with whom they'd been told they'd get on well. The women had been briefed to act in one of two ways: some were to seem easy to get (to accept the date immediately), others hard to get (not to be available for at least a week). What was the result? Some of the men (as the best-selling dating-manual *The Rules* might predict) did prefer the hard-to-get women. However, *just as many* preferred the easy-to-get dates. This suggests that the authors (and readers) of *The Rules* need to think again, remembering that most of us are attracted to warm, friendly, candid people. Nor, these days, does a girl need to be a virgin to attract Mr Right: Western males have no interest whatsoever in marrying virgins.

The *number* of previous sexual partners a woman has had does not affect her mate value. In fact, it's often good for relationships for partners

LIKE A VIRGIN

● virginity is on the rise for men: at age 20, 8.3% of US males are still virgins compared with 1.0%, 40 years ago

● 40 years ago 7% of men had their first sexual experience with a prostitute; that's now down to 1.5%

● virginity in women is also slightly more popular today: 5.8% of 20-year-old women are still virgins, compared with 4.6% , 40 years ago

● hysterical press reports of underage sex are greatly exaggerated: at age 16, 75% (14 countries were surveyed) are still virgins

FIRST DATE SEX

- 25% of men are turned *off* by sex on a first date
- 15% of men expect to have sex on a second date
- 15% of men prefer to wait more than a month before having sex
- 40% would agree to first-date sex but would also be prepared to wait if they thought they were with the right person
- only 1.4% of couples who eventually marry had sex within the first two days, compared with 13.7% of couples in very short-term relationships

to have had a similar number of previous lovers. But while men can have sex as *early* in any relationship as they like without risking their mate value, women have to be more careful, since the research shows clearly that the double standard is still in operation much of the time. But not always. Early sex doesn't put a woman's mate-value at risk when it's sex between equals: that is, when she and her partner are equally permissive about sex; when their commitment (or lack of it) to each other is at a similar level; when his overall mate value is no higher than hers (or is lower), and when her mate value doesn't depend mainly on her physical attractiveness. However, women have little to fear from 'holding back' on sex for a little while, if that's what they want to do: even among the current generation of young males, only 5% *expect* sex from a woman on a first date.

While men don't put their mate value at risk through offering, or agreeing to, early sex, they have to be on their guard in a different way: a man who reveals his 'vulnerable side' to his date early on seriously jeopardizes his mate value. Women who use dates as therapy sessions also act as passion assassins, but they can reveal personal vulnerabilities earlier than men without losing as much mate value.

Not all attraction proceeds strictly in accordance with mate value laws. A person can be highly desirable in Mate Market terms, yet totally fail to appeal to you personally. In the 'Lady Chatterley' effect', the usual mate value pattern is reversed, and a man or woman develops a deep passion for a person well below them in the Mate Market. The reasons for these violations of mate value laws are as varied as the couples themselves (they have mainly to do with our personal *love maps*, which are covered in Chapter 3). But they do not overturn the general rule, which is that for a relationship to be mutually satisfying and long-lasting, both partners

CLEVER CUPID

HERE'S LOOKING AT YOU SOME MORE

● in 11 countries across Africa, the Americas, Asia, Australasia and Europe, women whose waist measurement is about 70% of their hip measurement, have high mate value

● faces are as important as bodies and, in both sexes, are judged more attractive if they are symmetrical

● 'symmetrical' males lose their virginity younger, get women into bed more quickly, have more sexual partners, give them more orgasms – and are more likely to be unfaithful

● an irregular feature (e.g. a large nose) really does bring down a person's mate value

● while not the case in the gay community, heterosexual men's mate value is affected by their height

● however, relative height matters most: women ascribe all kinds of good qualities to even-slightly-taller men, seeing them as fearless, protective and ambitious

need to see themselves, and each other, as being of roughly equal value in the marketplace.

the hunt

It was seen earlier that a substantial number of both men and women *satisfice* (settle for less) when they come to choose a mate, and that this is a major reason that many relationships do not last. Although some people satisfice because their expectations are so unrealistic that no one can please them, more often the problem is that they don't have a large enough field of eligible potential mates to choose among.

In the normal course of daily life, without taking special steps to 'meet people' we may hardly ever come across even one person who would be remotely suitable as a life partner. 'I'm 17 and everyone seems to be taken,' one desperate girl complained on a teen-dating Internet site. Ridiculous? Not necessarily. Even in a college environment where there are great opportunities to socialize and potential mates on every corridor, people quickly develop a tight circle of like-minded friends (often of the same sex) with whom they spend most of our leisure time. And when

WHY FINDING PARTNERS CAN BE TRICKY

● smaller families mean smaller family networks

● more people can afford to live alone

● many leisure activities, particularly television, are now home based

● people live in big cities where they don't know their neighbours

● they may re-locate for work and have few contacts in the area

● unemployment isolates some people and over-employment (long working hours) isolates others

● most colleagues of comparable mate value may be of the same sex

● people may be keen not to settle down too young, then find that many among their circle are already spoken for

people travel around the country (even, sometimes, when they travel abroad) they often run into people they already know. Although this is described as an amazing coincidence, it rarely is because people self-select into a narrow band of obvious compatibles who tend to go to similar places and do similar things.

Researchers believe that many men and women could benefit from professional help with mate hunting, and that one day partner search will become big business. This is made more likely by the fact that people now have a number of mate hunting periods during their lives. They settle down later, divorce more often and live longer. Yet many people apply less ingenuity to choosing a mate than to choosing a new car. They set up their lives in such a way that they don't get much practice at relationships; or they complain that they never meet anyone, while continuing to look in the same places that have turned up little of interest in the past. 'Lovers,' scolds a US love-expert, 'often use search methods that are not in their own best interest.'

Which methods are? The most usual way for partners to meet has always been through personal networks, that is family and friends. Sticking to your own kind very often pays off, for the odds of finding a soul-mate among our nearest and dearest (provided you *like* your nearest and dearest) can be high. But the fact that by sticking too closely to your own kind you are passing up valuable opportunities becomes clear when something forces you out of your comfort zone into other people's networks. Perhaps you are a college room-mate from a different faculty; or you accept a job in a different city; or you answer a flat-share advertisement; and suddenly

SHOPPING CHANNELS
FAMILY AND FRIENDS

● 92% of people date someone they have met through family and friends

● 40% of people marry from within that mate-pool

● relationships begun this way bask in the glow of feeling 'normal'

● they often have a chance to develop gradually: 55% of married couples introduced this way knew each other for more than a year before they had sex

● only 10% of couples who met through friends and family had sex in under a month, compared with 40% of couples who met *outside* personal networks

you find yourself dating eminently suitable people you would never have met but for that chance life change.

One reason that mate hunting via personal networks pays off so often is that you are least likely to be messed around by someone introduced to you through friends and, particularly, family. After all, if a person is only in the market for a one-night stand, to pick on a family friend doesn't make sense: they'd do better to cruise an out-of-town bar. One study found that among very short-term relationships, not a single one had begun through a *family* introduction.

Mate hunting through personal networks is also (relatively) safe in that it helps to screen out weirdos and serious liars. It's also time efficient, in that the people you meet this way are likely to share many of your attitudes and expectations. And even if you don't find a partner, you haven't entirely wasted our time, as you will have been keeping up with people who are important to you. American experts Elaine Hatfield and Richard Rapson advise that, rather than looking desperately for a mate, a good approach can be to create a wide network of casual friends. 'Once people have established a network of friends it is a short and easy step to begin to find suitable dates.'

A theme that will come up again and again through this book is the importance of family approval to the success of a relationship. Research shows that if family (and friends) approve your choice of partner, the chance of a happy, long-lasting relationship is greatly increased. This is particularly relevant when it's the *woman*'s family who approve the match.

This doesn't mean that things go best when parents oversee their children's choice of mate. In the West, relationship *problems* can actually be

MAKING THE MOST OF PERSONAL NETWORKS

● think local: get to know your neighbours
● be friendly (smile) and be proactive (send emails to colleagues you fancy)
● accept invitations and invite people over
● get a life: go out and about, doing things that interest you
● change your 'beat' to new bars and restaurants
● get fit, walk the dog regularly in the same place and talk to people you see there
● if you don't chat easily, take a social-skills course
● think of each person you meet as the tip of a new contacts-network and then work it
● offer a luxury holiday to any friend who leads you to the partner of your dreams (one researcher did this, and it worked!)

ARRANGED MARRIAGES

● worldwide, 60% of marriages are currently arranged, either by parents or match-makers
● arranged marriages remain most stable when divorce is hard to come by (but this does not mean they are necessarily happy)
● arranged marriages where one partner comes from abroad (even if from the same cultural background) often fall apart
● arranged marriages decline swiftly as soon as young people are allowed free choice: among Indians in the UK arranged marriages have dropped from 75% to 25% in just one generation

predicted if parents play a great part in this. And couples who give parents' approval as a key reason for marrying are more likely than other couples to end up divorced. Nor are the outcomes necessarily better in countries such as Japan, China or India, where arranged marriages have been the norm. In all countries studied, break-up rates (though not necessarily *divorce*) are higher and general misery more common in arranged than in free choice partnerships. Although one small-scale study in Jaipur in India in 1982 found that while arranged marriages started out less happy than free-choice marriages, within 5 to 10 years they were happier; and a 1967 Japanese study found men (but not women) equally happy whether or not their marriages had been arranged. This was probably because parents consulted with sons but not with daughters when arranging the match.

Hobbies and sport can provide a useful mate pool, especially for less confident people who may feel more relaxed when focusing on an activity they enjoy. Eighty per cent of men and women have dated a partner met this way. As will be seen in Chapter 2, the value of shared interests cannot be overstated, and the most successful dating agency is one for classical music lovers. However, contrary to advice given in many dating manuals, attending events that bore you silly just to meet someone is a bad idea. Most people want a like-minded partner and men in particular rapidly go off dates who have pretended to enjoy an activity but whose true preferences become clear later.

Over half of all currently married Americans met at school or college. However as people settle down later this percentage is likely to fall, and love found through the workplace is likely to become more common. Currently, only 15% of men and women marry someone met at or through work. This isn't a hugely impressive hit rate, when you think how much time you spend there. In part it may be due to the fact that workplace-based love is not without its complications.

Church groups seem to provide a rich source of partners, at least in the US. Twenty-five per cent of Americans have dated someone met via a church group and 8% of smug marrieds met that way. This is a remarkable hit rate, given that lots of people never go near a church and that many of those who do spend very little time there. It's fun to speculate why churches are such hotbeds of romance. One probable reason is that you don't meet many

LOVE AT WORK
- 80% of men and women have dated someone met *through* work
- 40% of office workers have dated someone they work *with*
- 20% of men and women have had sex with a co-worker
- 9% of office workers have had sex in the office
- 1% have had sex with a client or with their boss

Workplace affairs are often short and sneaky, given that
- 75% of people think workplace sex leads to a bad atmosphere
- 94% of people disapprove of sex with the boss
- 33% of partners in extra-marital affairs are work colleagues

commitment-phobes there: people who attend church are more likely to be repenting of wild oats than sowing them. Wild-oat sowers do, however, tend to turn up at their friends' weddings. Relationships begun at other people's weddings can't be trusted, even if the wedding is held in a church. 'Too much sex in the air,' said one let-down lover, gloomily.

LOVE-TALK ...

A good place to meet a man is at the dry cleaner's. These men usually have jobs and are hygienically responsible.

JOAN RIVERS

love thy neighbour

Another reason for the relatively high hit rate of church-based romance is that churches tend to be local to where you live – love and locality are strongly linked. Even as late as the 1960s American couples had a 50% chance of finding a partner among people who lived within walking distance of their childhood home. Today people move more freely around the country and around the world, but many of them still choose partners from the part of the country in which they were raised or find a partner in their new locality.

A top UK dating agency, Drawing Down the Moon, reports that most of its successes are between couples who live less than eight miles apart. And we interviewed a couple who'd first met 300 miles from home, and then found that their parents lived within five miles of each other. Living

SHOPPING CHANNELS
LOVE AT FIRST BYTE

- 10% of Internet users have placed an online dating advertisement
- 11% have responded to such an advertisement
- 12% have had sex with someone met online
- dating invitations made by e-mail are as common (38%) as face-to-face invitations (40%)
- researchers estimate that by 2020 33% of couples will meet their life partner via cyberdating
- if so, things will have to change: www.match.com, a US site with 4 million subscribers claims 1,000 marriages – a 0.00025% success rate

nearby may say something about life-style preferences or perhaps it makes 'getting to know you' less pressured. Certainly, *not* living nearby when a relationship is deepening is a serious disadvantage, and helps explain why holiday romances rarely find a future back home. The importance of living near your partner while you are establishing a relationship (or, indeed, are trying to sustain one) cannot be overstated. This is one very good reason that Internet dating, particularly internationally, is unlikely to be an effective pathway to long-term love for most people.

shopping around

Although mate search through friends and family should be our first port of call, seriously combing (or creating) personal networks in order to ferret out potential mates doesn't suit everyone. Some people operate better in a more impersonal atmosphere. Of course once you begin looking further afield you're in a tricky landscape where poseurs, liars, cheats, users and abusers can all too easily come out to play. But that

HOT SAFETY TIPS
FOR INTERNET DATING

● Start slowly and e-mail only to start with. 'Listen' for odd behavior, inconsistencies, or someone too good to be true. If anything makes you uncomfortable, walk away.

● Guard your anonymity and never include identifying information in your e-mails. Stop communicating with anyone who pressures you for it.

● Do not trust easily, ever, but especially online. Your trust should be earned gradually through consistent, honourable, forthright behaviour. Someone you think is lying, probably is.

● Request a photo or several in many settings, including casual, formal, indoors and out. Photos can be cheaply scanned in anywhere, so suspect anyone who refuses.

● Talk via the telephone (after a while). A phone call shows communication and social skills. At first use only a cell-phone or a pay-phone, as their phone may display the number you call from.

● Meet when *you* are ready. Trust your instincts if you don't want to meet, and never meet anyone who pressures you to.

needn't put you off, provided you stick to sensible safety rules. Most people who try dating outside their network do so without ill effect, and many achieve positive results. In fact 10% of smug marrieds met in 'cruising' situations (on vacation, in a bar or on a business trip) or via an advertisement or agency. This is an impressive hit rate, given how little time most people spend on these activities.

Couples who meet outside personal networks are twice as likely as couples introduced by friends or family to have short-term relationships. But that's not because meeting outside networks is worse but because a substantial percentage of the people you meet outside your personal networks are likely to go ahead not just with a one night stand but with a *relationship* even when they know it won't go on for long. Researchers think that people recognize *within the first few moments of meeting someone* whether that person is a long-term love candidate or not. If not, and that person is *inside* their immediate circle, they usually don't attempt a relationship even if the person is relatively attractive and would do in the short-term. However, if the person is relatively attractive and is *outside* their immediate circle, they'll often have a fling, knowing they can bail out when they please without social embarrassment. Of course this wastes the time of a more genuine partner who is hoping for long-term love.

Another thing to look out for when dating outside personal networks is something researchers call romantic perfectionism. If a person proves to be a long-term user of advertisements and agencies, beware: their personality may make them unlikely to settle seriously with anyone. Some people advertise regularly for partners, typically meeting up with many potential lovers in an exhausting round of dating, and then rejecting them all because no one exactly matches an often unrealistic ideal. Commitment is eternally withheld in case a more attractive candidate appears. One surprised researcher noticed that a woman who'd received 150 replies from an advertisement, advertised again a few months later. Even among sincere advertisers, many are what researchers call game-players, people who are more interested in the hunt than the conquest (although they may not be aware of this themselves).

Another point to remember if you're hunting outside your personal network is the cost. This can be considerable, both in time (when you are cruising or pursuing ads or agencies, you aren't doing anything else remotely useful) and money. Bars and other cruising sites can involve substantial out-of-pocket-expenses. Placing and answering personal ads can be pricey if you do it a lot. Online agencies can charge as much as £699 for a year's membership, and one terrestrial UK agency charges

£2,000. But even people who try ads and agencies without hitting the jackpot often comment that they have a lot of fun. And if you really have exhausted your personal networks and are looking for tomorrow-love, what more important thing could you be spending your time or money on?

The way you approach an agency or an advertisement needs to be thoughtful. Dateline (who provide an advertising as well as an introductions service, both online and terrestrial) define their most successful ads as those that have attracted the most responses. But this is not the way

SHOPPING CHANNELS
ADS 'N' AGENCIES, THEN AND NOW

Even 20 years ago:
- more than one heterosexual in four admitted picking up someone in a bar
- one person in five had tried a personal ad
- one person in ten had tried a dating agency

Today
- every local newspaper carries columns of personal ads
- UK-registered terrestrial dating agencies have quadrupled in seven years, up from 159 (1992) to 698 (1999)
- agencies aren't just for the old or desperate: in 1997, 781,000 single women and 1,268,000 single men *aged between* 20 and 24 were registered with terrestrial UK agencies

SHOPPING CHANNELS
TOP TIPS FOR PERSONAL ADVERTISEMENTS

- personal ads can work particularly well for older daters
- advertise in a publication you read yourself
- where possible, advertise in a local publication
- never give out your real name or address
- quiz advertisers before you agree to a meeting
- remember that many aren't looking for long term love, and this is particularly likely in publications known for their jokiness
- even in serious publications, 68% of males (55% of females) are after a casual relationship
- sex-workers regularly use personal advertisements

it should work. Who wants to wade through hundreds of replies from unsuitable people? What you should be aiming for is an advertisement that attracts only a few responses, all of them from people you find truly interesting. One 53-year-old (female) British advertiser, who worded her advertisement in a very original manner and placed it in an entirely suitable publication, found that every single man of the five who replied was a possible.

A ground rule is to be honest – with yourself. Apparently advertisers all too easily lose touch with reality when writing self-descriptions and send out photographs taken years earlier. One man who characterized himself as 'fit, a lover of sport and travel' turned out to be a chain smoker who watched football on television and hadn't travelled anywhere since he was nine! In the US, you can hire people to help you write your advertisement, and they suggest you ask your friends to contribute suitable adjectives. ('However,' said one such ad-writer, 'if you're a woman you put "pretty" in *whatever*!')

agencies: the truth

How useful are agencies? On the whole, probably not as useful as personal advertisements, particularly for women over 40, who do *much* better to advertise. However, specialist agencies can be useful at all ages, and for younger women (under 35) general agencies may also be worth thinking about. They're allegedly oversupplied with men under 30 (who are often keen on slightly older women and may be working incredibly long hours, making it difficult for them to meet women in more ordinary settings). And since males over 40 may prefer women a few years younger, agency pickings for late twenties/early thirties females may be good.

Since agencies are not required to run police checks on clients, you should treat anyone you meet through them with extreme caution. And before handing over substantial amounts of cash to the agency, you should check out their financial position: agency bankruptcies are common. But the main problem with agencies is the size of their client pool. It's usually too small for appropriate matches to be made. One company estimated that if it signed up people at random, it would need more than one million subscribers before it could confidently match clients on even such basic traits as age, locality, race, class, religion, education and height. Joining an agency that caters for people of like

SHOPPING CHANNELS
AGENCY WATCH

● anyone can set up a dating agency, and among 40 surveyed in the UK, not one owner had worked in the industry before

● only one owner in five had a university education, and fewer than one in three had any relevant statistical training

● more than two-thirds of the agencies had no full-time employees

● 74% made up the questionnaires themselves

● 68% relied on personal hunch to match couples, and only five used any kind of formal psychometric assessment

● 11% admitted drawing names randomly from their pool, and most had too small a pool to produce appropriate matches

mind (Socialist Partners) or like body (Plump Partners, Herpes-Sufferers) can, by reducing the odds, be an inspired move. Look for them on the Web.

Dateline has the largest client pool and the longest questionnaire. This agency is targeted at Mr and Ms Average, and therefore suits many people. However, those who are less mainstream may find they simply cannot describe themselves accurately by ticking the Dateline boxes. If you find this with any agency questionnaire, it indicates that you are wasting your time and should not pursue it. An eco-warrior, having struggled on with the Dateline forms, found herself matched with a worker at the local nuclear power station she was campaigning to have shut down!

Researchers who've thought a lot about agencies come down in favour of one particular kind: local agencies which organize group lunch or dinner events for single people. These are on the increase. They are safe and search-efficient: in a short period, and in a relatively safe setting, you meet a number of people and can find out quite a lot about them. Back to friendship networks? It would seem so: this mimics the gathering of a group of friends, and extends your social circle most naturally.

While use of advertisements and agencies is very much on the increase, some people still feel that to consider such methods marks them out as socially inadequate. If that's your view, then you shouldn't touch them. Even couples who think they feel quite cool about advertising or using an agency, can actually feel bad about it underneath, and this can surface unhelpfully when the relationship hits a rough patch. That said, the more usual these search methods become (and

HOT SAFETY TIPS

MEETING YOUR AD/ AGENCY/INTERNET DATE

● Be safe and meet and have your first few dates in well-populated public places. Provide your own transport there and back.

● Never be collected from home or go on hikes, bike rides or in a car. When the date is over, leave on your own.

● Tell a friend where you are going and when you'll be back.

● Give them your date's name and number and (if you're away from home) your own contact details

● Be extra cautious outside your area; carry a cell-phone and don't say where you're staying. Rent your own car and never allow your date to meet you at the airport or train or bus station or arrange you somewhere to stay. Arrive early at the meet-point and if it looks dodgy, leave.

● Get yourself out of a jam. Never do anything you feel unsure about. If you feel uneasy slip away, call a friend for advice, ask someone on the scene for help or if you feel you are in danger, phone the police. Never worry or feel embarrassed: your safety is much more important than one person's opinion of you.

they're becoming *very* usual in some places and among some age groups) the fewer esteem problems there'll be. Internet dating may already be different. Internet couples may see themselves, and each other, as exciting and adventurous. Certainly, people who meet via the Internet often actually boast about it.

One day, private enterprise (seeing a business opportunity) or governments (grappling with family breakdown or low birth rates) may seek to help men and women widen their search pool. Indeed, in Singapore this already happens. A government agency (the Social Development Unit) creates dating opportunities for its citizens and is credited with the recent marked rise in the marriage rate. Singaporeans like to use the state agency, because they know it can check out applicants for criminal records, and establish whether or not they are already married.

Today, in most countries, if you want to extend your field of eligible partners beyond your personal network you must carry out your own research, make your own contacts, run your own security checks. Above all, you must make sure your mate-search is efficient. That means, firstly, preparing your 'self' (as you might your body) by making sure that you are *fit and ready to love*: if you're anxious or depressed or racked with low

SHOPPING CHANNELS
NEW IDEAS

Dating agencies (like travel agencies) could be required to:

● register with a central body
● run security and marriage checks
● publish details of their client pool
● reveal their employees' qualifications
● describe their matching-methods and security procedures

Scientifically proven 'compatibility' tests could be:

● provided free to high-street shoppers
● offered to couples renting or buying property together
● given out along with pregnancy testing kits
● provided to couples marrying in church or registry offices

MORE HOT SAFETY TIPS
WHEN STRANGER-DATING WATCH OUT FOR

● refusal to speak on the phone before meeting
● being significantly different from online/telephone persona
● attempts to pressure or control you
● intense anger or frustration or heavy sulks or passive-aggression
● demeaning or disrespectful comments and physically inappropriate behaviour
● failure to provide direct answers to direct questions
● failure to introduce you to friends, colleagues or family members

self-esteem you'll probably make stupid choices. Secondly, being *realistic* about your position in the mate-market, rating yourself neither too high nor (just as important) too low. Thirdly, *investing in your search* with time, energy, ingenuity and (if necessary) money to create a substantial pool of possibles. Fourthly, *wasting a minimum of time* on relationships that feel wrong or don't seem to be getting very far. And finally, *recognizing a good match when you see one*. What this will look like, is the subject of the next chapter.

love busters

Use these lists differently, depending on whether your relationship is still in the early stages or is deeply entwined (e.g. you have had a child together).

● **Early stages** If even one negative statement below applies to you, think carefully: you will already have some sense of the relationship not being right, and this may help you understand why. However, if there are also many positive reasons for being together (see Love boosters) then the negative(s) may be cancelled out. Good endings can come from bad beginnings.

● **Deeply entwined** If one or more of the negative statements below applied early on in your relationship and you still went on to create a partnership, this suggests that even if you are currently not happy, your relationship also has many strengths. Before giving up on it, you need to explore these strengths further.

A relationship is less likely to last happily if it begins when you ...
● are physically agitated through such things as exercise (jogging/the gym), drugs, loud music, an exciting/competitive/illicit atmosphere
● are emotionally agitated: anxious, jealous, frightened, lonely, embarrassed, unhappy
● have gone to an event you aren't interested in, in order to meet someone
● are in the middle of your monthly cycle (women)
● are at a transition point in your life
● are feeling under great pressure to find a mate
● have made a serious compromise choice: this mate is far from ideal
● have, within the previous 12 months, lost someone who meant a lot to you (partner, parent, child, close friend)
● have, within the previous 12 months, suffered a big disappointment or other stress (been seriously ill, had a friend/relative who has been seriously ill, lost money, been in trouble with the law, failed to get a job, a promotion, exam-success)
● have, within the previous 12 months, experienced a big positive change (come into a lot of money, worked on an exciting project, been promoted)

A relationship is less likely to last happily when you ...
● feel a sense of competition with your mate
● continue, after the first little while, to feel that that love 'hurts'
● experience many highs and lows in your relationship

● place high importance on physical attractiveness (which may also be expressed through focus on clothes, including being a shopaholic)
● are in competition with many others over relatively few sexual partners
● are unusually close to your parents (men particularly)
● are financially intertwined with your parents (both sexes)
● have family and friends who strongly disapprove of your partner
● think mainly of external reasons why you should be together (your families like each other, your partner earns well, your partner is physically very attractive)

love boosters

You are more likely to find a mate when you ...
● cultivate a wide circle of friends
● are realistic about your position in the Mate Market (rating yourself neither too high nor, just as important, too low)
● are proactive in seeking contact with potential partners
● invest seriously in your mate search, in terms of time, money, energy and intelligence
● are a warm, friendly, candid person
● use search methods appropriate to your age, location, culture and class
● move on quickly from relationships which aren't going anywhere, or about which you have serious doubts
● find out why you always choose unsuitable partners (if you do)
● really are ready to settle down

A relationship is likely to become 'serious' when you ...
● become committed at approximately the same rate
● recognize early on that this relationship could be important
● don't use early dates as therapy sessions (men particularly, but women also)
● don't offer sex too early (women only)
● are introduced via family and friends
● live close to each other geographically
● don't become dependent too soon

A relationship is more likely to last happily when you ...
● experience strong 'in love' feelings (fondness/admiration) for your mate (men particularly)

● experience strong friendship feelings alongside physical attraction, from the beginning
● are of similar mate value to our partner
● are similarly physically attractive (particularly important for gay couples)
● are physically very attractive *and* assertive
● have high self-esteem
● have had similar numbers of previous sexual partners
● are no more or less committed to your partner than they are to you

THE LOVE QUIZ

TEST RESULTS

TEST 1:
READY FOR LOVE?
Your total: ▢   Your partner's total: ▢
A score of 24+ indicates low readiness for love: this person isn't in the market for a serious relationship.

TEST 2:
PASSIONATE LOVE
Your total: ▢   Your partner's total: ▢
A score of 36+ counts as a high passionate love score. If both partners feel this way, the omens are good. A person with a generally pragmatic approach to life may not score highly here, but may nevertheless have a very satisfactory relationship.

TEST 3:
LOVE OR LUST?
High scores on three or more of these questions indicate lust rather than love. Could be fun but don't count on the future.

TEST 4:
REAL LOVE?
Your total: ▢   Your partner's total: ▢
An overall score of 24+ (or a very high score on any question except question 3) indicates a compromise relationship that is unlikely to last happily (although it may last).

TEST 5:
PAINFUL LOVE?
Your total:

Been together more than two weeks? Your overall score is 24+? Forget this relationship: it's not going anywhere.

TEST 6:
MATE VALUE: PART A
Your total: Your partner's total:

A score of 32+ suggests a mate-value imbalance, from your point of view. Comparing and contrasting answers here can be useful: your partner may see things differently. If you both agree there's a big mate value difference, then there could well be trouble ahead.

TEST 7:
MATE VALUE: PART B
Your total: Your partner's total:

A score of 36+ suggests a mate-value imbalance, from your point of view. Comparing and contrasting answers here can be useful: your partner may see things differently. If you both agree there's a big mate-value difference, then there could well be trouble ahead. Or you can take steps to reduce the imbalance.

2
matching

love maps

star-gazing

fatal attractions

match making

birds of a feather?

a love less ordinary

couples who play together

family values

a divorce gene?

godly love

'my partner, my self'

love busters

love boosters

love maps

Why do you fancy the people you fancy? Partly (as we've seen) because they have the looks, personality or status that other people also find attractive. But of course this isn't the whole story: a person others find dazzling can leave you cold, and you can be transfixed by someone other people hardly notice. The reason for this lies in a personal 'blueprint' for desirability that each of us carries within us, and which is known by sex researchers as our *love map*.

Is everyone's love map *entirely* individual? No. Because people absorb the sexual guidelines of the community in which they live, many elements of their love maps are shared. For example, most women in Western society are more turned on by sexy pictures of women than they are by sexy pictures of men. This is not because all women are inherently lesbian but because they have grown up with sexy images of women around them. Nevertheless, each person's life path is different, and each individual absorbs and interprets society's sexual guidelines slightly differently, and this accounts for the specialized design of their love map: an image here, a voice there, a smell, a touch, a sensation, a dream, an atmosphere – all contribute.

The programming of your love map begins well before you are born, when sex hormones flood the developing brain. Programming continues through infancy and childhood until, by puberty, your love map is in place. At this stage, it contains all the major topics of your adult sexual life, including whether you are gay, straight or bisexual, and the beginnings of any fetish. As you become sexually active your love map is gradually revealed but little can be done to change it: adult sexual experience mainly reinforces themes that are already present.

You *know* when your love map is activated: you say the 'chemistry' is right, and often recognize that something about your lover feels familiar. This isn't always to your advantage: for example, women whose fathers were alcoholic have a much higher than average chance of marrying an alcoholic. Nevertheless, your love

SEX-TALK ...

Like native language, a person's love map ... bears the mark of his own unique individuality, or accent ... it is usually quite specific as to the details of the features, build, race and colour of the ideal lover, not to mention temperament, manner and so on.

JOHN MONEY

FAMILY MATTERS

● partners from similar-sized families often choose each other

● committed couples often find out later that features of their child-hoods are strikingly similar

● a first child/second child combination is common and often works well: one partner is used to making decisions, the other to being looked after

● choosing a partner because we hope they'll be different from some-one who hurt us in the past often fails: they may turn out to be simi-lar, either because we have gone for what feels familiar or because our expectations of them stimulate such behaviour

map cannot be ignored. There's no use telling yourself you *should* fancy a perfectly nice and suitable person if you simply don't. Your love map sets out clear parameters within which you must operate if the sexual connection is to be satisfactory. For some this means being attracted to a series of clones (Kirk Douglas's first and second wives look astonishingly alike) but most people have more flexible patterns: your love map allows you to appreciate a wide range of looks and personalities.

It's often said that we choose partners who remind us of our opposite-sex parent. Is this true and, if so, does it bode well? The answers are, not usually and not particularly. You may recognize in your partner some qual-ities that remind you of your opposite-sex parent but are as likely to see qualities reminiscent of your *same-sex* parent. In fact, we rarely see big similarities with any member of our close family, possibly because love-map programming usually makes us sexually indifferent to people we are raised with. Israeli children brought up in *kibbutzim* almost never marry each other (even though their parents often want them to) although when babies adopted away from their birth-parents meet them as adults, sexual feelings on both sides are common.

When a lover strikes you as strongly similar to a parent, this is often because that parent failed you in some way. Researchers are certain that unfulfilled longings for important people from our past (not just parents, but people such as high-ranking school-mates you longed to be close to but who ignored or teased you) often leave traces in your love map. 'Each time we lose someone, we internalize those attributes that appealed to us, and eventually build up, usually unconsciously, a composite of the attributes of which we have been deprived in the

THE BUSINESS STORY

● since the mate is regarded as a business partner, money, social status and management skills are highly valued

● partners are expected to perform their duties and responsibilities according to their 'job description'

● if one partner holds more power, an unequal boss/employee situation can develop

past,' writes Professor Sternberg of Yale University. Professor Sternberg believes this doesn't just direct people to certain types of lovers, but to certain types of love *stories*.

Professor Sternberg has developed a list of the 25 most common love stories. Each provides a set of assumptions about what love should be like and how it should progress. There's the Teacher–Student Story (where one partner instructs and the other learns); the Sacrifice Story (where giving up something for the sake of your partner is seen as a sign of true love); the Government Story (which can be democratic – power is shared – or autocratic – one governs, the other is governed) and so on. Some people, as mentioned in Chapter 1, see love as a game of which the hunt is the high point; for others (particularly very anxious types) love is a tale of romance or self-sacrifice. Yet others take a more practical view: romance leaves them cold, and their priority is to find a good team-mate.

At different life stages people may be looking for love to fulfil a different function. They may regard it as a game when they are not ready to settle down (or are with a partner they know isn't suitable in the long term). They may seek a good team-mate after they have had their fill of romantic and sexual adventure. Both young people and late-middle-aged people often incline towards romantic stories.

When someone says that a relationship didn't work because the timing wasn't right what s/he sometimes means is that an otherwise compatible couple were operating ill-matching love stories *at that time*. However, while love stories can change over time they do not simply disappear. They are embedded in your love maps, and you change them by elaborating on them, rather than by replacing them with something brand new. Some people repeat exactly the same love story over and over again.

The love story idea helps to explain how you can be attracted to people who, in the most obvious ways, are very different from each other. They resonate with your love map not because their looks or personal qualities

LOVE STORIES

THE WAR STORY

- the partners prefer arguing to compromise
- their regular battles help keep their relationship interesting
- this story is dangerous unless it is equally balanced
- after a 'good fight' partners must feel revitalized, not devastated or else they will find themselves in a Horror Story

match those of some internalized ideal *lover* but because you can cast them in the same role in your favourite love *story*.

It's not only your lover you cast in your stories – you also cast yourself, often with no conscious realization that you are doing so. For example, a woman who repeatedly falls for men who are unavailable may harbour assumptions about women being 'taken over' by love. Unconsciously fearful of this story line, she may be side-stepping close involvements, even though she believes she longs for them. We interviewed a 55-year-old career-minded woman who was in a very stable and happy relationship – the first she had ever had, and which had begun after her menopause. Only when children were no longer a possibility (she later realized) had she felt safe enough to 'get really close', since now 'too much' (giving up her career for motherhood) could not be demanded of her.

Just as you can find more than one type of person attractive, so you can operate in more than one type of love story, but most people usually have a Top Story that they tend towards. When you take some time to discover that a particular person is 'right' for you, this may be because you can't cast them in your Top Story. You may later alter this to accommodate them (as Harry did in the film *When Harry Met Sally*) or tune in to a story lower down your hierarchy, and cast both protagonists in that. This may work well enough; however, there is always the possibility that you will later meet someone who fits your Top Story better. Professor Sternberg believes that this is often what has happened when quite a good relationship unexpectedly goes down the tubes, to the puzzlement of friends, family and the deserted partner.

The match between a couple's love stories has to be good. A couple may fight bitterly and be the despair of all their friends, yet stay together for life because they are working on a common story such as the Horror Story (in which one partner terrorizes and the other is terrified). By contrast, a couple who are wonderfully well suited in other ways can come unstuck because one partner's dominant love story is suppressed:

perhaps this is the Pornography Story (they need to be treated as a sex toy, or treat their partner as a sex toy) or the Mystery Story (they need their partner to exude an air of mystery). Some stories, such as the Fantasy Story (in which a relationship is expected to carry on like a fairy tale) or the Collection Story (in which someone needs a collection of different partners) of course bode badly for long-term love.

When you inspect your lover's love history, you need to be very aware of their dominant love stories. If, for them, love repeatedly doesn't work out *for the same reason* then you should be on your guard: it is unlikely that you will be able to write a new story with them. You also need to realize that, as your lives progress, you are co-author (with your partner) of an ongoing love story. You create that story through your daily behaviour, and must be aware that there are huge in-built expectations to any story. For example, if you have co-authored a Garden Story, you can't simply drop it once a baby is born; if you have co-written and co-lived the House and Home story, then you need to tread softly if one partner develops outside

LOVE STORIES
THE GARDEN STORY

● the relationship is viewed as a garden that needs to be continually watered and tended

● sometimes one partner cares and the other is cared for

● the strength lies in the partners' watchfulness and the attention lavished on the relationship

● one potential disadvantage is that boredom and lack of spontaneity may develop

LOVE STORIES
THE HOUSE AND HOME STORY

● the home the couple creates together becomes their focus

● doing things for the home feels like doing things for the relationship

● some 'house and home' couples have trouble showing affection towards other people

● these relationships work most smoothly when both partners are 'caretakers'

● similar stories sometimes operate where the couple focus on pets or on a joint project, such as a yacht or a classic car

interests (perhaps returns to college or furthers their career). You need to honour the expectations that each love story brings and negotiate from them with warmth and understanding, as you develop a new tale of love.

star-gazing

When a couple is said to be well matched this doesn't only refer to their love stories or their mate value. It means there is an easy meeting of bodies, minds, values, interests, personalities and dreams – a general and complex harmony which will ultimately allow each person to refer to their partner as 'my other half'. Modern researchers recognize this and call it relationship fit, and 2,500 years ago the Ancient Greeks had also spotted it. They saw that some couples seemed to fit together seamlessly, as if they had been born for each other. From this they developed the theory that human beings had once been four-legged, two-headed creatures who had been cut in half by an angry god and sent to wander the earth in search of their 'divided selves' – the perfect and original match who would make them whole again. Interestingly, the Ancient Greeks didn't think that everyone would always, or even mostly, search for a partner of the opposite sex. In their view, the severed 'other half' was just as likely to be someone of the *same* sex.

The more average you are, the less challenging your hunt for a mate is likely to be. 'Standard' men and women, by definition, share similarities with many people and so have a greater chance of bumping into similar others. However the oddballs of the world need not despair: once an unusual couple does pair up, their relationship often lasts quite well, not because it is better but because alternatives are fewer. For example, gay couples stay together longer in the country than in town, and a major reason for this is that the number of gay people in the countryside is tiny.

What strategies can you use to find your perfect match? Claims are made for many methods. *Personology* claims you can discover your partner's love and lust style in just six seconds – it's written all over their face; *physiology* maintains that if your bodies aren't compatible, you won't connect emotionally or sexu-

> **LOVE-TALK ...**
> I can't understand why more people aren't bi-sexual. It would double your chances for a date on Saturday night.
> **WOODY ALLEN**

ASKING ASTROLOGERS
- 93% of Westerners know their star signs
- 20% believe in a 'special harmony' between certain signs
- 5% chose their partners with star signs in mind
- in India, people of all classes compare horoscopes before contracting marriage and astrologers choose the wedding date

ally'); *numerology* states that you should add up all the numbers in your partner's date of birth – January equals 1, February equals 2, etc – then match them with your own; *Chinese astrology* nominates an animal for each birth year, and 'guarantees' successful outcomes for particular pairings such as the Rat (1960, 1972]) and the Snake (1965, 1977); and last, but by no means least, there is *Horoscope Analysis*.

Until now, it's been easy to make claims on behalf of any of these matching methods because no one has followed their predictions up scientifically to measure whether or not they come true. But that has recently changed – for Western astrology at least. In the mid-1990s a Swiss researcher named Gunter Sachs carried out a huge survey to establish whether there really is a link between star signs and human behaviour. As part of his project, he examined the birth, marriage and divorce records of almost 400,000 of his countrymen, looking for particularly

TRADITIONAL ASTROLOGY
There are four 'compatibility' groups:
- Fire: Aries, Leo, Sagittarius
- Air: Aquarius, Gemini, Libra
- Earth: Taurus, Virgo, Capricorn
- Water: Cancer, Scorpio, Pisces

Lovers from within each of these groups should get on very well.

There are also three serious 'incompatibility' groups:
- Aries/Cancer/Libra/Capricorn
- Taurus/Leo/Scorpio/Aquarius
- Gemini/Virgo/Sagittarius/Pisces

Lovers from within each of these groups should get on badly.

STAR SIGN FINDINGS
COUPLE MOST LIKELY TO GET TOGETHER

- Aries/Aries
- Taurus/Taurus
- Taurus-man/Libra-woman
- Gemini/Gemini
- Leo-man/Aries-woman
- Virgo/Virgo
- Libra/Libra
- Scorpio-man/Pisces-woman
- Sagittarius/Sagittarius
- Sagittarius-man/Aries-woman
- Capricorn/Capricorn
- Aquarius/Aquarius
- Pisces-man/Scorpio-woman

enduring (and particularly short-lived) pairings, which he categorized according to the signs of the zodiac.

Sachs' conclusions shocked and upset zodiac believers because his findings did not support most of their claims. There was no comparable reaction from zodiac doubters, who mostly paid no attention to Sachs at all – and perhaps should have. For Sachs' research *did* show some links between marriage, divorce and partners' star signs, even if these were not always as traditional astrologers would have predicted.

Interestingly, traditional astrology doesn't say much about matches between couples who share the *same* star sign (e.g. an Aries/Aries partnership) although clearly these couples will be within a compatibility group, so you'd think they'd get on well.

Zodiac believers say that star signs alone are only part of the picture: 'rising' planets, for example, are said to exert an influence, as is the 'Age' (it is currently the Age of Aquarius). But, as Sachs pointed out, in such a large survey as his, statistically significant findings should emerge from star-sign matching alone, if particular star signs really are especially compatible or incompatible.

As the above box shows, of the couples most likely to get together, Sachs found that 12 were from within the astrologers' compatibility groups. At first sight this is an amazing hit rate. However, closer examination reveals that 8 of the 12 couples don't just come from within the same astrological compatibility group – they actually share an identical star sign. This is a thumbs-down for astrologers, who wouldn't have predicted this at all, and don't like it. Even more fascinating is the fact that the odds of this happening by chance are 1:6,700,000.

As far as the Sachs research goes, you need to be aware of two things. Firstly, this research was conducted in one country only. The same results might not be found in China or India or Australia, or even in Germany next door. Secondly, a measurable *link* between star signs and mating behaviour doesn't mean that one *causes* the other. Sachs' finding that many Swiss couples have identical star signs (that is, have birthdays within a couple of weeks of each other, though usually a year or two apart) may have nothing to do with zodiac influences but may stem from shared life experiences, say, from age-positioning within the school year.

What did Sachs find when he checked out the Swiss couples *least* likely to get together? As the box above shows, 6 out of the 12 (that is, 50%) were from within the astrologers' own *incompatibility* groups. This should be considered a big thumbs-up for astrologers. The likelihood of this happening by chance is 1:433.

Having established that there are clear, if sometimes unexpected, links between some people's star signs and mutual *attraction*, Sachs looked for the relationships most likely to *last*.

STAR SIGN FINDINGS
COUPLE LEAST LIKELY TO GET TOGETHER

Out of a possible 72, 12 combinations have an above-average likelihood of *not* getting together:

- Aries-man/Scorpio-woman
- Taurus-man/Gemini-woman
- Taurus-man/Leo-woman
- Cancer-man/Aries-woman
- Leo-man/Aquarius-woman
- Scorpio-man/Gemini-woman
- Sagittarius-man/Pisces-woman
- Sagittarius-man/Capricorn-woman
- Aquarius-man/Scorpio-woman
- Aquarius-man/Taurus-woman
- Pisces-man/Virgo-woman
- Pisces-man/Libra-woman

STAR SIGN FINDINGS
RELATIONSHIPS
MOST LIKELY TO LAST

- Aries/Aries
- Gemini-man/Taurus woman
- Taurus-man/Cancer-woman
- Capricorn-man/Pisces woman
- Pisces-man/Scorpio-woman

Of these only Pisces-man/Scorpio-woman is one that an astrologer would predict (i.e. is from one of the astrologers' compatibility groups). Sachs then turned his attention to the relationships *least* likely to endure.

STAR SIGN FINDINGS
COUPLES LEAST
LIKELY TO LAST

Five pairings proved to have very little staying power. These were:

- Aries-man/Leo-woman
- Gemini-man/Capricorn-woman
- Libra-man/Aries-woman
- Scorpio-man/Gemini-woman
- Sagittarius-man/Gemini-woman

Two of these especially *un*stable relationships – Libra-man/Aries-woman, Sagittarius-man/Gemini-woman – are from the astrologers' incompatibility groups, and therefore would accord with their predictions. The others, however, would not.

Sachs then combined his data. The most *successful* relationships, he reasoned, would have two features: above-average attraction (marriage rates) and below-average break-up (divorce). While three pairings meet those conditions (see box below), only one would be predicted by traditional astrology. Sachs also looked for particularly *unsuccessful* partnerships (which he reasoned would have low rates of attraction and high rates of break-up). Again there were three, and only one would be predicted by traditional astrology.

Where does all that leave us? Intrigued, certainly, but not relying seriously on traditional astrology to predict your perfect match. If the Swiss

STAR SIGN FINDINGS

Most likely to get together, least likely to split:

● Pisces-man/Scorpio-woman: clear above-average marriage rates, slightly below-average divorce (three cheers for astrologers – they'd predict this)

● Capricorn-man/Pisces-woman: slightly above-average marriage rates, sharply below-average divorce (thumbs-down for astrologers – not from their compatibility groups)

● Gemini-man/Taurus-woman: average marriage rates, sharply below-average divorce (thumbs-down for astrologers – not from their compatibility groups)

Least likely to be attracted, most likely to split:

● Libra-man/Aries-woman: slightly below-average marriage rates and sharply above-average divorce (three cheers for astrologers – they'd predict this)

● Aries-man/Leo-woman: slightly below-average marriage rates, sharply above-average divorce (thumbs down for astrologers – not from their incompatibility groups)

● Gemini-man/Capricorn-woman: below-average marriage rates, above-average divorce (thumbs down for astrologers – not from their incompatibility groups)

can't look to the stars with any real confidence, neither (it would seem) should you. To find our perfect mate we must consider other things.

fatal attractions

One area that can provide useful clues as to whether love will last is a phenomenon researchers call *fatal attractions*. Here turn-on factors (qualities that attract you to someone) become turn-offs and are given as reasons for the relationship breaking up. For example, you may go for a partner who is successful and focused but later see them as workaholic. Or you may find someone's youth and innocence refreshing, later to complain that they lack maturity. Or you may be attracted by someone's devotion, later to find them obsessive (and possibly violent – see Chapter 5).

Fatal attractions are amazingly common, being given as reasons for break-up by almost one couple in three. Women are more likely than men to say they have experienced a fatal attraction, which may mean that men spend less time analyzing the

THEY SAID IT ...

A man who will only eat in Italian restaurants with his back facing a wall probably has a few enemies.

RITA RUDNER

whys and wherefores of break-ups or that they put disenchantment down to something less specific, such as personality or looks. However, it may also be that women are less good at judging character at first sight, which is a distinct possibility.

It might be thought that falling heavily and passionately in love makes fatal attractions more likely, because 'love is blind'. In fact, research shows that love is rarely blind. Even when you are wild about someone, you're usually aware of their faults. You just choose to ignore them or tell yourself that they don't matter. Even lust isn't blind to qualities you may later find irritating, although it can blind you to the *absence* of qualities that you will one day wish your partner had, such as intelligence or a bright personality. This is really important, because it shows that most fatal attractions could be recognized in advance. The issue is not so much whether you notice them (you almost certainly do) as whether you see them for what they are. You may ignore warning signs if, for the kinds of reasons outlined in the last chapter, you have a strong wish to convince yourself that everything will be OK. But wilful blindness isn't always your

STUPID CUPID

HIGH-RISK QUALITIES FOR FATAL ATTRACTIONS

- your lover is highly *attentive, romantic and committed* (later *possessive and smothering*)
- your lover is *highly protective* (later *controlling*)
- your lover is greatly *funny and fun* (later *superficial*)
- your lover is a *party animal* (later a *drunken clown*)
- your lover is *strikingly spontaneous* (later *chaotic*)
- your lover has a *very strong character and beliefs* (later *pushy, loud or domineering*)
- your lover has *charming eccentricities* (later *irritating habits*)
- your lover is *self-sufficient and reserved* (later *cold and uncaring*)

THE LOVE QUIZ

TEST 8: SOCIABILITY

Rate each statement below. Enter the total in the box on page 103. Now get your partner to do the same.

6	5	4	3	2	1
Not true		Neutral			True

1 My partner and I have at least one major shared interest
2 We like to spend similar amounts of time together – and apart
3 We both like being around other people to roughly the same degree
4 We are similarly adventurous or unadventurous in exploring the world
5 We like to be outdoors/indoors to much the same degree

problem; you may not know what a fatal attraction looks like because no one has ever told you.

Warning bells should ring whenever an attracting quality is *extreme* or when its opposite quality is missing: when, for example, a person is highly organized but not flexible. You also need to be on your guard when the attracting quality is one you don't believe you have yourself, and would like to have.

Another type of fatal attraction can occur when partners who are very *different from each other* team up. The reality is that while opposites may attract, they don't stay together nearly as long or as happily as more similar types.

This may come as a surprise, since it is popularly believed that love works best when partners are different: one a leader, the other a follower; one chatty, the other silent; one rational, the other emotional; and so on. Researchers all over the world have been carrying out experiments to test this theory and are united in their findings: it doesn't usually work. Opposites don't stay together as long or as happily as more similar couples.

match making

What do we mean by similar and different? People can be similar (and different) in many ways. Some similarities are more important than others and others can be downright destructive. Some differences don't matter and others can even be helpful. While similarity has been called the glue of romantic relationships, it has to be thoroughly investigated if you hope to use it as a crystal ball.

Physical similarity between couples was first recorded in 1903 when researchers brandishing tape measures found partners matching in height, arm span and length of left forearms. More recently, similarity in earlobe length has been noted! In one fascinating study researchers laid out individual photographs which, when put together, made up real life, engaged couples. People who'd never met the people or seen their photographs were told to put them into pairs. Going solely on looks, these complete strangers matched a remarkably high proportion of the couples accurately. When they didn't and their first-choice match was not correct, their second-choice match almost always was.

Looking like another person can be a predictor that you'll get together with them. Think Brad Pitt and Jennifer Aniston, Kate Winslett and Jim Threapleton, Iman and David Bowie, Styler and Sting. However, there's no evidence that look-alike couples have longer-lasting or more satisfying relationships than look-different couples. Certainly, in build and facial features David Bowie looks like his second wife, but he looked even more like his first.

While look-alike couples don't do better than the average, couples whose *level of attractiveness is similar* do. In fact, similarity in attractiveness is so important that manuals for relationship counsellors often

SIMILARITY

LOVE NOTES

- if partners look very different other areas of similarity tend to be particularly strong
- similarity is more highly valued in the US and Western Europe than in Japan or Russia
- when a couple are good communicators, similarity doesn't matter so much
- the higher a person's self-esteem, the more likely they are to choose a partner who is like themselves

THEY SAID IT ...

I think about people as if they were those many-faceted mirrored balls that reflect the light in nightclubs. Each one of us has many, many facets like that. And if someone matches us on some critical number of these facets, they can be right for us. But it doesn't necessarily have to be any particular combination of facets. It just has to be enough of them.

HAMBURG

warn them to take note if one partner in a troubled pair is markedly better looking than the other: this can be a cause of their difficulties. It's actually quite rare to meet a couple whose level of physical attractiveness is *not* similar. This is because, as we go about the business of choosing a mate, our wish to better ourselves is balanced by fear of rejection and most of us end up settling (after a couple of false starts) for someone whose attractiveness is on a level with our own.

We also tend to settle for a partner whose *personality* is similar to our own. In fact, within eight weeks of a first date similarity in personality is an even more reliable predictor of continuing attraction than similarity in level of attractiveness. It's also a reliable predictor of *continuing* satisfaction. A year after moving in together, couples with similar personalities show up as happiest when scored by researchers.

What does it mean to be similar in personality? Systems for categorizing people's behaviour (popularly known as personality tests) are becoming familiar as more and more people take them at work. Employers use these tests to weed out problem job applicants, match particular people with particular jobs and help team members accept and deal with their own (and their colleagues') funny little ways: if one team member can think that a

INTROVERTS:
- like to relax by being alone
- enjoy constancy and routine
- think before they act
- listen more than they talk
- have a few close friends
- process information and feelings by thinking in private
- don't volunteer information – they need to be asked
- are 'dark horses': what you see isn't necessarily what you get

EXTROVERTS:

- like to socialize with a wide circle
- enjoy variety
- act before they think
- talk more than they listen
- like to discuss things — that's how they find out what they think!
- often change their minds after a discussion
- don't mind being the centre of attention
- easily express emotions: what you see is what you get

second takes time to respond because he's a typical *introvert* (rather than because he's a sulky bastard) business may run more smoothly.

Probably the most widely used psychological test of the last ten years is the Myers-Briggs Type Indicator. Although the 'Myers-Briggs' (as it is known) is mainly used at work, three of the four personality dimensions it describes are relevant to romantic relationships too.

The first of these looks at where people get their *psychological energy*: if from other human beings, they are called *extroverts*, if from within themselves they are called *introverts*. Although most people fall mainly into one or other category, they are likely to show some characteristics from the opposite category, some of the time. A few will be genuine half-and-halfers, which can be a good way to be, but being extremely one or the other (rampant) isn't helpful since extreme personality traits make couple relationships difficult.

The second relevant Myers-Briggs dimension reveals how people make decisions. If they do this mainly on the basis of rational thought, the Myers-Briggs categorizes them as *thinkers*. But if they prefer to let emotion and hunches drive them, then they are called *feelers*.

The third Myers-Briggs dimension which has impact on the success or failure of people's love lives has to do with the *degree to which they try to control life events*. Here they may be a *planner* (licking everything into shape as they go along) or an *optionizer* (hating to come to decisions too early and preferring to keep their options open). In this dimension differences will be seriously problematic: a *planner* matched with an *optionizer* will usually end up tearing their hair out.

One really important point is that no category is better than another. Each has advantages and disadvantages. For example, a rampant *planner* can insist on more structure than is actually needed, while an *optionizer* drives everyone mad by losing interest in a project when it is only half

PLANNERS:

- look to the future more than the present
- are uncomfortable without established routines
- collect information methodically before they make decisions
- once they have the information, make their decision quickly
- regularly draw up 'to do' lists
- do what they say they'll do (when they say they'll do it)
- usually see work as more important than leisure

completed or by refusing to book a holiday until all the best are taken. Yet *optionizers* can be a lot of fun and are sometimes right to leave things to the last minute: a decision made early may not be the best decision.

Most of us have a vague idea of the categories we fall into, but thinking them through carefully (and working out how your partner fits in) can be very useful, because it can help us explain and tolerate behaviour which we find surprising, and enables us to devise strategies to handle clashes. It can also stop us taking disagreement too personally. And if we understand how personality matching works, we can make a quick exit from any new relationship that we judge is going to cause us grief.

We don't necessarily settle any more willingly for a partner whose personality is similar to our own than we settle for someone whose attractiveness level is similar to our own. Our first preference may be for someone whose personality we see as different – and more desirable. For example, introverts are often more attracted to extroverts than they are to other introverts. However, they are less able to hang on to them, often being successfully elbowed out of the way by other extroverts.

OPTIONIZERS:

- prefer a flexible lifestyle over routines
- like to 'go with the flow' to see what will happen
- put off making decisions because something better might turn up
- put off making decisions because they don't yet have enough information
- meet their deadlines in a last-minute rush
- make last-minute changes
- often give play priority over work

THINKERS:

- do not avoid conflict
- are happy to listen to fair, honest criticism
- can be blunt – they see truth as more important than tact
- become upset and irritated if rules aren't followed
- enjoy debate
- refer more often to facts than to feelings
- see flaws and tend to be critical
- will rarely say 'I love you' or 'you look great' because they assume you know how they feel about you

Extroverts tend to think they are superior to introverts. This is partly because 75% of the population are extroverts (so extroverts are seen as the norm) and partly because the Mate Market pecking order favours people with bright, sociable personalities. But in fact, extroverts don't operate more effectively than introverts; they just operate *differently*. Even though introverts are so often drawn to extroverts they do much better to stick to their own kind. The research shows clearly that couples who enjoy a similar amount of social excitement (that is, interaction with people outside the relationship) tend to do best in the longer term.

Although *thinkers* and *feelers* are at opposite ends of their personality dimension, they quite often get together, probably in the hope of getting a good balance in their lives. (It is worth remembering that feelers are just as able to make rational decisions as thinkers but simply choose not to.) Provided that a thinker/feeler couple is prepared to handle disagreement over potentially sparky issues such as money and raising children, their combination can be a good one. The thinker (being direct, upfront and brave about conflict) can see that troubles are ironed out, while the feeler works towards harmony and compromise, monitors the emotional temperature and boosts their partner's confidence.

Whether the thinker or feeler is male or female can be quite important. There are more thinkers than feelers in the population, and more men tend to be thinkers. On the whole, males find relationships with rampantly feeler-females difficult, preferring female partners who are thinkers or half-and-halfers. By contrast, females can be exasperated by extreme thinker-males: they tend to prefer their men either to be rampant feelers or half-and-halfers. A thinker-female/ feeler-male combination can be especially good.

FEELERS:

- like to please others
- say 'yes' to keep the peace
- don't like disagreement
- imagine other people's feelings to be hurt if their own would be
- do something if it feels right
- want to be treated kindly
- tend to avoid giving or receiving criticism

One way of looking at personality that has attracted a lot of attention over the years has been the categorizing of people as Type A or Type B. Type A people are high achievers while Type Bs are more laid back. Type A people get a lot of the good things (wealth, success and acclaim). They also get a lot of the bad things (migraine, heart disease, stroke). Since high-achieving people often have high mate value, Type As can be sought-after. But how will they shape up as love partners? At first sight, not well. The partners of Type As are often unsatisfied with their relationships, *particularly if they themselves are Type Bs*. Apparently Type As let work impinge badly on home and, as partners, are neither thoughtful nor positive.

However, a closer look at Type As shows two major sides to their personality, one of which is more troublesome than the other: *achievement/striving* and *impatience/irritability*. It's not the *achievement/striving* that's the problem, although it does make them take on too much, which can infuriate their partner and has often been an issue when couples split up. The more serious problem lies in the *impatience/irritability* element

CRAZY CUPID

TYPE As TEND TO:

- shout at other drivers
- eat quickly
- don't take exercise (so often get fat)
- usually try to do several things at once
- hurry other people and interrupt their sentences
- become irritable when kept waiting
- feel guilty when relaxing
- die prematurely

of the Type A's personality, which can come out in a lecturing, blaming, demanding and criticizing attitude, and causes most of the health problems. Type As who learn to control their impatience and irritability, or who leave it at work, can make quite good life partners (although you shouldn't bank on retiring with them since they may well be dead by then). The atmosphere they work in can make a difference. Type As working in a culture that encourages competition, conflict and deviousness are more at risk of couple problems than Type As working in kinder atmospheres. In some companies, more than 65% of the staff will be Type As.

birds of a feather?

One realization that has recently dawned on researchers is that it is not so much that similarity draws couples together, as that *dis*similarity turns them off. Everyone has begun a conversation with an attractive person, only to lose interest seconds later when they prove to 'come from a different place'. When one person quickly loses interest in another, the rejected one usually feels they've failed, that somehow they weren't good enough. That's often not so. They have simply proved to be too *different*.

When unalike couples are happy together, it tends to be in spite of their differences, or because they are similar in other ways, or (and this can be a big one) because they *see themselves as similar.* When couples were measured as either leaders or followers, it was discovered that many leader-type people were happier with a partner who was a follower (this doesn't mean that a leader/follower combination would be good in the long term, only that in the short term these couples got on better). But here was the really interesting part: the happy leaders didn't actually see their partners as followers, but as leaders like themselves!

Where partners see one aspect of each other as similar, they'll often see other aspects as similar, too. And when they see themselves as different, they can deny similarities that seem obvious to everyone else. As the marriage of the Prince and Princess of Wales disintegrated, onlookers were transfixed by the powerful and increasing similarity of many of their core values and concerns, while the unhappy pair seemed only able to grasp their differences. It's interesting that most unhappy couples cannot even agree about why their relationship doesn't work. Each gives different reasons.

An important similarity issue is similarity in intelligence. This is *not* the same as similarity in education, although the two often go together.

Similarity in communication-style is important, too. As will be covered in more detail in Chapter 5, couples who communicate in similar ways find it easier to resolve differences. This is worth serious thought, and rather blows out of the water the idea that the only couples destined for marital bliss are those who can talk the hind leg off their relationship. Men and women of few words can do very well together.

Early on, the similarities people look for in a partner are the obvious ones: race, age, class, religion and education. People with disabilities (such as deafness) tend to mate with each other, not just because they tend to understand and accept each other but also for a more mundane reason: they meet each other socially. Younger couples of all kinds are more 'surface similar' than older couples, partly because they tend to meet near their parents' homes or at places like college where they mix with many people

---

LOVE NOTES

SIMILARITY INSIDE-OUT

From the inside:
- couples who are seen as similar *by themselves* are more approving of each other
- they also feel more secure in their relationship
- when they disagree, they may behave less touchily, which helps them reach productive compromise

From the outside:
- couples who are seen as similar *by others* get a great deal of support
- when partners are seen as similar, outsiders actually like each one of them better as an individual
- relatives and friends tend to encourage the match

CLEVER CUPID

LIKING AND BEING ALIKE

- researchers who sent pairs of 'similars' and 'dissimilars' off on blind dates found that the similars got on much better, even to the extent of standing closer together
- the children of 'similars' may exhibit many of the same characteristics, leading to easy family harmony
- randomly paired couples share an average 43% of genetic markers
- sexual partners *and close friends* share an average 50%

from backgrounds similar to their own. Younger people may also have a greater need than older people to reinforce themselves by mating with someone similar.

However, while all happy-together couples share many obvious similarities, these do not *in themselves* predict long-term happiness. Couples (particularly younger couples) who split up often started out as surface similar as couples who have stayed together. In fact, couples from very *different* backgrounds may make *fewer mistakes* in judging compatibility, because in order to get to know each other they have to do a lot of talking and explaining. Surface similarities are more important to men than to women, and this means that a woman whose lover's background is very different from her own should need extra convincing of his sincerity.

> **THEY SAID IT ...**
>
> As a general thing, people marry most happily with their own kind. The trouble lies in the fact that people usually marry at an age when they do not really know what their own kind is.
>
> **ROBERTSON DAVIES**

a love less ordinary

As people increasingly find mates from outside their cultural group, a big issue becomes when and whether a relationship between two people from seriously different backgrounds will survive. In a sense, of course, every relationship is cross-cultural, since every family has its own culture (rituals and values), which the new couple must integrate if their partnership is to succeed.

At the present time couples are much more likely to break up if partners are from different races. Different values and expectations will often play a part, but family resistance may be more crucial. The so-called Romeo and Juliet effect, in which parents' opposition is supposed to make love stronger, hasn't been borne out by research: when family and friends oppose a match, it is much *less* likely to succeed. Family opposition to mixed marriages is lessening in countries such as the US and the UK. In 1985, 50% of white British people said they'd mind if a close relative were to choose a mate from an ethnic minority group. The disapprovers are now down to 25% (although just over 50% still think that other people would mind). This growing tolerance mirrors changed attitudes to Catholic/Protestant matings which, just a generation ago, were frowned upon in these countries. Yet now, in all but a few places, these barely raise an eyebrow.

In trying to predict whether or not a mixed-race (or mixed-religion) partnership will last, the couple needs to be ruthlessly honest about their compatibility: their interests, values, attitudes and beliefs. They also need to pay special attention to why they themselves have made an unconventional choice. Just as a person with low self-esteem will often choose a partner who is very different from themselves, so a person who feels uneasy in their own family may choose a partner from a different race, religion or country. Such choices can be liberating. They can also, of course, be unsustainable acts of rebellion. Signs that the rebel will end up back in the fold, with their relationship on the rocks and tug-of-love children sobbing in international airports, include continuing to have lots of friends from their own family background and seeing value in children being brought up in their family tradition.

Whenever being different is a major reason for partner choice the outlook for the relationship is not good, unless the partners are seriously compatible on many other levels. In particular, partners should pay attention to how much *both* families support them, and be on the look out for any of the Killer Habits (see box below), which all predict very strongly that relationships won't last.

Some of the trickiest mixed marriages are not between couples from different *cultures* but between couples from different *classes.* You can have more in common with a different-race person of your own class than with a same-race person of a different class. Hindu parents often worry as much (or more) about their children marrying outside their *caste* as outside their race. And researchers looking at the way American families

MIXED-RACE COUPLES

● 50% of British-born Caribbean men (33% of women) have white partners

● 90% of 20-year-old British Caribbean males who have girlfriends have *white* girlfriends

● 19% of British-born Indian/African-Asian men (10% of women) have white partners (these ethnic groups came to the UK half a generation later than Caribbeans)

● in the UK virtually no Pakistani and Bangladeshi (Muslim) males or females have yet married out

STUPID CUPID

THE SEVEN HABITS OF HIGHLY UNSUCCESSFUL RELATIONSHIPS

- physical violence or domineering behaviour
- infidelity (particularly early on)
- spending money foolishly
- heavy drug/alcohol use
- intense jealousy
- finding personal habits in your mate extremely 'irritating'
- negativity/moodiness

operate have found that class is more important than race in predicting how parents will treat their children. This is important, because agreement/disagreement over approaches to raising children is a serious issue for couple compatibility.

Any match that doesn't follow a conventional pattern will be more challenging. This doesn't mean that it will be worse, only that it will be trickier. This rule applies whether the less ordinary love is between mixed-race or same-sex partners, disabled partners or ethnic minority partners, partners of very different ages or from strikingly different classes or cultures. Even quite standard couples can end up with a 'love less ordinary' if they embrace an unconventional lifestyle, such as a dual-career partnership, where both have demanding jobs.

When a partnership follows a well-worn path it is buoyed up by warmth and approval, and this *really helps it along*. When it breaks a mould it becomes a tale of the unexpected, with many twists and turns and expectations for the couple and their families to negotiate. This offers huge potential for conflict and misunderstanding. One researcher was fascinated to

THEY SAID IT ...

I came home glowing because I'd just landed a really juicy account for my firm. I started to fold the laundry, and suddenly my mother-in-law is crooning over me about the ironing – a job I hate and never do, because it stinks of the drudgery I'm determined to escape. I exploded:'It's not my job to do the ironing!' My father-in-law looked at me like I was going mad for shouting at this poor woman who's just trying to help. But the assumption that it was my job to do the ironing sent me over the edge.

find that even a strongly feminist mother-in-law will not support her daughter-in-law's career if she thinks her son is not being properly looked after, and her disapproval can quickly translate into lack of support for the relationship.

Disapproval by the *wider society* (a cross that has been borne by mixed-religion partners and still weighs heavily on same-sex partners and partners from different racial groups) can prove almost as destructive as family disapproval because it can set off a lot of conflict within the couple. It is sad that less ordinary lovers so often have a hard time of it, especially since many are trailblazers, creating new definitions of love that will one day liberate the rest of us. But they face special pressures which, the research shows, they must acknowledge and address if they are not to go under.

Even couples from the *same* minority group face extra pressures when compared with mainstream couples. Because they share a common (and relatively unusual) background they can be fooled into thinking they're more similar than they really are. This illusion can persist until children come along and decisions have to be taken about how to bring them up. Partners can then find that they have quite different attitudes to their shared background, one, perhaps, wishing to celebrate it, the other to play it down. Same-sex couples, too, can easily assume they're more similar than they actually are.

You'd think that if men were 'from Mars' and women 'from Venus' same-sex couples would be the stars of the mating game (especially lesbians, since women are supposed to be intuitively better at relationships). In fact, as the box below shows, gay couples (*particularly* lesbians) break up more often and more quickly than do most straight couples. The reasons for this will come clear in this book. They include such things as the fact that so many gay people have to go to bars or use 'lonely hearts' advertisements to meet, with the result that they are much

LESS ORDINARY LOVE

- couples experiencing social disapproval may not recognize it
- instead, when the going gets tough, they may turn on and blame *each other*
- feeling defensive, they may *idealize* their relationship, refusing to acknowledge (and work on) difficulties that exist
- or they may feel so *pessimistic* that they give up at the first sign of trouble

BREAK-UP RATES

Couples who had been together 2 years or less:

Married: 4%

Cohabiting: 17%

Gay male: 16%

Lesbian: 22%

Couples who had been together between 3 and 10 years:

Married: 6%

Cohabiting: 12%

Gay male: 16%

Lesbian: 20%

Couples who had been together more than 10 years:

Married: 4%

Gay male: 4%

Lesbian: 6%

less likely than straight couples to mate with people *like themselves* – that is, from a similar background. Killer Habits are also very common among gay people and this is due in part to the pressures of growing up gay in a straight society.

Same-sex relationship research highlights the ways in which each sex's gender training can hinder love in *all* relationships. Generally one person (often a woman) is alert to signs that a relationship is slipping and takes steps to pull it back. In a male/ male partnership, neither partner may take this job on, and then the relationship can be said to suffer from a double dose of man. Far from being supersensitive, gay men can be so scared of being labelled effeminate that they won't express feelings of need or vulnerability, or take care of these in their partner.

Lesbian relationships are at risk in a different way. Often neither partner will be up-front about what they want or need. Very feminine women (gay or straight) tend to be unassertive. An important element in femininity (so-called because people used to think that only women had such qualities) is finding connection with others terribly important. Because of their strong need to feel connected, people high in femininity can be scared to push openly for what they want in case their partner dumps them. Instead, they manipulate. They deny problems, fail to solve them and don't take their partner's views and feelings seriously. When both partners do this, the relationship can be said to suffer from a double dose of woman. Highly feminine gay *males* don't tend to be so bad. Maybe

MASCULINE/FEMININE

To be masculine means being strongly self-directed and able to take the initiative (it used to be thought that only men could be this).

To be feminine means being expressive and connected with others (it used to be thought that only women could be this).

● in fact, anyone (male and female) can be high or low in both masculinity and femininity

● people who are good at relationships are often high in both masculinity and femininity

● couples (gay or straight) with one highly feminine and one highly masculine partner often run into difficulties

their conditioning as men helps them be more assertive, so they can go after what they want in a more open and healthy way, while still valuing their connectedness to others.

couples who play together

A key predictor that a relationship (gay or straight) will last, and last happily, is *similarity in leisure interests*. Early on this predictor can be surprisingly hard to spot. This is partly because new lovers tend to do things that most people can enjoy without being deeply interested in them (like eating out); and partly because when a relationship is in its early stages a woman who is in love often shows enthusiasm for activities dear to her lover's heart. She doesn't do this to trick him; she does it because she finds that when she joins in the activities he enjoys, he rewards her both by feeling more love for her and by expressing his affection more openly. A man isn't similarly tempted to join so enthusiastically in a woman's favourite activities because she isn't nicer to him if he does.

At the early stages, a woman's feelings for her lover aren't noticeably influenced by whether he shares her leisure interests or not. However, within a year of living together or being married, the outlook changes. Women's love for their partners is increasingly affected by the sharing of leisure interests. Also by this stage, a man whose partner's early enthusiasm for snooker or football has begun to fade is feeling let down. The important thing for shared interests is that the enjoyment really does have to be *mutual.* When the researchers have looked closely at shared interests, they've found that doing things as a family or doing things as a couple doesn't benefit the relationship in the long term unless everyone involved in the joint activity is really getting something out of it.

Couples who share major leisure interests are often (but not always) on the same *wavelength*. When a couple are on the same wavelength their key *attitudes, beliefs* and *values* are compatible. At the beginning of a relationship this can be even trickier to gauge than shared interests, as people play down difference and play up similarity to smooth the pathway to intimacy. In fact, your own core *values, attitudes* or *beliefs* may not even be obvious to yourself (let alone to your partner): sometimes they only become clear when you are put on the spot.

Of course a partner with different *values, attitudes* or *beliefs* can be your salvation. Their perspective may offer you a new way of seeing and of living. But a little of this goes a long way. Even if your core beliefs are 'bad' for you, they are an integral part of who you are and you may regard any challenge to them as the deepest of personal attacks. This is especially so when the challenge comes from your life partner, who is supposed to accept you warts and all and be your greatest ally. Without quite a lot of shared values, you probably won't be in a relationship, but if there are lots of disagreements about values or bitter disagreement in an area that's important to you, then this points to serious problems ahead.

CLEVER CUPID

SHARED INTERESTS

● a joint passion for music, art, travel, good food, dancing, stamp collecting, doing up old houses, etc., should never be underestimated as relationship 'glue'

● a shared passion for active sports doesn't bode so well: in later life, couples who relied on this for togetherness often go their separate ways

● most couples who are happy together have at least one genuinely shared interest; and when this runs out of steam, they develop another

● a shared activity is particularly important if one partner has a time-consuming interest (this may include their work) which their partner does not share

THE LOVE QUIZ

TEST 9: KNOW YOUR PARTNER'S VALUES

6	5	4	3	2	1
Upsetting disagreement		Strong disagreement		Mild disagreement	

1 Consider each of the topics below. Choose up to four where you and your partner don't agree. Rate the disagreement using the scale above. Enter the results on page 103.

- religion/spirituality
- politics
- race
- social justice
- abortion
- immigration
- homosexuality
- families
- crime
- drugs
- social class
- education
- 'the environment'
- 'tradition'
- men/women(roles/duties)
- men/women (differences)

2 Note other topics of disagreement to which you and your partner keep returning. List up to four. Rate your disagreement using the scale above. Enter the results on page 103.

3 Choose a topic where you feel there is substantial disagreement between you. Then ask of this topic:

(a) Whose fault is it?

(b) What should be done to fix it?

Rate your different approaches to (a) and (b) using the scale above, and enter the results on page 104.

Another important area for couple similarity is *life organization*: how tidy you are; whether you like your home dark or flooded with sunlight; whether you're a 'night person' or a 'day person'; and whether we like to sleep with the window open or closed. These *life-organization* topics can easily shade into *wavelength* issues, as for example, over taste in furniture or pets, or preferences for town or country living. No couple expects to match on all or even most of these, but heavy disagreement should never be ignored: the second most important causes of arguments between couples (after money) are personal habits such as tidiness or hygiene.

Lovers who look at the world in a similar way *and* like to organize their lives in similar ways find, as one researcher puts it, 'when they're at home they feel like they're on vacation'. Most of the time these deeply compatible couples do not experience their relationship as hard work. Indeed, researchers are beginning to suggest that the rather grim notion that marriage is hard work arises from generations of ill-matched couples struggling on together when divorce was out of the question.

You'd think that by the time couples actually got married they'd have realized whether or not their interests, values and tastes matched well enough, but apparently not. Among divorcing *parents* (that is, couples who once considered themselves sufficiently compatible not only to marry but also to have children together) 54% of women and 33% of men cite 'serious differences in lifestyle and/or values' as one of the top reasons for the break-up.

Pre-marriage questionnaires which oblige couples to check for (among other things) similarity in interests, goals and values can now predict with more than 80% accuracy which couples will stay together happily, and which won't. Among the engaged couples who take these tests, around one in five calls their marriage off. In some US cities this has led to a 35% drop in the divorce rate, in just two years. You might think that doubting couples would be the least likely to accept an offer of a test, but that's not so. Where at least one partner is already feeling uneasy, the couple is more likely to agree to take a love test.

THE LOVE QUIZ

TEST 10:
DAILY LIFE

Rate each statement below. Enter the total in the box on page 104. Now get your partner to do the same.

6	5	4	3	2	1
Not true		**Neutral**			**True**

1 Our standards of neatness/cleanliness are similar
2 We are similarly careful/careless in looking after our own possessions
3 We are similarly interested in living healthily
4 Our standards of personal hygiene are similar
5 We place similar importance on creating a comfortable home
6 Our preferences as to where to live are similar

THE LOVE QUIZ

TEST 11:
KNOW YOUR PARTNER:
AMBITIONS

Write down answers to the following questions and get your partner to do the same. On each question, rate the degree to which your want undermines or supports your partner's.

6	5	4	3	2	1
Undermines		**Neutral**		**Supports**	

1   I want enough money to ...
2   I want enough power to ...
3   I want enough time to ...
4   In my life, I most want to be ..
5   In my life, I most want to do ...
6   In my life, I most want to have ...

If a discussion on any issue becomes *heated* double your score on that question. Now enter your joint score on page 104.

family values

A hot topic for many couples is the way earning and caring will be shared out. When society's expectations were clear, couples didn't have to think twice about who carried the briefcase, cleaned the bath or took care of the children. Today, when there are no set rules, agreeing who does what at home can prove a minefield. The most recent generation of newlyweds argue most about two things: like their parents and grandparents before them – *money*; and *un*like their parents and grandparents before them – *the division of household labour.* It is thought that this last is one major reason why the divorce rate has rocketed in recent years: disagreement between couples over housework and childcare is a major divorce predictor.

    The study of 'early nesting' couples mentioned in Chapter 1 found that similarity between the couples' *parents* here could be important. The young wives stayed more satisfied with their marriages if both their father and their father-in-law had similar education levels. The young husbands were happier if both their mother and their mother-in-law had (or hadn't) worked outside their homes. In 'late nesting' couples this pattern wasn't found. This suggests that for couples who get together when they're young, similarity between each partner's inherited family values can be particularly important.

Around 30 or 40 years ago, men and women who operated 'traditional' roles (home for her, work for him) tended to have the best marriages. In fact, a direct link could be traced between divorce and a woman going out to work. There were several reasons for this. One was that some husbands got cross when their wives took jobs; another was that some wives only worked when they were already planning to leave. As for women earning more than their husbands, that was unusual and (in many people's minds) unthinkable. Even 20 years ago, couples were more likely to break up if the man said his wife was ambitious or if he thought she wasn't doing her fair share of the housework.

Times have changed. Today a *man's* not pulling his weight at home is the better predictor of divorce, and couples who believe that earning and caring should be shared rather than divided up in the traditional way, feel more positive about long-term relationships than couples who believe women should care and men should earn. What's more, the link between women, work and divorce is no longer found. Indeed, when a woman

THE LOVE QUIZ

TEST 12:
FAMILY BUSINESS

Rate each statement below as you believe it applies to you as a couple Enter the total in the box on Page 104. Now get your partner to do the same.

6	5	4	3	2	1
Not true		**Neutral**			**True**

1 My partner and I agree on how much time to spend with our own families

2 My partner and I agree on how much of our private business to tell our own families

3 We agree about the number of children we'd like to have, and when to begin our family

4 We agree about who should look after the children

5 We agree about who should earn money for the family

6 We agree about who should do what around the house

works the quality of her relationship tends to *improve*. This is partly because the family has more money and partly because she's less likely to be depressed than if she's not working. There are still some issues, though. When *mothers of very young children* work full-time both they and their partners tend to be less happy with their relationship than where mothers work part-time (although the couples don't actually fight more and are *not* more likely to break up). Interestingly, when the children's father shares responsibility for organizing childcare, many of the problems experienced by these dual-career couples disappear.

Today, when careers can blossom or wither unpredictably and jobs can disappear overnight it can be hugely advantageous for a couple when both partners can provide for their families. Perhaps for this reason, recent research shows that *flexibility* in terms of who cares and who earns bodes well for the future of relationships. Couples living together are massively more likely to split when a woman *doesn't* work than when she does. And even among smug marrieds (who tend to be older and more conventional than couples who live together without marrying) when a wife earns even *twice* as much as her husband the divorce risk now barely rises at all. A predictor of a relationship lasting *and* of the male partner being healthy, is that he regularly does some housework. Such men are also less likely than so-called traditional men to be overwhelmed by their partner's emotions or to shy away from conflict.

Disagreement over house and home activities may be at the root of some of the problems faced by *differently aged* couples. Younger women rate older male partners as less into sharing family responsibilities, more sexist, more conservative, more authoritarian and less sexually liberated. Older man/younger woman partnerships are most likely to break up when the woman was young when the couple got together. Once the younger

LOVE NOTES

WOMEN, CHILDREN AND DEPRESSION

High depression levels are found among:
- non-employed mothers
- employed mothers who are solely responsible for childcare

Low depression levels are found among:
- employed women without children
- employed mothers who have no problem finding childcare (and whose partners share responsibility for sorting it out)

partner is over 40, however, age differences don't seem to matter: these relationships are not usually at risk.

Why should relationships between older women and younger men be more likely to succeed even than same-age partnerships? It may be that this (relatively) unusual set-up makes couples think carefully before committing themselves, or that the kinds of men who seek older partners may be especially home focused. In any case, this arrangement is perhaps not as unusual as has been thought: in Britain before the Industrial Revolution, one bride in four was older than her husband. One reason was that most women worked, and an older woman was likely to be richer (and have higher mate value). Today, as women earn independently, the older woman/younger man scenario is likely to become quite common again.

a divorce gene?

It's easy to understand how relationships can run aground on differences. But similarities can also cause problems. Why should this be? Too much similarity can be stultifying, and if you married a clone you would probably die of boredom. Most of us, except the most fearful, have a strong internal 'push' towards growth and development. In a sense we 'marry to expand our souls' (as one researcher puts it) and if you don't have that opportunity inside your relationship you will often look for it outside.

Some people place a very high value on the safety of apparent similarity; others find the excitement of apparent differences more appealing. Neither way is right or better than the other. The trick lies in recognizing the category you fall into, and the category your partner falls into, and noting when difference is being experienced as a positive (or as something that genuinely doesn't matter to either partner) and when it is causing ongoing conflict or anxiety.

A big danger when similarity is very great is that it creates a zone that is taken for granted and therefore never addressed or explored, so that when differences do develop you may repress them. Repressed differences keep you more separate from, and unknown to, your partner than the obvious differences that you fight over. Partners (particularly lesbian partners) who experience powerful initial attraction based on such feelings as 'we are so alike' or 'I feel joined with her' need to be particularly on the alert. When one wants to explore differences or even spend a little time alone the other often assumes they want to end the relationship and goes off in a huff. Researchers have also identified *Babes in the Wood* partners who view the outside world as hostile, spend most of their leisure time together and never criticize each other. They can appear very happy until the moment when they realize that they have begun to experience each other as *dull*.

While some aspects of your partner need to be as familiar and comforting as known parts of yourself, it is through being different that excitement and interest are generated. Routine quite literally desensitizes people: if your touch, taste, sight, hearing and smell receive little stimulation they half go to sleep. One reason a new lover can appear so inter-

CAPRICORN MAN
is perceived as very dull:
He is hard working and ambitious. He wants to get married and raise a family. He has no problem with the concept and implementation of commitment ... Finally – a man who takes relationships seriously! Blessed with the sensitivity of a tax inspector, the humour of an IBM clone and the heart of a merchant banker, a Capricorn man takes everything seriously.

LANG & RAJAHA

esting and exciting is that their newness awakens your senses, as do the new places you go with them and the novel things you do together. One way of keeping established relationships fresh is for the partners to keep introducing variety into their lives: when retired couples travel the world together, this may be precisely what they are doing.

Differences between partners can usefully modify the way both behave, as, for example, when a financially cautious person puts the brakes on a spendthrift and a spendthrift loosens up their other half, but there are likely to be many rows in the process. Here the big thing will be how well the couple manage those differences (see Chapter 4). Warning bells should sound when any difference strikes you forcefully, particularly if it makes you cross or contemptuous. This is most likely to happen when differences are extreme, or are in an area that is particularly important to one partner.

An area where similarity bodes badly, is when people with *similar problem backgrounds* pair up. Perhaps both lost a parent; both had depressed mothers; both had parents who fought a lot or drank heavily or used drugs; or both (and this is common among lesbians) were sexually abused. At the beginning, these couples are often bowled over by a sense of recognition and acceptance. But this can be another kind of *fatal attraction* because neither may be emotionally equipped to handle the other's neediness or distress. People from problem backgrounds do better to choose people from happy homes as their life partners.

People whose parents split up (or never lived together) are more likely than people from two-parent families to remember their childhood as unhappy and so it comes as no surprise to learn that they themselves are seriously at risk of divorce. In fact the prognosis for them is even worse than the figures in the box below suggest. This is because official statistics measure only *divorce*, and many people whose parents split up don't get married – they just live with (cohabit with) their partners, and cohabiting relationships break down a lot more often than marriages. People whose parents split up after years of vicious fighting may actually be less of a divorce risk themselves than those whose parents seemed reasonably OK until one met someone else and the affair led to break-up.

The second generation divorce risk is especially high when *both* partners have divorced or separated parents. And, interestingly, it isn't lessened if parents waited to split up until their children were

> **THEY SAID IT ...**
>
> A difference that makes no difference is no difference.
>
> **WILLIAM JAMES**

WHEN PARENTS HAVE SPLIT UP

● in the US women with divorced parents are 60% more likely than other women to end up divorced
● US men with divorced parents are 35% more likely to divorce
● in the UK, the increased risks are 50% for women and 100% for men
● even when the fact that the children of divorce often grow up poor and/or enter relationships young is taken into account, a 25% increased risk remains

grown. This may be because their adult children come to look back on their whole life as having been built on a lie (the lie of their parents' happiness) and so may be especially mistrustful in their own relationships. What's more, people whose parents found it impossible to reconcile their differences may not have learned, first hand, some of the basic skills that make for successful partnerships. Or when they do experience difficulties, they may make no attempt to solve them, believing (as one of our interviewees put it) that 'unhappiness is normal'. They may also see break-up as the natural solution when the going gets tough.

So excited have researchers been by the findings on second-generation divorce, that some have spent considerable time trying to track down a 'divorce gene', so far without any success. However, there is a sense in which divorce *is* 'genetic': identical twins (who have the same DNA) are more prone to divorce than non-identical twins (whose DNAs are different). It may be that identical twins share some of the negative personality traits that make romantic relationships less likely to succeed (see Chapter 5).

A key reason that people from unhappy homes are a high divorce risk is that they tend to rush into relationships young. People whose parents parted are five times more likely than people whose parents stayed together to get into a serious live-in relationship before the age of 25. Being in a relationship young makes you high-risk as a love partner, whether your parents are still together or not.

One study has shown that if children of divorced parents nevertheless had good relationships with their parents *during their teenage years*, they have as much early success in love as people whose parents had stayed together. Maybe this means they learned relationship skills through the way they related to their parents, or perhaps they felt happy at home and

STUPID CUPID

BABY, BABY

● 50% of teen brides are separated by their tenth anniversary, compared with 25% who married in their early twenties and 16% married after the age of 30

● *domestic violence* is most common among young couples

● for every year of increased age at marriage, couples report 21% fewer problems due to *infidelity* and 11% fewer problems due to *jealousy*

● for every year of increased age at marriage, couples report 7% fewer problems with *drink and drugs*

so didn't need to rush into a relationship young (and create a home of their own) and before they were ready.

Young couples are especially likely to have no money (and to have problems managing what they do have) and this leads to another important divorce predictor: growing up poor. This is often connected with having divorced parents: half of all US single-parent children are rated poor compared with just one in ten whose parents live together. Even young people who remain well off after their parents part are twice as likely as their classmates to drop out of school, and so are at risk of being poor themselves as adults. Most people whose parents parted are determined not to repeat their mistakes. Certainly finding a truly compatible partner is an important task, but that's not where it ends, or even begins. The children of divorced parents do best when they come to terms with their relationships with their parents; make conscious efforts to learn how to handle relationships well; don't form their own families young; and get good qualifications and jobs so they aren't dependent on their families or stuck in the poverty trap. If they take care of all that, then the odds for their own relationships are good. In their later-life partnerships, they are no more likely to break up than people whose parents stayed together.

THEY SAID IT ...

I do not believe in recovery. The past, with its pleasures, its rewards, its foolishness, its punishments, is there for each of us for ever, and it should be.
LILLIAN HELLMAN

godly love

Belonging to a particular group within society can make someone high, or low, risk as a love partner. In the US if you're a New Age type or a Baptist or have no religious connections you've a higher chance of breaking up with your partner than if you're a Jew or a Catholic or a mainstream Protestant. If you are a *regular* churchgoer in almost any faith, you're a lot more likely to stay married than a person who never goes to church, or only does so from time to time. Church-going couples report a lot of intimacy, respect and agreement, and *all seven* of the Killer Habits are less common than average in their households, except for infidelity (of which more later). However, the news isn't entirely good: being a regular churchgoer is also a risk factor for being long but *unhappily* married.

Why do churchgoing couples tend to last longer together than non-churchgoing couples? Are they better people? Does God smile on them? No: they're embedded in communities that enforce rules of good behaviour and offer support when things start to go wrong. Churchgoing couples are also self-selecting: that is, wild types (whose bad relationship records would bring down the average of any group) tend to keep away from churches. The churchgoers most likely to stay happily together are couples raised in the *same* religious tradition, who are close to a parent who holds the *same* religious beliefs and who remember their childhood as *happy*.

Understanding the divorce risk factors within any community helps people to grasp the extent to which every private relationship is embedded in a public system, which supports or undermines it. For example,

LOVE NOTES

LOW BREAK-UP RISK IN UK PAKISTANI AND BANGLADESHI FAMILIES

- divorce is frowned upon
- organized religion is influential
- older generation controls mating (for example, young couples often live with the male's parents)
- children generally stay with their father's family if the mother leaves
- few women are sufficiently educated to live independently
- communities are self-contained with few escape-routes for unhappy partners (for example, few use welfare benefits)

being African American (or, in the UK, having parents or grandparents from the Caribbean) makes you *very* high risk indeed as a love partner, whether you mate *outside* your own racial group or *within* it, and this is particularly so if you are *male*. Being a white Northern European (or North American) makes you a moderately high love risk. And coming from China or from the Indian subcontinent makes you very low risk, even when your family is not at all well off.

Why should African Americans/Caribbeans be so high a risk? When there's a man shortage (or woman shortage) in any community, break-up rates in that community will be high. This is partly because the mate value of the sex in short supply becomes inflated, and members of the other sex may need to poach to get a partner. This is now the situation in African American districts in the US, where women greatly outnumber men. This is not because more girls are born but because boys are more likely to partner outside the black community, to die young (due to drink, drugs or street violence) and to be unavailable through being in hospital or in prison. Between 70% and 80% of heterosexual African American men are unfaithful to their live-in partner, a similar rate to white homosexual males. Even among middle-class families, African American men and women separate at twice the rate of white Americans.

Like family histories, cultural histories can affect whether a relationship is likely to last. Most African communities outside of Africa were established as a result of the slave trade. Slave masters actively broke up slave families, so stable man/woman relationships were discouraged and women learned to create family groups made up of themselves and their children. It's worth noting that African people who came to Britain

SOME REASONS FOR *MEDIUM-HIGH* BREAK-UP RISK IN WHITE NORTHERN EUROPEANS (AND NORTH AMERICANS)

- the culture supports the search for self-fulfilment in love
- life-long emotional intimacy is expected
- organized religion has relatively little influence
- divorce is no longer considered disgraceful
- many women are educated and able to live independently
- most women keep the children after divorce
- state benefits are available to single mothers

SOME REASONS FOR *HIGH* BREAK-UP RISK IN UK CARIBBEAN AND AFRICAN AMERICAN COMMUNITIES

● lone-parent grandmothers and mothers are plentiful, providing role models for women to 'go it alone'

● daughters often have babies young

● mothers keep the children when relationships break down

● mothers and their adult children are often interdependent

● there's a big mate imbalance among younger age-groups: as a higher proportion of young men from the black community die young, are ill or caught up in substance abuse

● the community is as willing as the white community to use welfare benefits (so women *can* go it alone)

directly from Africa (for example, from Nigeria) and from communities that were *not* slave based, are not so high risk in the separation stakes.

Researchers have interviewed African American men to see whether they start out as committed to their mates as men from other cultural groups, and it seems that they do. Their relationships are undermined by the kinds of things listed above, and (of course) by racism. Africans/Caribbeans suffer hugely from racism and this easily translates not only into feeling bad about yourself (and your partner) but also into being poor. Black men are usually 'last in, first out' in the job market (if they get a job at all), and most black women earn very little. For African American couples, a major predictor of a long, happy partnership is the *male's* commitment to being a parent and sharing care of the children. It may be that since so many African American couples break up (or never live together), the couples that make it are those who both find family life especially rewarding.

'my partner, my self'

Important and illuminating as these love-risk categories are, they only provide averages. Against the odds, people from the low-risk groups can have spectacularly *un*successful relationships, just as people from high-risk groups can do wonderfully well. What is clear from the research is that no risk factor (or even cluster of risk factors) dooms a love affair: it's what you do with them that counts. Nor does a good or bad partner match only happen in ways that are obvious to the naked eye. A lot of the matching happens unconsciously, and in ways that can be difficult to spot.

Everyone sees how partners play to their strengths in daily life – the one who feels confident with electronic equipment programmes the video, the one who drives most confidently takes the wheel. Similar processes operate in people's emotional lives. The partner who is a natural leader (perhaps a first-born child) sets the pace; the partner who is more passive, or more wary (often a second-born child) obeys instructions. This kind of division of labour (whether practical or emotional) can be satisfactory and efficient, and many couples construct their identities around it. But it can be dangerous: there is a fine line between playing to our strengths and being boxed in. If you never programme the video you don't learn how to (you may even begin to think you are stupid or no good at technical things). If you always drive, and your partner gets no practice, then you *have* to drive even when you are very tired: the car won't be safe in your hands.

Here the *fatal attraction* phenomenon raises its head, only this time it's not an attracting quality that, on closer examination, has proved to be uncomfortably extreme. This is *fatal attraction by stealth*, a gradual process by which partners gradually develop polarized ways of operating: loud/quiet; strict/lenient; generous/mean; sexually aggressive/sexually passive. As each drifts towards the opposite corner of the boxing ring, a couple who once saw themselves as quite similar (and were not wrong about this) start to see themselves as different – and incompatible. A clue that this is happening, or has happened, is the thought, *'how did we once think we were so well suited, and get it so wrong?'*

But there can also be something more subtle operating – something deeper than simply playing to your strengths. This occurs when people behave in a particular, rigid way not only because such behaviour comes naturally or is efficient, but because they are *afraid to do anything else.* Then something spooky can happen: you can uncon- sciously export *into your part- ner* feelings or personal quali- ties that you don't want to see in yourself. As if by magic, your partner starts to feel them *for you*, and may begin to act them out.

> **THEY SAID IT ...**
>
> Some men are too polite. I was trying to lift weights at the gym and the guy next to me kept saying, 'Here, let me get that for you.'
>
> **RITA RUDNER**

CLEVER CUPID

HOW PEOPLE IMPORT/EXPORT FEELINGS OR QUALITIES

● a woman who despises her own feelings of aloofness chooses an aloof lover who acts out aloofness for both of them, while she remains feminine and clingy

● a man who believes he is devoted to his ill mother (but who, in fact, feels seriously burdened by her) chooses a partner who doesn't like his mother and will express the aggression he feels but can't bear to acknowledge

● a woman who is secretly terrified of losing control chooses a wild partner in whom she sees the compelling out-of-control part of herself of which she is frightened

Researchers don't know how we manage to export feelings out of our own psychological system into that of another person. They only know, by direct observation, that we do it, and that we do it *often*. We do it most obviously when, feeling guilty or upset, we blame someone else. As the person we have blamed absorbs our guilt and upset, we feel relief. If they don't accept our guilt and upset, and turn them back on us, we feel miserable again (we have imported the uncomfortable feelings back into ourselves). Unhappy couples do a lot of this passing of feelings backwards and forwards in tit-for-tat fights. Another way exporting can work, is that we locate in our partner *personal qualities* that we find unacceptable. For example, someone who finds it difficult to be looked after, chooses someone who wants to be looked after. The strong partner locates their own need to be looked after in their weak mate, and proceeds to look after both lots of neediness at once – their partner's and their own.

To recognize when you are *importing* someone else's feelings isn't easy. A trick is to note if you feel a sudden surge of negativity (anxiety, fear, sadness or anger) when this isn't what you were feeling a minute ago. It may be that some or all of these sudden feelings are really *your partner's*, which you have just absorbed from them. And if they consistently behave in a too-good-to-be-true way (for example, always being kind and thoughtful) while you find yourself behaving in the very opposite way (being critical and edgy) what may be happening is that you are doing the bad stuff for them. Or, of course, they may do the same for you, while you skate through the day full of smiles.

Some researchers have called this import/export business the 'secret contract of marriage.' (The 'contract' is not said to be secret because we hide it from other people, but because we hide it from ourselves.) Sometimes the couple exchange feelings; at other times just one partner exports, and the other imports. As the years pass, partners create entire *systems* through which they do this, and some researchers believe that the so-called 'chemistry' of love may be the unconscious recognition that a particular partner is going to be willing to accept and act out feelings or qualities that we want to get rid of.

The brilliant thing about exporting feelings into our partner and getting them to carry these around with them, is that they *are not lost*. We can remain in touch with them without finding them overwhelming, although we will become very scared if our partner tries to leave (after all, they are carrying a part of our 'self'). If, over time, our partner manages to embody your exported feelings in a non-scary way (and the relationship is a truly happy one) then the feelings or qualities we once felt the need to get rid of may begin to seem acceptable, and we may be able to absorb them back into our self.

Although this sounds like some bizarre science-fiction fantasy, it really does happen: counsellors often watch, with fascination and amazement, as couples 'heal' each other through this unconscious process. But the outcome can be less happy, and often is. Each partner begins to dislike the other for embodying the feelings they fear and despise in themselves. Or one partner starts to change and mature, and has no need to play the old game any longer. At this point the other may redouble their efforts to keep the delicate balance of that secret contract in place. Then the relationship is likely to polarize, and fall apart.

CRAZY CUPID
THE REAL LOVERS' VOWS

'I promise that I will attempt to be some of the many important things you want of me, even though they are some of them impossible, contradictory and crazy, if you will be for me some of the important, impossible, contradictory and crazy things that I want of you. We don't have to let each other know what these things are, but we will be cross, sulk, become depressed or difficult, if we do not keep to the bargain.'

PINKUS AND DARE

THE LOVE QUIZ

TEST 13:
IMPORT/EXPORT

1 Think of a quality or feeling your partner has that:

(a) seems more extreme than the average; and

(b) is something you rarely experience yourself; and/or

(c) is the opposite of a quality you have

(d) is a quality or feeling you: don't like, get annoyed by, get upset by, find difficult to handle

2 Think of a quality or feeling that you have that:

(e) seems more extreme than the average; and

(f) is something you rarely see in your partner; and/or

(g) is the opposite of a quality your partner has

(h) is a quality or feeling your partner doesn't like, gets annoyed by, gets upset about, finds difficult to handle

Turn to page 104

love busters

Use these lists differently, depending on whether your relationship is still in the early stages or is deeply entwined (e.g. you have had a child together).

● **Early stages** If five or more of the negative statements below apply to you, think carefully: you will already have some sense of the relationship not being right, and these may help you understand why continuing with it may be a mistake. However, if there are also many positive reasons for being together (see love boosters) then the negative(s) may be cancelled out.

● **Deeply entwined** No single negative indicator (or even a cluster of negatives) should be taken as a cue to give up on your relationship. Understood in the context of this chapter, they may help you grasp some of your dissatisfactions and prompt you to work at these areas, in order to create a more satisfying partnership.

Your relationship has a below-average chance when you ...
● differ from your mate in the degree to which you like to plan ahead
● differ significantly from your mate in IQ
● come from very different backgrounds (young couples mainly)
● have consciously sought a partner who is very different from yourself

- have very different views as to how to spend money, bring up children, or divide housework, childcare and paid employment
- have different cultural backgrounds
- are part of a social group greatly disapproved of by society
- believe you and your mate think and feel as one (gay women particularly)
- felt strongly that you are so alike at the first meeting (gay women particularly)
- have an identical twin who is separated or divorced
- have separated/divorced parents
- *both* have separated/divorced parents
- had parents who were very unhappy together
- grew up very poor
- are under 25
- are very disappointed with the amount of money you have
- find any of your mate's personal habits intensely irritating
- have seriously unequal incomes (lesbian couples mainly)
- are highly feminine (women) or highly masculine (men)
- continue to be very close to your parents (men only)
- are financially dependent on your parents (or have a parent who is financially dependent on you)
- like to challenge authority
- are a member of the Armed Forces (men)
- were unemployed in the first year you were together (men)
- do not work outside the home (female cohabitors)
- work full-time *and also organize all the childcare* (mothers)
- have recent African/Caribbean ancestry (men particularly)
- are more than three years older than your partner (men only)
- are more than three years older/younger than your partner (except heterosexual women if they are the older partner)

love boosters

Your relationship is more likely to become 'serious' when you ...
- look like your partner in facial features or physique

Your relationship has an above-average chance when you...
- are non-standard people
- are similar to your mate in terms of personality (warm/cold, extroverted/introverted)

● enjoy being with people about as much, or as little, as your mate
● judge yourself similar to your mate in the areas of life that are most important to you both
● come from similar backgrounds (young couples only)
● share leisure interests which *both partners* genuinely enjoy (sex and hands-on parenting included)
● have few serious conflicts in terms of attitudes, beliefs, values and lifestyle preferences
● are flexible about which partner works inside/outside the home
● have similar personal habits in terms of tidiness and personal hygiene
● pool finances (gay couples particularly)
● have parents who come from China or the Indian subcontinent
● regularly do housework (men)
● are particularly committed to being a parent and sharing the care of children (African/Caribbean males particularly)
● are more than two years older than your (male) partner (women)
● have had sudden financial success (men)
● are the better educated partner (men)
● are financially dependent (women)
● are highly expressive (one or both of you)

THE LOVE QUIZ
TEST RESULTS

TEST 8: SOCIABILITY

Your total: [ ]   Your partner's total: [ ]

The lower your score, the better. If your score is 20+, be afraid. If there's also a big difference between your score and your partner's, be very afraid.

TEST 9: VALUES

1 Topic 1: Your score: [ ]
   Topic 2: Your score: [ ]
   Topic 3: Your score: [ ]
   Topic 4: Your score: [ ]
2 Topic 1: Your score: [ ]
   Topic 2: Your score: [ ]

Topic 3: Your score: ☐

Topic 4: Your score: ☐

3 (a) Your score: ☐

(b) Your score: ☐

The point about this test is to get you thinking and talking. The scores aren't so important, but any 40+ score should be worrying.

TEST 10:
DAILY LIFE

Your total: ☐   Your partner's total: ☐

The lower your score, the better. A big difference between your score and your partner's on any question spells trouble. Differences here can often be covered by, for instance, hiring other people in to do your cleaning. A score of 30+ is cause for concern.

TEST 11: AMBITION

Your total: ☐   Your partner's total: ☐

The point about this test is to get you thinking and talking. The scores aren't so important, but any 30+ score should be worrying.

TEST 12: FAMILY BUSINESS

Your total: ☐   Your partner's total: ☐

Although an overall score of 24+ is cause for concern, these are such fundamental issues that a very high score on any one question should be taken seriously, as should any marked variation between partners' scores. If you can't resolve these differences through talking and nego-tiating, then this could be a moment to look for short-term coun-selling. It's important always to find a counsellor who is experience in working with couples.

TEST 13:
IMPORT/EXPORT

This is an exercise to get you thinking and talking. Positive answers to one of these questions suggests that one partner is 'owning' qualities/feelings the other doesn't like in themselves. Positive answers to both indicate that qualities/feelings are being swapped. Watch out for distress. Simply understanding what's going on may be enough, or one or both of you may need to work on 'taking back' uncomfortable feelings/qualities so that polarization doesn't take place.

3

mating

commitment

Similarity in commitment is an important predictor of relationship success. This sounds obvious, but how many people have spent months or even years trying to convince a half-hearted lover to commit? Such efforts are generally wasted. Even if wedding rings are eventually forced on to fingers divorce will often follow, sometimes many years down the line. In a relationship with a bright future commitment usually develops *at pretty much the same rate on both sides*, although in the very early stages small imbalances don't matter. At that point extra efforts by a slightly more committed partner can boost the other's commitment.

What does 'to commit' mean? If a partner asks you to commit, they are asking for evidence that you see your relationship as having a future. If you won't do this, then it probably doesn't, but even if you get engaged or married, nothing is guaranteed, for commitment can never be a once-and-for-all promise. That's because it waxes and wanes in response to three fundamentals: how satisfied you are with your relationship; whether you can see a satisfactory alternative to it; and whether moving on would cause you to lose a lot of things you have 'invested' in it.

Proof that this rather unromantic process truly is the way commitment works is shown by the fact that most people who stay in unhappy relationships don't do so because they are great at commitment but because they can't see a real alternative: they tend to have few friends and few outside interests, don't believe they can control what happens to them in life, and were often sexually and romantically inexperienced before their present relationship.

Younger people regularly quit relationships that by the standards of older couples are actually quite satisfying. This is partly because they see many more alternatives, and partly because they don't have so much *invested* in a shared life. But even quite heavy investment (such as a joint mortgage, or children) doesn't have a huge hold on younger people if they're unhappy inside their relationship. For them, satisfaction is of overriding importance. However, although investing in a shared life doesn't usually keep young couples

TEST 14: INVESTMENT

To measure your partner's investments in your relationship, rate each statement below as it applies to them. Enter the total in the box on page 143. You probably don't need to do this quiz to sense your own.

6	5	4	3	2	1
Not true		Neutral			True

1   My partner is spending less time with people who get in the way of our relationship.

2   My partner is disentangling emotionally (and if relevant legally) from a previous partnership

3   My partner has introduced me to friends and family: our relationship is becoming 'public property'

4   My partner has made life changes to bring us closer together geographically, or give us more time together

5   We are beginning to develop a shared life: e.g. moving in together, doing up a place of our own

6   We have talked about how many children to have and when to have them, and our ideas coincide

7   Our finances are gradually becoming less separate

8   We are getting married

together, *failure* to invest should be regarded with deep suspicion, for it is a serious break-up predictor. The degree to which investment is occurring is *the most powerful predictor of all* (even more powerful than *satisfaction*) that a dating relationship will continue. This means that a non-investing partner should be considered a poor bet however intense their passion and however loving their words.

love and money

One of the strongest of the ties that bind is money. Joint ownership of property, shares and savings makes partners think twice about bailing out when they are going through a rough patch. Pooling cash is a serious indicator that you are investing in your relationship. Cohabiting couples are less likely to pool than married couples. Sometimes this is because they have doubts about the partnership (in which case failure to pool is, of course, a sign that it will not last). However, if they aren't pooling because the relationship is new or because they value a sense of independence, then not pooling does *not* necessarily mean trouble ahead. Women are less likely to want to pool than men, but this may not be because they are keeping their options open for a quick getaway, but because they fear their money will be swallowed up in household expenses. Gay couples are less likely to pool than straight couples. Some gay couples stay financially semi-detached because they believe 'gay relationships never last'. Sadly, thinking like this can be a self-fulfilling prophecy. Pooling cash and buying property together may be especially important for gay couples, since so many don't have children to act as a reason for staying in a relationship and so helping them weather a storm. As time passes, most couples (gay and straight) tend to move towards pooling or to become so financially intertwined that whether or not they have separate bank accounts no longer matters. Getting the balance between wanting to stay and having to stay is tricky: no one wants to be locked in to a miserable relationship, but unless you are tied in to some extent, you may not see the difficult times through.

THE LOVE QUIZ

TEST 15: MONEY

Rate each statement below. Enter the total in the box on page 143. Now get your partner to do the same.

6	5	4	3	2	1
Not true		Neutral			True

1   I am rarely puzzled or bothered by the purchases my partner makes
2   I am rarely puzzled or bothered about how seriously my partner considers major purchases before making them
3   My partner and I have similar attitudes towards building up credit card or other debt
4   My partner and I agree on the approximate amount we like to save
5   My partner and I generally agree on how much financial risk to take
6   My partner and I generally agree on who should have the 'final say' when we buy something jointly
7   My partner and I generally agree on how fully to consult with each other before one of us spends money.

CLEVER CUPID

LOVE AND MONEY

- a man being unemployed in the first year a couple live together doubles the risk of break-up
- worrying about money can cause people to act inflexibly and negatively
- UK couples jointly earning less than £10,000 a year are twice as likely to argue every day as couples earning more than £20,000
- poorer people tend to be more concerned that their partner agree with them, and are less able to resolve their differences

Couples are especially likely to split if, together, they're poor. What do have they to lose by separating? Quite a lot of love seems to be cupboard love – women, in particular, are more likely to stay with a mate who is doing well financially, and are more likely to leave him when he's doing badly. Among lesbians, unequal *incomes* predict that the relationship is less likely to last. One reason that being poor is such a serious divorce predictor is that having no money can damage the *quality* of the relationship. When couples are disappointed with the amount of money they have, they tend (*except for lesbians*) to find their entire relationship less satisfying. They also tend (*especially same-sex couples*) to blame each other for the short-fall, rather than seeing the cash crisis as a joint problem. The biggest cause of arguments (cited by 40% of all couples) is money and between 25% and 33% of couples rank money as their primary problem.

How we administer our money can also point to whether love will to last. Break-up is likely when partners argue a lot about how money is *managed.* Although couples have many and varied ways of organizing their finances (sometimes with one partner in charge, sometimes with responsibility shared) couples who feel they have equal control over how money is spent have more tranquil relationships and are less likely to split.

When people are poor, each generation can need the other's financial help to get by. In the West, this can seriously endanger love. Researchers are convinced that a young couple's first task is to create a strong 'couple identity' separate from their families. To do this they must be selfish with cash, time and loyalty, spending these on each other, rather than on their parents. But if children have to support their parents financially, or if parents are supporting their children, separating out can be difficult. Where parents and children (*sons* in particular) remain closely intertwined, a young couple's relationship will be at risk.

LOVE NOTES

MEN, WOMEN AND MONEY

● when the male partner has sudden financial success, the break-up risk for a couple drops

● when the female partner has sudden financial success the relationship isn't harmed – but it's not improved, either

● where the man is the better educated (and therefore likely to be the higher earner) a couple are 31% *less* likely to part than a couple with the same level of education

● when the woman is the better educated a couple are 43% *more* likely to part than a similarly educated pair

While money can't buy love, it can do a lot for it, and not just because it makes life less stressful. Couples see money as a symbol of their success. They equate it with goodness, ability, talent, drive, even moral uprightness, and often see it as a joint accomplishment – as proof that they chose each other well. In love, the saying 'to those who have shall be given' is painfully true: success in life breeds success in love. The better your education and your job, the richer you tend to be and the more likely you are to be lucky in love. Doing well in the world helps you feel good about yourself, positive about others, purposeful about life and willing to face new challenges – all great qualities for making the most of love, too.

unpacking satisfaction

How *satisfied* you are with your relationship is a major predictor of whether it will last. This sounds obvious, but it wasn't always so: in the past, couples who were miserable often stayed together for life, and though some still do this, it's becoming less common. Research also used to show that women were, on average, less satisfied with their marriages than men. That's changed, too; now it's men who are more likely to report feeling dissatisfied – and no one knows why. Perhaps family life more often runs to the woman's agenda. There's clear evidence, for instance, that women in their twenties and early thirties often feel ready to have children, and that this is the time most couples do have their babies. Men, left to themselves, become interested in having children about a decade later. However, as women delay child-bearing, men's and women's baby agendas may move closer together.

Another reason why men report more relationship dissatisfaction than women may be because when they feel unhappy, they are less likely to leave. Men generally spend less time in the house than women do. Diluting their unhappiness with outside interests may make them able to bear at-home unhappiness for longer. Women being more focused on house and home, may feel at-home misery more acutely, and so be driven to bail out. They may also feel they have less to lose. In most countries women have a pretty shrewd idea that they will keep the children; men who are fathers may stay home unhappily for longer because they fear losing close relationships with their children, a reasonable fear since after divorce, most do. US States that have changed their custody laws have discovered that women also stay longer in unhappy relationships when keeping their children isn't a foregone conclusion.

Although, as mentioned in Chapter 1, one couple in ten becomes increasingly more satisfied with their relationship as the years pass, an early *drop* in satisfaction is much more usual – even among couples who will stay together happily. On average, relationship satisfaction falls over the first three or four years by about 3-4% per year. This gentle but steady decline is the single most regularly documented finding in all the couple research, and it *doesn't* mean that a relationship is on the way out. Researchers consider it so normative that they suggest weddings should come with health warnings: *you will feel increasingly dissatisfied over the next three or four years. Everyone does. Stick with it.*

LOVE CONNECTIONS
LOVE AND DISSATISFACTION

● when a woman is dissatisfied with the relationship, her male partner usually is too

● when a man is dissatisfied with the relationship, his (female) partner may not be

● a man's dissatisfaction is a better predictor than a woman's that a relationship will end, even though 3 out of 4 people who file for divorce are women

● 7% of couples are in miserable relationships from which they do not see a potential way out through separation or divorce

TEST 16:
HOW SATISFIED ARE YOU?

Rate each statement below as it applies to you. Enter the total in the box on page 143. Now get your partner to do the same.

6	5	4	3	2	1
True		**Neutral**		**Not true**	

1 I often share my goals and plans with my partner

2 I often share my feelings with my partner

3 I am greatly satisfied that my partner is my life-companion

4 I am greatly satisfied with the support my partner gives me

5 I have a great deal of respect for my partner as a person

6 My partner is an excellent companion in leisure activities

7 I feel that my partner values me as much as I value them

8 I feel that, all things considered, I get no less than I give

9 I feel that, all things considered, I get no more than I give

10 I rarely fantasize about a better relationship

Although a gentle decline in satisfaction isn't cause for alarm, in that early period you do need to look out for *sharper* drops in satisfaction. These don't bode well and need to be dealt with before they get out of hand. Similarly, if the gradual decline in satisfaction continues beyond the first three or four years, you ought to take action: in relationships that are going to stay happy, dissatisfaction levels out after the first couple of years. It is worth noting that men and women may define relationship satisfaction differently: men look mainly at the quality of the relationship; women also take into account how well they interact with other people as a couple.

do virgins do it better?

One of the most important elements of relationship satisfaction (and, therefore of course, commitment) is sexual satisfaction. In the West, this began to be openly acknowledged about 70 or 80 years ago, when virginity in women was still highly valued. Later, in the 1960s, when Western girls in large numbers began sleeping openly with their boyfriends, the whisper was that immoral as this was, it might at least help courting couples discover whether or not they were sexually compatible. What was meant by this? A similar enthusiasm for sex was implied, but many people also thought that for sex to be satisfactory the actual physical fit of the partners' genitals was crucial. This made sexual satisfaction in marriage a serious lottery for the pre-maritally chaste, since they couldn't test for this physical fit until *after* they'd said 'I do'. This *sexual* compatibility was believed to be quite separate from *relationship* compatibility.

Today, the idea of delaying sex until after marriage is again becoming popular, driven partly by nostalgia, partly by fear of AIDS and partly by a belief that if people don't have sex before marriage, they're less likely to be unfaithful afterwards. Attractive as this notion may be (to some) it is seriously misguided: if young Westerners were to insist on embracing virginity, it's probable our divorce-rate would rise. That's partly because sexual incompetence would increase, and this would lead to widespread sexual unhappiness. When divorce was considered shameful and was hard to come by, sexually miserable people often suffered in silence. Now that divorce is relatively simple, they leave.

Another reason that widespread sexual misery would be guaranteed if virginity were again to be heavily promoted is that it would bring together couples who were genuinely ill-suited sexually. That's because virginity always ends up being seen as more of an issue for women than for men. Many of the women who manage to hang on to their virginity (and so are rated as high value) can only do so because, by nature or upbringing, they aren't very interested in sex. Starting sex late is, for women, quite a strong indicator that it will not be hugely important to them in later life, while one of the major predictors that women will really enjoy sex and rate it important, is that they start being sexually active relatively young.

Unlike the high value (often sexually indifferent) virgin female, the high value male is unlikely to be a virgin. In fact, due to looks, cash and (often) charisma he will probably be unusually sexually experienced. So when the two get together the resulting mismatch often leads to a partnership that is not very physical. When there are a lot of these around (as was the case in Victorian England) this triggers the

SEX TALK ...

Couples who are on the same *wavelength* and who like to *organize their lives* in similar ways (but who are not *sexually well-matched*) will only be happy if sex is unimportant to both partners. Because, otherwise, they will feel that life is passing them by.

HAMBURG

expectation that men will 'get what they need' through infidelity. In Japan, where virginity has traditionally been highly prized (to the extent that there's been quite a trade in 'sewing women up again') 70–80% of married men surveyed in the 1980s had had sex with women other than their wives.

Nowadays in most communities in the West both sexes are allowed to be sexually skilled before they settle down. This has led to less anxiety about sex in marriage and, in a sense, to less focus on it. There is now more concern with the quality of other aspects of the couple's relationship. In fact, the pendulum can be said to have swung too far, with too little investigation often carried out into what's going on (or not going on) in the bedroom. So total has this turnaround been, that in the US, Europe and Australia there's a shortage of recent major sex-behaviour surveys, while many books tackling relationship issues barely mention sex at all.

This is surprising, even alarming, given that one of the two main predictors of a relationship lasting (and lasting happily) is how sexually satisfied the partners are. This holds good for both men and women, and for every kind of couple – gay, straight, married or cohabiting. Where sex is not a happy experience, partners will generally describe their relationship as unhappy; and when they say they have a good relationship they will mostly say that their sex life is good too. While there can be good sex in a bad relationship, consistently bad sex in a good relationship is less common, and one of America's leading relationship specialists believes that without a sexual relationship that is satisfying to both partners, very few Western couples today will stay together.

Whether you'll find sex satisfying can be heavily influenced by both when and where you live. Two out of ten Japanese women in stable relationships have never experienced orgasm during intercourse, compared with one in ten such women in the West. Here the 'sexual revolution' has done a lot for both the sexes. Even by 1970, couples of all ages were

> **SEX TALK …**
>
> Couples who are *sexually well-matched* and are on the same *wavelength* but who like to *organize their lives* in different ways will often have tempestuous but long-lasting relationships.
>
> **HAMBURG**

> **SEX TALK …**
>
> Couples who are *sexually well-matched* and like to *organize their lives* in similar ways (but who are not on the same *wavelength*) can be happy if they do not expect deep companionship from each other.
>
> **HAMBURG**

having sex around once a fortnight more than their equivalents in the early 1940s. And things have gone on improving: Finnish researchers, who in 1971 had asked men and women how much they enjoyed intercourse and how satisfying their relationships and their sex lives were, found a 1992 sample happier and more satisfied in every category. There had also been a gender catch-up, with the women in 1992 as generally satisfied with sex as the men (though still not quite as likely to describe the last time they had sex as being pleasurable).

Since achieving satisfaction is closely connected with what your expectations (and comparison with previous lovers is inevitable), sex needs to be as fulfilling and exciting as *you know you are capable of having*. This requires a kind of brutal honesty. If sex with your current partner is markedly less inspiring than sex you have enjoyed with someone else *over a sustained period of time* this bodes badly for the future of your new relationship, particularly if sex is very important to you. That said, even the most wonderful sexual connection will not be enough if the other major areas of compatibility are missing.

Sexual comparison based on what you think sex *should* be like (rather than on how you have actually experienced it) causes a surprising amount of trouble. People whose sexual expectations are very high report a lot of sexual dissatisfaction whoever they are with. Most couples with sexual problems have too many requirements for a sexual experience to be 'right'. Most couples with sexual problems have too many requirements for a sexual experi-

> **SEX TALK ...**
>
> Couples who are *sexually well-matched* but are on different *wavelengths* and like to *organize their lives* in different ways will become so irritated with each other on a daily basis that even sex will gradually become impossible.
>
> **HAMBURG**

ence to be 'right'. They often believe that sex should only arise out of love and won't have sex when they're feeling exhausted, unhappy, angry or distant. In fact, since sexual arousal produces a powerful hormone, oxyciton, which encourages humans to form strong emotional bonds, love often arises out of sex and the chances of having highly erotic or romantic sex increases when we're prepared, at other times, to have less than perfect sex: half-hearted sex, tired sex, dutiful sex, silly sex, tension-releasing sex, sad sex, angry sex, and so on. As the experts put it: Couples who allow themselves a wide range of sexual expression have fewer conflicts and better relationships.

To experience your sex life as satisfying you don't have to experience it as deeply amazing and wonderful. You only have to experience it as not

TEST 17:
SEX BELIEFS 1
(STRAIGHT RELATIONSHIPS)

You must be ruthlessly honest which of these statements rings a bell with you, even if you'd say they were absurd. Score each of them individually, and enter the scores on page 143-4. Your partner may like to do the same.

6	5	4	3	2	1
True		Maybe			False

1 For great sex, all that's really needed is a big penis
2 A woman who doesn't want sex doesn't love you
3 A man won't fancy you if your body's full of flaws
4 Hard-driving sex is the most likely to send women wild
5 Weakness, fear and vulnerability aren't acceptable in men
6 The man should always take charge of sex, and orchestrate it
7 Real men want sex all the time, and are always ready to perform
8 Cuddling, hugging, kissing, holding and caressing are mainly for paving the way to sex
9 A 'real' woman wants less sex than her partner
10 When sex is good, it flows naturally: there's no need to correct or explain

*dis*satisfying. For this reason, *low* sexual expectations aren't necessarily a problem, as long as both partners have them. In China, as in the rest of the world, sexual satisfaction for both men and women is strongly linked to how often they 'do it', how much foreplay there is and how consistently they achieve orgasm. Since foreplay and female orgasm are somewhat lacking in China, the relatively high levels of sexual satisfaction reported by Chinese women greatly surprised Western researchers, until they realized that state propaganda had been describing sex as unpleasant, presumably in an attempt to keep China's birth rate down. In light of this, the women's 'satisfaction' can be seen less as an expression of sexual rapture than surprised relief. 'Sexual satisfaction,' writes one researcher, 'is found where sexual expectations are met.'

sexual synergy

Does sexual *compatibility* exist? If so, what does it consist of and what part does it play in sexual *satisfaction*? Researchers have found answers to these questions, and the first idea they've knocked on the head is the old notion of sexual compatibility as some kind of miraculous genital 'fit' which will be revealed (or not) on your wedding night.

Sexually experienced women will sometimes tell you they've found achieving orgasm during intercourse especially easy with a particular partner, their theories as to why ranging from 'my clitoris seemed to rub against him' to 'he smelt right' to 'I was totally in love' to 'I didn't like him so I wasn't worrying about *him* at all' (women who feel powerful and in control

THE LOVE QUIZ

TEST 18: SEX GAMES

Rate each statement below as it applies to you. Enter your responses on page 144. Now get your partner to do the same.

10	9	8	7	6	5	4	3	2	1
Must have				**Really like**			**Can enjoy**		

As part of a sexual relationship I like to:

(a)   give oral sex

(b)   receive oral sex

(c)   engage in mutual masturbation

(d)   have sex in lots of different positions

(e)   have sex in lots of different places

(f)   dress up/have my partner dress up in sexual outfits

(g)   use sex toys

(h)   look at (or listen to) mainstream erotic images or stories

(i)   look at (or listen to) hard-core erotic images or stories

(j)   talk about my sexual fantasies

(k)   act out my sexual fantasies

(l)   have heterosexual sex outside my main relationship

(m)   have homosexual sex outside my main relationship

(n)   have group/triadic sex

(o)   take part in sado/masochism

(p)   cross-dress

TEST 19:
READY FOR MONOGAMY?

Rate each statement below as it applies to you. Enter the total in the box on Page 144. Now get your partner to do the same.

6	5	4	3	2	1
True		Neutral		Not true	

1 I've found it easy to stay faithful to a partner

2 I feel I've done enough and seen enough sexually

3 I don't have a strong wish to have sex with more people before I settle down

4 Long-term sex with a previous partner has not been more rewarding than sex with my current partner

5 With my current partner, I feel I'm getting what I need sexually

6 The idea of never having sex with anyone else for the rest of my life doesn't bother me.

are often highly orgasmic). This is as may be (and it's noticeable that many of these theories have nothing to do with physical fit and everything to do with 'relationship') but the sexual compatibility the researchers have uncovered is of a different kind. They've discovered that 'chemistry' apart (see later) a good sexual match has as much to do with how you think and feel about sex *in general* as with how you think and feel about sex with a *particular partner*. This means that many couples could get a fairly good idea of how sexually compatible they'd be without actually laying a finger on each other (as long as they'd laid a few fingers on other people, and so were aware of their own likes and dislikes).

In *sexual* compatibility, as in the compatibility dimensions covered in Chapter 2, similarity rules. Partners who are generally similar (in background, personality, interests, values, etc.) also tend to be the most satisfied sexually. As for sexual *attitudes*, *interest* in sex and *taste* in sexual activities, when these are similar, partners not only get more satisfaction, they also tend to get more horny more often and to enjoy oral sex more. As with other kinds of couple similarities, it may not be so much that sexual similarities boost sexual interest as that sexual differences erode it.

An important issue for sexual compatibility (that is, lots of sexual satisfaction and few complaints) is how ready both partners are for *monogamy*. Satisfaction with your sexual relationship (as with any kind of relationship) depends on the ratio of benefits to costs. The benefits of having sex only with your live-in partner have to be offset against the costs of forsaking all others. If you don't find that difficult you will see your relationship as rewarding. If you do, then however well you and your partner get on and however sexually compatible you are, you will still be dissatisfied.

An excellent predictor of sexual compatibility is how well a couple communicate *about sex*. Communicating well about sex functions as an aphrodisiac: it leads to more sex, to more satisfying sex and to more orgasms. Women who communicate well about sex are rated sexually compatible with a greater number of partners. Communicating well about sex isn't as usual as you might think, for although most people say they wish their partner would tell them what they like, few do. Researchers now think that a lot of so-called sexual incompatibility may really be failure to communicate about sex. For example, it's quite common for women who've recently been pregnant to feel self-conscious about having put on weight, and so they either avoid sex or seem half-hearted about it. Unaware of the real reason, their partners tend to read their reluctance as meaning 'she's gone off me' and either withdraw sexually themselves or continue to press resentfully for sex. After a while, one partner (and it's usually the woman) may conclude that, as a couple, they are sexually incompatible.

Nor is it communication just *about sex* that matters: couples who communicate well in other ways have better sex in the long term (though not necessarily early on in their relationships). This suggests that if people who've undergone communication skills training at work were to apply the techniques at home, their sex lives (along with their career prospects) might improve.

SEX FACTS

COMMUNICATION SKILLS THAT LEAD TO BETTER SEX INCLUDE:

- expressing affection
- resolving conflict
- solving problems
- revealing personal information
- revealing your feelings
- asking for what you want and need
- giving praise
- giving constructive feedback

TEST 20:
SEX COMFORT

Rate each statement below as it applies to you. Enter the total in the box on page 145. Now get your partner to do the same.

6	5	4	3	2	1
Not true		**Neutral**		**True**	

1 When it comes to sex, my ideas and values are very like my partner's

2 I am satisfied with the variety in our sexual life

3 Neither one of us knows much more about sex than the other

4 Neither one of us is greatly more interested in sex than the other

5 I can talk easily with my partner about what appeals to me sexually

6 I feel comfortable during sex with my partner

7 My partner and I rarely argue about sex

Another major area of sexual compatibility is how *comfortable* both partners feel about sex. Most people become sexually more at ease as they get older, but some are pretty easy to start with and others have loads of sex yet never really feel comfortable. 'Sexual comfort' levels stem from a mix of things: personality, past lovers, religion, the media and (above all) how parents felt about sex – if talking about it was discouraged or just not done, and parents had a traditional 'she cares/he earns' relationship and believed in strict discipline, you are very likely to feel uncomfortable about sex. This is a shame since discomfort (or guilt) about sex strongly predicts that sexual relationships will not be happy, while feeling sexually at ease not only increases enjoyment but can actually *boost self-esteem* – and as we've already noted, people with high self-esteem are more likely to make a success of love.

Difference in partners' sexual comfort levels is dangerous since it leads to sexual loneliness and resentment. The sexually comfortable partner feels frustrated, disappointed and deprived; their sexually uncomfortable mate feels pressurized, guilty and inadequate. Small differences can be fine, as long as the less comfortable partner is reasonably comfortable. But if one partner is seriously uncomfortable about sex (or about an aspect of it that's important to their mate) then it's best if the other is too. They may not have a great sex life by other people's standards, but they will both feel *safe*.

feeling you – feeling me – feeling good

Linked with sexual comfort is *sexual adventurousness*. Although sexually adventurous couples have more and better sex, similarity is, once again, more important. How sexually adventurous someone will be can often be figured out from their general attitudes: sex in the missionary position is more likely when a woman feels she has little power in the relationship, the couple have traditional ideas about men's and women's roles and/or the woman is physically not very attractive (as rated by herself and her partner). A major reason that a woman's weight gain can be bad for a couple's sex life is that it often makes her less willing to engage in adventurous sex. Men tend to be more sexually adventurous than women, so it comes as no surprise to learn that sexually adventurous women are rated sexually compatible with more men.

The ultimate in sexual adventurousness is open marriage. Although couples who are more relaxed about infidelity are more likely to break up than couples who are not, the higher break-up rate among couples in open marriages (32% versus 18%) seems mainly to be related to the kinds of people they are – less conventional, more sexually experienced before they got together, and so on. In fact, among married couples who've been together longer than two years, an agreement (spoken or unspoken) that, under certain circumstances, one or both partners may have 'outside' sex is *not* a predictor that the relationship will break up. This is not the case among lesbians and cohabitors, for whom such an agreement predicts break-up at all stages. For all couples, outside sex in

---

SEX FACTS
SEXUAL ADVENTUROUSNESS

- 2–4% of married couples have engaged in 'swinging'
- fewer than half of these have done it regularly
- 9 out of 10 straight couples have oral sex
- 50% of (married) couples experiment sexually some of the time
- 2 out of 5 bath or shower together
- 1 in 10 tries anal sex
- 1 in 5 swims nude together, watches X-rated videos, buys sex-toys or sexy underwear or makes love out-of-doors

the first two years bodes very badly, particularly when the person having it is male.

In established open marriages, jealousy doesn't seem to be a major problem (nor is it a big deal for most of the four out of five gay males who have outside sex). When it does become a problem, most of the open marrieds stop having outside sex (although a few continue secretly). What people say and what they do isn't always related – couples who approve of open marriage don't always do it, while many couples who don't approve of the idea, do.

Swinging (where a couple has outside sex together, with another single or pair) seems to be a truly shared activity. Swingers go on picnics and on vacation with other swingers, and swinging can definitely improve their sex lives. However, about half of all swinging couples only try it once or twice, and it has its dark side: feelings of jealousy, inadequacy, guilt and rejection are common; and sexual problems and divorce can follow. A big danger of having sex regularly outside your main relationship is that it can cause you to disassociate sexual arousal from your partner so that home gradually becomes a sex-free zone. This often seems to happen among the many gay couples who have a lot of outside sex.

To understand why the de-sexing of love can be so dangerous, we need properly to understand what sex is *for.* Around 80% of both men and women report that when they first have sex with someone this tends to boost their feelings of love; and the more they like the person before they have sex, the more their loving feelings are boosted by it. Among men, even generalized sexual arousal can heighten loving feelings. When researchers handed one group an erotic story to read (and others a relatively dull essay on the mating behaviour of herring gulls) those who read the erotic story gave their regular partners higher marks in both 'love' and 'liking' immediately afterwards.

One reason people focus so much on sex is that it's the way our species reproduces itself. However, there's more to it than that. We are powerfully drawn to experiences that make us feel good, and sex delivers multiple 'feel goods', both bodily (through physical pleasure and release) and emotionally (as we disclose to another human being a part of ourselves we normally hide). Associating such experiences with our partner boosts our positive regard for them, and when sex goes

SOME 'FEEL GOODS' DELIVERED BY SATISFYING SEX

● satisfying sex helps partners feel *loved and valued*

● satisfying sex helps partners feel *competent* (if you feel you are a good lover you often feel you're a good partner in other ways)

● satisfying sex helps partners feel in *control* (i.e. that if they hit a bad patch they'll be able to get back on track)

● satisfying sex helps couples feel *emotionally close*

● satisfying sex helps people see their partner as *supportive*: in fact, how *supportive* you believe your partner to be is more closely linked to satisfying sex than to anything else — even how s/he behaves towards you during a fight

AWOL, so does an important way of feeling good. *Not* having sex at home also removes a major source of shared activity: sex counts as one of the *shared leisure activities* mentioned in Chapter 2 which help keep relationships on track.

One way of spotting whether a relationship is happy is to count the expression of 'feel goods' each partner directs towards the other in the form of appreciative words, actions, looks, touches, smiles and so on. When things are going well, partners will give out no fewer than five of these positives to every one negative (sneer, sigh, frown, etc.). Interestingly, this is the same ratio that builds self-esteem: people with high self-esteem see themselves as having one failure to five successes, as they go through life. Among couples who have been together for some years, a low level of positives is a bigger indicator than anything else that the partnership is on the way out.

This means that if you want to stay happy you have to think more about making your partner feel good, than about not fighting with them. Not fighting can mean you are not engaging, and a middle path seems to be ideal: while lots of arguments (about sex and other things) are associated with less satisfaction and with less satisfying sex, many couples who *never* argue about sex have no sex at all. One rather interesting, and surprisingly accurate, way of establishing how happy a couple are together, is to count the number of times they have sex over a particular period, and deduct from it the number of arguments they have. When there are more sexual events than arguments, the couple will rate as happy.

THE LOVE QUIZ

TEST 21:
SEXUAL SATISFACTION

Rate each statement below as it applies to you. Enter the total in the box on Page 145. Now get your partner to do the same.

6	5	4	3	2	1
True		Neutral		Not true	

1 The chemistry between us is right
2 I find my partner sexually attractive
3 I feel attractive to my partner
4 My partner makes it clear that s/he enjoys sex with me
5 I am satisfied with the intensity of our sexual connection
6 On the whole, I'm satisfied with how often we have sex
7 Within this relationship, I can enjoy my favourite ways of having sex
8 I usually feel fulfilled and relaxed after sex with my partner
9 When either of us refuses sex, it's generally not a problem
10 Although I enjoy sexual fantasies, I don't think seriously about having sex with other people
11 Masturbation is a pleasant addition to our sexual life

getting satisfaction

How important to sexual satisfaction is physical *release*? It is often assumed that women don't care much about this. Indeed, one probable reason lesbian couples have relatively little sex is that partners may not take their own, or their lover's, need for orgasm seriously enough to feel obliged to work on the sexual connection.

In fact, while women (like men) give emotional closeness as an important reason for having sex, women of all ages also name physical release as a major (often *the* major) sexual motive. Women's orgasm even plays a part in keeping couples together. Women who rarely have orgasms with their primary partner, very often regard both their sexual relationship and their wider relationship as dissatisfying. The more *reliable* and *frequent* women's orgasms are, the more satisfied they tend to be with their sex lives and with their relationships. Orgasm doesn't have to occur through intercourse (70–80% of women have trouble regularly achieving orgasm through intercourse alone) but women are actually more likely than men to say that satisfying sex helps them feel happy with their relationship, and that unsatisfying sex damages it. Giving up on sex is a bad strategy: an especially strong link between good sex and good love is made by lesbians and by cohabiting straight couples (both the men and the women).

How important is sexual release to men? The way some people talk would make you think orgasm is all they are ever in it for. In fact, only men under 25 name physical release as their primary reason for seeking sex. Above this age 'showing love for partner' becomes men's main motive. This is more than mere words: the most powerful predictor of how often a couple will have sex is the man's *feelings of love* for his partner. Since most men can take orgasm for granted (just 0.2% of men never orgasm, and three out of four men, compared with only one out of four women, achieve orgasm every time) orgasm itself isn't such a marker of the 'joy of sex' for men. Despite almost universal orgasm, only 48% of males declare themselves usually physically extremely pleased with sex with their mate.

Do men need their *partners* to have regular orgasms? Certainly men (like women) enjoy seeing their lovers have a good time, and men whose mates orgasm easily and often tend to regard their sexual relationships as particularly rewarding. However, it's our own (rather than our partner's) orgasm that really concerns us, neither men nor women find sex *dis*satisfying if their partner doesn't climax regularly, as long as he or she seems

---

SEX FACTS

FEMALE ORGASM AND SEXUAL SATISFACTION

● women who achieve their first orgasm after their male partner report less satisfaction than women who achieve it before or simultaneously with him

● multiply orgasmic women are not especially satisfied with their sexual relationship

● in the US, African American women (38%) and Hispanic women (34%) are more regularly orgasmic than white women (26%)

● in both Finland and the US, high-school educated women are more regularly orgasmic than college-educated women or women who did not complete high school

● 40% of women declare themselves usually physically extremely pleased with sex with their primary partner

ORAL SEX AND SEXUAL SATISFACTION

● heterosexual men who give and receive oral sex are happier with their sex lives than those who don't

● gay men also like oral sex, but it's not such a marker of a happy sex life

● lesbians who give and receive oral sex are more satisfied with their sex life *and their relationship* than those who don't

● heterosexual women who give oral sex are more likely to be sexually compatible with their partners

happy about it. So perhaps women don't need to fake it nearly as often as they think they do.

The way relationship satisfaction and sexual satisfaction are linked isn't a one-way street, it's a loop. Although relationship problems are more likely to cause sexual problems than the other way around, tension and arguing both spring from, and result in, little or no sex. Good sex is often linked to a sense of fairness. People who feel they are getting as much (or more) out of a relationship as they are putting in report more relationship satisfaction, more sexual satisfaction and more sex. This is why women are often heard to say 'if he'd clean the toilet, I might think about sex'.

Couples also use sex as a *measure* of how well their relationship is going (middle-class couples in particular see satisfying sex as proof that they are close). So when sex isn't satisfying (or isn't happening) irritation and anger may arise as much from fear that the relationship is in trouble, as from physical frustration. And when your partner gets on your nerves for other reasons, sexual problems suddenly start to matter: you are most likely to blame your partner for too little sex when you're also blaming them for other things. While even happy-together couples regularly report sexual difficulties or sluggish sex lives, the difference between happy and unhappy couples is that unhappy couples report more (and more upsetting) sexual problems more of the time.

The most striking finding from all this is that, for both sexes, love and sex are thoroughly intertwined. To say that women want love while men want sex doesn't accord with the clear findings that, in committed relationships, love is fed by sex, and sex is fed by love. It's interesting that older couples who aren't having intercourse often have regular episodes of sexualized caressing and cuddling – an important acknowledgement that the physical side of a relationship contributes in a major way to the love connection.

Research also shows that men and women are turned on by pretty much the same things. Given that anxiety is such an aphrodisiac, it's no surprise to learn that both sexes are aroused by the forbidden both in reality and in fantasy. No one should feel guilty about that: it's the way people are made. Also, most people almost always fantasize while they're having sex and about 50% of men and women report *never* having fantasies that include their partner. That doesn't mean that people really want to do outrageous sexual things (wanting to fantasize about them is very different from wanting to do them) or to have sex

MEN'S SEXUAL COMPLAINTS

In unhappy relationships:
- his partner is not very enthusiastic (54%)
- sex is too infrequent (44%)
- his partner does not always achieve orgasm (40%)
- his partner achieves orgasm too slowly (40%)

In happy relationships:
- his partner is not very enthusiastic (21%)
- sex is too infrequent (21%)
- his partner does not always achieve orgasm (26%)
- his partner achieves orgasm too slowly (27%)

WOMEN'S SEXUAL COMPLAINTS

In unhappy relationships:
- there is not enough foreplay (42%)
- he ejaculates too quickly(39%)
- her partner wants sex too often (28%)
- there is not enough tenderness during sex (27%)

In happy relationships:
- there is not enough foreplay (9%)
- he ejaculates too quickly (23%)
- her partner wants sex too often (23%)

N.B. In happy relationships it is never reported that there is not enough tenderness during sex.

with lots of people (both sexes experience monogamous sex as the most satisfying) but it does suggest that if sex is to remain satisfying in the long term, you can't rely on love or romance to get you going: erotic sex needs to be a focus in itself, within the general framework of a loving relationship.

It used to be thought that women were sexually aroused by romance and men by impersonal sex (Erica Jong's 'zipless fuck') but properly conducted experiments now show that women do not respond *sexually* to romance. Women who emphasize affection and closeness as their motive for sex actually report low sex interest, low frequency of arousal and low enjoyment of sex. Both sexes are aroused by erotic materials, and are most aroused by erotic materials combined with a touch of romance (the zipless fuck with just a hint of the personal). For women, saying they want sex for affection and closeness may actually be code for saying they are not very interested in sex.

One last surprise finding about sex is the role physical attractiveness plays in how satisfying people find sex. In Chapter 1 we pointed out that physical beauty was *the* major attractor for both women and men. Indeed, one in six men (gay and straight) and almost one in ten straight women (but few lesbians) actually tell researchers that 'movie star' good looks in a partner are important to them. Yet while many more people are happier with their sex lives when they rate their partner very attractive, an astonishing number are perfectly content even when they rate their partner seriously *un*attractive.

One partner wanting more sex than the other is the most common reason couples rate themselves sexually incompatible. How often people want sex can vary enormously, because their levels of sexual desire are affected by all kinds of things. Some are permanent (e.g. your personality),

SEX SURPRISES...

● around 4 out of 5 people (gay, straight, men, women) are satisfied with the quality of their sex life when they rate their partner *very attractive*

● around 2 out of 3 people (gay, straight, men, women) are satisfied with the quality of their sex life when they rate their partner *moderately attractive*

● around half of all people (gay, straight, men, women) are satisfied with the quality of their sex life even when they rate their partner *unattractive*

● gay men and women who think others see them as less good looking than their partner fight more *about sex*

WHO WANTS IT?

● in the US blacks, whites, Protestants and Catholics have sex about as often as each other

● Hispanics and people with no religious beliefs have sex slightly more often in the US

● college-educated people have less frequent sex than high-school-educated people.

● men who never completed high school have the least sex of all, whatever their race

● couples who have sex within one month of meeting have sex almost twice as often *when they are living together later* as couples who waited six months or more for sex

but many are temporary (e.g. how sad or happy you feel). And while personal stuff (such as your attitudes or physical health) affect your sex interest, so does relationship stuff (how similar you are to your partner; how well you are getting on, etc.). Nor is *desiring* sex the only reason people *suggest* it. They propose (and refuse) sex for all kinds of reasons: to keep the peace, to reward (or punish) a partner, to dominate them, to bribe them, to stop them leaving or because they believe that sex helps keep the relationship on track.

Although the same person can have sex more frequently with one partner than with the next, everyone has a base-rate of sexual interest that they tend towards and which remains fairly similar from one relationship to another. A person who has experienced low sexual desire with one lover will often end up, after an early sexual flurry, equally sexually lethargic with the next. Since most couples have enthusiastic sex when they first get together, a mismatch in desire levels won't be immediately obvious. At that stage most people are getting *enough* sex, and only the man's dissatisfaction with the *quality* of the sex should be seen as signifying trouble ahead.

gender tending

A good match between a couple's sex interest is central to sexual compatibility and this is becoming increasingly important as women feel more comfortable about sex. There's evidence that women adjust their desire levels to suit their partner, but the adjustment has to be pretty mild or there'll be trouble later. Difference in sex interest causes the most grief when the woman's sex interest is the stronger, both because it's physically more difficult for her uninterested male partner to perform, and because (as in other areas of life) desires that go against the social grain cause the most ructions.

A man whose (female) partner doesn't enjoy sex a great deal or want it as often as he does may feel frustrated and angry but he won't have to feel insecure about *himself*. He can shrug and say 'women are like that'. Similarly, although his less-sexual partner can feel invaded or even disgusted, she can feel OK about *herself* and say 'men are like that'. But when the tables are turned, there can be shame as well as frustration: he fearing he's not a 'proper man'; she that she's an 'animal'.

Overall (and particularly when they are young) men are more concerned with sex than women: they pay more attention to sexual things; they masturbate more often; and, as teenagers, are aroused several times a day and more intensely and distractingly than teenage girls (who report arousal only a couple of times a week). Gay male couples have sex more often than all other couples; and at all relationship stages lesbian couples have sex less often than all other couples.

THE LOVE QUIZ

TEST 22:
SEX BELIEFS 2

Rate each statement below as it accords with your beliefs. Enter the total in the box on Page 145. Now get your partner to do the same.

6	5	4	3	2	1
False		Neutral		True	

1 It's natural for men to want sex more than women
2 It's OK to use sex to punish or reward your partner
3 Sex when either partner is angry or upset is a bad idea
4 Sex when either partner doesn't feel like it is a bad idea
5 Sex should only happen when the woman really wants it
6 Sex has been a failure if both partners are not totally satisfied
7 Sex between committed partners should always be loving, erotic and special
8 If either partner masturbates between sex, it means that their sex life isn't satisfactory

WHO DOESN'T WANT IT?

● while 40% of *young* women report periodic absence of sexual desire, so do 28% of *young* men

● among cohabiting couples 43% of women (22% of men) say they are the partner more likely to refuse sex

● when men want more sex than their partners, they only (on average) want it once or twice a month more

However, it would be wrong to put this down simply to women being less sexual. Sexual abuse can lead to low sexual desire – and many lesbians have been sexually abused. And the common belief that *'nice girls don't want sex'* can cause gay women (and straight women, too) to feel uncomfortable about pushing for sex even when they'd like to. If infrequent sex really were what women want, lesbian women should be ecstatic. They aren't: most complain bitterly.

Men's apparently greater sex interest is very much age related: by middle age, women want sex as much as men; in older age they are sometimes *more* interested in sex. And, recently, even the existing desire gap between younger men and women seems to be closing. Over the last 40 years, Western women have been wanting more sex, having more sex, masturbating more often and enjoying more orgasms. Researchers who studied Canadian students on a beach holiday found that similar percentages of girls (13%) and boys (15%) had casual sex. The only difference

SAYING 'YES' ... SAYING 'NO'

● women refuse sex more often than men, but this is mainly because men ask for sex more often than women

● the *ratio* of sex refusals is the same for women and men: i.e. both sexes refuse the same percentage of sex-requests

● men are more upset by sex refusal than women

● women are more upset by sex demands than men

● partners who refuse sex about equally are happier together and have more (and more satisfying) sex

● when the man refuses more often than the woman, the relationship is heading for trouble

was *why*: the boys who had casual sex had gone on holiday with plans to have it but among the girls it was more a spur-of-the-moment thing (but not because they were seduced). Girls were most likely to have casual sex if their girlfriends did.

The idea that men, compared to women, are sex obsessed may partly stem from the fact that women's desire often goes unrecognized – even by themselves. When men listen to erotic tapes while wired up to arousal-measuring machines (which chart pulse rate, skin moisture and so on) they don't need to check the machines to know when they're turned on, but although women wired up in the same way and exposed to pornography become as physically excited as men, they can be astonished when the machines reveal the truth. Another reason women may fail to notice their own desire is that because men tend to initiate sex, many women may get it before they really want it (a bit like eating before you're properly hungry), and so may rarely experience intense sexual longing.

start-ups

Is sex always instigated by the person with the higher sex drive and refused by the partner with the lower sex drive? No. It's often initiated by a more *expressive* partner (who is warm, emotional and aware of other people's feelings) and refused by a more *powerful* partner (the richer or better-loved – being better-loved always gives you power). Research shows consistently that when at least one partner is highly expressive, the outlook for the relationship is improved: one reason may be that the expressive partner takes care of the couple's sex life.

A big imbalance in power is very bad for sexual satisfaction. While less powerful partners are reluctant to refuse sex (they may feel that to refuse

---

SEX SURPRISES

WHY MEN AND WOMEN DON'T WANT SEX IS BECAUSE THEY ARE:

● too tired (most common)
● not feeling well (second most common)
● feeling tense or preoccupied (third most common)
● angry with their partner (fourth most common)

SEX IN THE FIRST TWO YEARS

Three times a week or more:

- 67% of gay male couples
- 61% of cohabiting heterosexual couples
- 45% of married couples
- 33% of lesbians

Between one and three times a week:

- 27% of gay male couples
- 31% of cohabiting heterosexual couples
- 38% of married couples
- 43% of lesbians

Once a month or less:

- 3% of gay male couples
- 1% of cohabiting heterosexual couples
- 6% of married couples
- 5% of lesbians

is not an option) this doesn't mean they initiate it. They tend to express little or no interest in sex. In fact people who feel dominated or overwhelmed by their partners often develop chronic low sexual desire. However, some researchers have pointed out that the partner who is least interested in sex gets extra power through not needing it because their partner has to ask. These researchers suggest that women's general powerlessness relative to men's may have caused them over the centuries to suppress sexual desire in order to gain a bit more power.

Why do sexually uninterested partners agree to sex? Sometimes they use it as a bargaining chip, sometimes because giving in is easier than having a fight and sometimes because they fear that if they refuse, their mate will look elsewhere. Among heterosexual couples who have been together a long time, women agree to sex when they quite strongly don't want it about 25% of the time, men 15% of the time. People rarely enjoy sex if their partner engages in it unwillingly, particularly if their attitude is 'all right, but you'll have to do all the work'. However, sex can be surprising: in about one fifth of cases where one partner wasn't keen, they ended up turned on and having a good time after all.

How often do couples have sex? Sexual frequency at the time of marriage or setting up home together is on average just over four times per week. That frequency should be reckoned to be about double your *long-term base rate*. This is because, over the next 12 months (that is, over the first year of settled domestic life) the amount of sex couples have will almost certainly *halve*. On average this will mean sex settling down to about twice a week, although many couples will do it more (and many less) often.

The good news is that it's not downhill all the way from here – or, at least, not yet. After that first year the average fairly happy couple find the decline in how often they have sex slowing down. In fact, allowing for the sexual ups and downs associated with having children, falling ill and coping with other major other life events, sexual frequency should take a full *20 years* to halve again, from whatever its level was at the end of that first domestic year. Therefore on average this means that, 20 years on, sex will have dropped to an average of once a week. Again, there'll be many couples who are more (and less) sexually active than this.

Why does sex drop off so quickly, for *all* couples, at the very beginning?Boredom doesn't seem a likely explanation as at this stage partnerships have been on the go for months, not years; however, physical habituation almost certainly plays a part. Familiarity with anything makes your senses shut down slightly; and as you feel safer and more at ease with a partner your anxiety levels drop. Both of these will lead to lower levels of physical arousal, which you will experience as reduced sexual desire.

When one partner begins an affair or behaves rejectingly, it is common for the rejected partner to feel sexually aroused and, if they have been experiencing low sexual desire, for this to vanish overnight. If the couple get back together again, sex may even become, for a while, as frantic and

SEX AFTER 10 YEARS

Three times a week or more:
- 11% of gay male couples
- 18% of married heterosexual couples
- 1% of lesbian couples

Between one and three times a week:
- 34% of gay male couples
- 45% of married heterosexual couples
- 26% of lesbian couples

Less than once a month:
- 33% of gay male couples
- 15% of heterosexual couples
- 47% of lesbian couples

LOW SEXUAL DESIRE
OFTEN RESULTS FROM

● physical causes, including illness (particularly if it affects parts of the body seen as sexual), some medications, alcohol and narcotics abuse

● body-self-consciousness, perhaps brought on by weight gain, particularly in women

● traumatic personal history, e.g. sexual abuse

● sexual orientation problems, e.g. operating straight when you're really gay

● unhappiness and depression in men and women

● exhaustion, particularly new mothers

● feeling less loving, for men particularly

● feeling powerless in the relationship, for both men and women

● feeling angry, for both men and women

frequent as when they first met. Given the role anxiety plays in physical arousal, this makes complete sense. But one thing is clear: desire will return to base rate once the emotional stuff has settled down.

The fact that couple sex is just that – sex between a couple – means that it cannot be separated from other couple issues: power, territory, possession, fair trade and so on. These will make themselves felt as the relationship deepens, and may complicate sexual desire. The carefree and *frequent* nature of early sex may in part be due to the fact that such complex issues haven't yet crawled out from under the bed. Also, after the first year or so, you may feel less need to prove yourself sexually, and so may start having sex more in accordance with your genuine levels of interest. It's interesting that while *general* boredom is given as a major reason for terminating *dating* relationships, and three out of four unfaithful men say they started their affair out of sexual boredom at home, sexual boredom is almost never given as the reason for not wanting sex *with our partner*, even when we've been with them for many years.

sex as a barometer

Sex, when properly understood, can be a great relationship barometer. *How much sex you are having* can tell you a lot about how *well you are doing* as a couple. As long as you know what's right for you and what's usual or possible at any life stage, you can use that knowledge to help decide when change in your sexual pattern points to problems and when it doesn't. Any marked variation from the norm (your own norm and, to a lesser extent, other people's) needs to be thoroughly explored and understood: if you are having sex much less often this month than last month or this year than last year, or if sexual problems seem to be on the increase, you need to find out why. For example, low sexual desire often sets in when you are repressing feelings, most commonly anger. It seems that when people repress one type of feeling, other types of feelings (including sexual ones) can also disappear.

What is usual or possible at the different life stages? The most powerful predictor of the amount of sex couples have is not how happy they are (although this is a serious contributing factor); it is age. Younger couples have much more sex than older couples. And though people who get together when they're older have quite a lot of sex to start with (like all those who are newly together), this soon drops back nearer to the level expected for their age. The length of time you have been with your partner also has a big effect: couples who have been together longer have less sex than those who have been together for a shorter time in the same age-bracket.

For obvious reasons, the amount of sex a couple has is largely dictated by the amount the male wants and feels able to have. What an older man will be up for can be quite strongly predicted by how important sex was to him when he was young, and how much of it he had. Another predictor is the couple's *beliefs* about sex and ageing. If occasional sexual difficulties are interpreted as sex winding down then they may give up or become so anxious that real problems do set in. By contrast, if sex problems are regarded as temporary then they'll often pass.

GETTING OLDER

Average number of times a month a married couple has sex:
- ages 19–24: 11.7 times per month

Then gradual reduction e.g. :
- ages 30–34: 8.5 times per month
- ages 50–54: 5.5 times per month

Now sharp reduction e.g.:
- ages 65–69: 2.4 times per month
- ages 75 or older: 0.8 times per month

SEX FACTS

SEX AND SATISFACTION – A 'VIRTUOUS' CIRCLE

- happy couples have sex more often than unhappy couples
- satisfaction with the relationship leads to greater desire for sex
- greater desire for sex leads to making more opportunities for sex
- more frequent sex leads to couples being happier with their relationship
- happy couples have sex more often than unhappy couples

Being unable to get an erection or have an orgasm is *not* part of the normal ageing process and is usually caused by such ills as depression, anxiety, sickness, medication or too much alcohol. Among couples who have been together for some time, sex seems to fall off in fits and starts. A couple may go through a low sex stage because they're worried or tired, or one partner is ill, or they're not getting on well. But when they are feeling better or the relationship has picked up again, the sex may not: they've become used to having less of it. This trend can usually be reversed by a sex 'blitz': consciously doing it a lot over a short period such as a couple of weeks. After this, having sex more often may well become the norm again.

As has been said, emotional closeness is a good predictor of *how satisfying* a couple will find sex. It is also a pretty good predictor of *how often* they'll have sex (the closer they feel, the more likely sex becomes). Next to age, happiness is the best predictor of sexual frequency. For example, couples who agree about money tend to have more sex than the average. But there's a 'ceiling' here: after true intimacy is established, sex doesn't become more frequent and, after the first couple of years, intense togetherness can actually be a sex destroyer. This has been noticed a lot among

SEX FACTS

WHO DOES IT?

- *people in second marriages* have sex more often than people in first marriages (perhaps bad sex first time around causes them to pay more attention to sexual compatibility when they choose their new partner)
- *cohabiting couples* have more sex than married couples, however many years they've been together (perhaps due to the fact that they are more likely to hold liberal views and less likely to feel guilt about sex)

lesbian couples, where those who have no personal space at home, and who share hobbies, activities, belongings, clothes (and even sometimes complete each other's sentences) often have very little sex. Sex may become more frequent once the partners learn to live more separately. However, frequency of sex isn't always linked to how happy a couple are. Violent couples have sex more often than many non-violent couples (the violence may force the sex to take place) but the partners are less satisfied and more likely to split up.

baby business

The frequency with which sex takes place may not make partners *equally* happy. In the first year of marriage, the men *most satisfied* with their sex lives often have the *least sexually satisfied* wives. Perhaps these men are getting sex as often as they want it, but more often than their wives want it. After a baby is born, the tables are turned. Now many women say their sex lives are just fine (maybe it's dropped to a level they feel comfortable with), while the men are more likely to complain that both quantity and quality have slipped badly.

Interestingly, the 'baby effect' on sex may be less than is believed. While new parents are usually exhausted (and often have lacklustre sex), by the time a baby is a year old, most couples are having very little less sex than they were before the pregnancy. They are also having as much sex as couples that have been together for the same length of time *without* having children. However, parents (fathers in particular) *believe* that, due to the children, they are having less sex, which is probably as damaging as if this really were the cause (and, clearly, it sometimes is). Sexual dissatisfaction after childbirth (which is not the same as having very little sex – it means having a great deal less sex or less high quality sex than one or both partners wants) shouldn't be brushed aside but should be regarded as a *serious* relationship issue.

When a woman returns to work soon after a baby is born, is the couple's sex life less satisfying? No. Whether she's a home-maker or is working part-time or full-time how *much* sex the couple has, how *satisfying* they find it and how *little* they want it varies hardly at all. There is one exception to this: new fathers tend to be slightly less satisfied with sex when their partners work 'high full-time' – that is, more than 45 hours a week. Men's sexual satisfaction tends to be linked to how interested their *partner* is in sex, and new mothers' interest in sex isn't much affected by whether they are in paid work. This is because exhaustion is the main cause of their sexual indifference, and home-maker mothers tend to be just as tired as working mothers. A woman's *attitude* to work is a better predictor than *whether* she works or the *time* she spends working, of whether or not she'll enjoy sex. New mothers who are at home full-time but would rather be working (or vice versa) will often find sex unsatisfying.

Men's experience of work is also a massive predictor of their enjoyment of sex, and *quality is more important than quantity.* Men who work more than 45 hours a week have no less (and no less enjoyable) sex than men who work fewer hours unless their long working hours stress them out. Men's sex satisfaction, like women's, suffers when, for *whatever* reason, they find work stressful (including when they don't enjoy it). When both partners work, the most sexually satisfied men tend to be those who enjoy their work *and* have partners who enjoy theirs, while the least satisfied tend to be men who don't like their jobs, but whose partners love theirs.

Among couples in general, one partner being in a very demanding job reduces the amount of sex the couple has, *even if the other isn't work-*

> ## SEX FACTS
> # HOW 'NORMAL' IS NO SEX
> ● 4% of couples aged under 30 had no sex in the previous month
> ● 6% of couples aged 31–35 had no sex in the previous month
> ● 8% of couples aged 36–45 had no sex in the previous month
> ● 10% of couples aged 46–49 had no sex in the previous month
> ● 17% of couples aged 50–54 had no sex in the previous month
> ● 43% of couples aged 65–69 had no sex in the previous month
> ● 73% of couples aged 75 or older had no sex in the previous month

ing. In the main, though, lack of opportunity for sex doesn't hold people back as much as they think. People who really want to have sex find the time, and complaining that they are too busy for sex may often be a smoke screen for relationship difficulties. Nor is it only the DIDS (double-income, double-stress) couples who face this: one survey of *college students* found that 43% said they didn't have enough time for sex.

Most couples in long-term relationships regard gradually diminishing amounts of sex as little cause for alarm and are satisfied with only moderately active sex lives. Infrequent sex can be fine as long as there are good reasons for it, the relationship registers as satisfying in most other areas *and* it's genuinely not an issue for either partner. This is so in gay, as well as straight relationships, and is particularly clear among lesbians in relationships lasting more than ten years. Yet while all that is true, you should never forget that happy couples generally have more sex than unhappy couples and that partners who don't have much sex often fight a lot. Dissatisfaction and fighting *about sex itself* are common in relationships that are going to break up.

love busters

Use these lists differently, depending on whether your relationship is still in the early stages or is deeply entwined (e.g. you have had a child together).

● **Early stages** If five or more of the negative statements below apply to you, think carefully: you will already have some sense of the relationship not being right, and these may help you understand why continuing with it may be a mistake. However, if there are also five or more positive reasons for being together (see Love boosters) then it may be possible to work on some of the negatives.

● **Deeply entwined** No single negative indicator (or even a cluster of negatives) should be taken as a cue to give up on your relationship. The relationship undoubtedly has strengths, or you would not be as deeply connected as you are. Understood in the context of this chapter, the negatives you have picked up on may prompt you to work at these areas, in order to create a more satisfying partnership.

A relationship has a below-average chance when ...
● one person forces the other into a commitment, before they're ready
● one partner is not visibly investing in the relationship
● you are dissatisfied with the relationship (men particularly)
● you are sexual perfectionists
● you become rapidly dissatisfied once you start living together
● after three years, you are still growing more dissatisfied
● one or other partner doesn't feel ready for monogamy
● one or other partner doesn't get their sexual needs met in the relationship
● one partner feels guilty about sex
● you operate an open relationship
● you allow at-home sex to become very infrequent
● the male partner is unfaithful within the first two years
● you report a lot of sexual problems a lot of the time
● you say you mainly like sex 'for affection and closeness' (women)
● the woman's interest in sex is noticeably greater than her male partner's
● the man refuses sex more often than the woman
● sexual refusal is a big deal (either sex)
● sex only or mainly happens because of violence
● you are dissatisfied with your sex lives
● you argue a lot about sex

love boosters

Your relationship has an above-average chance when you ...
● have invested a lot in your shared life
● don't see a better alternative
● find life together highly satisfying
● were sexually and romantically inexperienced before this relationship
● have not had very much better sex in a previous relationship

- have your sexual expectations met in this relationship
- have similar sexual attitudes
- have similar levels of interest in sex
- have similar levels of sexual inhibition
- find your sexual relationship reasonably satisfying
- communicate well about sex
- communicate well about other things
- over a month, fight less often than you have sex
- regularly have orgasms with your partner (women)
- give and receive oral sex (lesbians particularly)
- feel you are getting as much out of the relationship as you are putting in
- feel we are getting more out of the relationship than we are putting in (men)
- sometimes make erotic sex your focus (using fantasy, sex toys, etc.)
- enjoy a wide range of sexual expression
- consider your partner very attractive
- refuse sex about as often as your partner
- feel you have equal influence within your relationship
- when sexual difficulties arise, you regard them as temporary
- have sex more often than the average for your age/stage in life
- give each other space and live independently in some ways (lesbians particularly)
- work out why your sex life has gone off the boil and take steps to remedy the situation (if appropriate)

THE LOVE QUIZ

TEST RESULTS

TEST 14: INVESTMENT

Your partner's total: ▢

Low scores signify commitment. Not all these steps need to have been taken if the relationship is in its early stages. However, a process of commitment needs to be measurable. High scores on four or more topics is cause for concern.

TEST 15: MONEY

Your total: ▢   Your partner's total: ▢

An overall score of 28+ is cause for concern. Remember that disagreements over money often figure in break-up. Disagreements over money often mean that one partner is living for today, one for tomorrow. If you can balance this, you may develop a middle way that is helpful to both partners. Or are disagreements about money really reflecting the fact that you don't have enough of it? Debt counselling may be indicated. If money disagreements are bitter, look for professional help.

TEST 16:
HOW SATISFIED ARE YOU?

Your total: ▢   Your partner's total: ▢

50–60: You won't do better than this.

40–49: Fine, if you both like personal 'space'.

30–39: There are difficulties: look carefully at answers with a very low score.

below 30: You are seriously dissatisfied and probably need professional help.

Be worried if you have low scores on questions 5 and 7, and/or a big difference in scores on any questions

TEST 17:
SEX BELIEFS (1)

1.   Your score: ▢   Your partner's score: ▢
2.   Your score: ▢   Your partner's score: ▢
3.   Your score: ▢   Your partner's score: ▢
4.   Your score: ▢   Your partner's score: ▢
5.   Your score: ▢   Your partner's score: ▢

6.	Your score:		Your partner's score:	
7.	Your score:		Your partner's score:	
8.	Your score:		Your partner's score:	
9.	Your score:		Your partner's score:	
10.	Your score:		Your partner's score:	

These are called 'dysfunctional' beliefs about sex because when they are strongly held by either partner, they can get in the way of satisfying sex. Every one of these statements is dysfunctional, so if your (or your partner's) score is high on any of them, you need to think seriously about where you got the idea, and talk it over with your partner. Three or more dysfunctional beliefs will seriously hamper your sex-life.

TEST 18:
SEX-GAMES

(a)	Your score:		Your partner's score:	
(b)	Your score:		Your partner's score:	
(c)	Your score:		Your partner's score:	
(d)	Your score:		Your partner's score:	
(e)	Your score:		Your partner's score:	
(f)	Your score:		Your partner's score:	
(g)	Your score:		Your partner's score:	
(h)	Your score:		Your partner's score:	
(i)	Your score:		Your partner's score:	
(j)	Your score:		Your partner's score:	
(k)	Your score:		Your partner's score:	
(l)	Your score:		Your partner's score:	
(m)	Your score:		Your partner's score:	
(n)	Your score:		Your partner's score:	
(o)	Your score:		Your partner's score:	
(p)	Your score:		Your partner's score:	

This is a test your partner needs to do too. Here you are looking for scoring differences. Serious areas of incompatibility will be immediately obvious.

TEST 19:
READY FOR MONOGAMY?

Your total: [ ]   Your partner's total: [ ]

A 26+ score indicates that fidelity for life is a reasonable goal for you. A lower score means you probably aren't ready to settle down at this time.

TEST 20:
SEX COMFORT
Your total: [　　] Your partner's total: [　　]

Two kinds of scores could indicate problems: very different scores on any individual question; or either partner scoring 21+ overall. This is very much a test which requires you to talk things over, since you can't *assume* you know your partner's feelings. This is a test you should take *together*, discussing things the whole way through.

TEST 21:
SEXUAL SATISFACTION
Scoring:

50–60 Most people would envy you.

40–49 You'll probably get by, if you're happy with the rest of your relationship.

30–39 There are difficulties: look carefully at answers with a very low score,

below 30: Your sexual satisfaction is low and your relationship is at risk.

TEST 22:
SEX BELIEFS(2)
1. Your score: [　　] Your partner's score: [　　]
2. Your score: [　　] Your partner's score: [　　]
3. Your score: [　　] Your partner's score: [　　]
4. Your score: [　　] Your partner's score: [　　]
5. Your score: [　　] Your partner's score: [　　]
6. Your score: [　　] Your partner's score: [　　]
7. Your score: [　　] Your partner's score: [　　]
8. Your score: [　　] Your partner's score: [　　]

These are called 'dysfunctional' beliefs about sex because when they are strongly held by either partner, they can get in the way of satisfying sex. Every one of these statements is dysfunctional, so if your (or your partner's) score is low on any of them, you need to think seriously about where you got the idea, and talk it over with your partner. Three or more dysfunctional beliefs will seriously hamper your sex life.

4

lasting

being and becoming

However well-matched a couple are, major incompatibilities (meaning differences or similarities that cause conflict) are not only likely – they are *guaranteed.* Researchers know this because they've worked it out mathematically. In one experiment they studied 168 well-established couples and found that only 59% had similar leisure preferences, and only 56% were in agreement as to the 'proper' roles for men and women. Taken together, this meant that only one couple in three was compatible in both these seriously important dimensions. The researchers then added another topic, and found that now just one couple in six rated as well matched. They didn't investigate any more topics because it was already plain that if they were to measure even five or six, most couples would be shown as incompatible.

But if you were to assume that, as the years pass, only the 'on paper compatibles' will do well (and the 'on paper' incompatibles will all do badly) you'd be wrong. When researchers tracked American couples (gay

THE LOVE QUIZ

TEST 23:
MANAGING CHANGE

Do you manage change well? Rate each statement below. Enter the total in the box on page 189. Now get your partner to do the same.

6	5	4	3	2	1
False		Neutral		True	

1 When we disagree, I often find it hard to understand where my partner is coming from
2 When you're really compatible with someone, you shouldn't ever disagree about important things
3 Really happy couples don't ever have to struggle to keep their relationships on track
4 Many of the problems we have are caused by my partner
5 We'll never solve our problems until my partner gets their act together
6 When my partner is unavailable to me, I find it very difficult to manage
7 I'm very busy: I don't have much time to put into this relationship

and straight) across six years of their relationships, they found that the most important happiness predictor wasn't initial compatibility (although, of course, this helped). Nor could lasting love best be predicted by the partners' personalities, how in love they were, or similarity in their backgrounds. What proved to be most telling was how effectively the couple managed *change*: the *changing circumstances* they were faced with; and the *personal changes* they had to make, to bridge their incompatibilities.

It's been said that being the right person in a relationship is as important as finding the right person, but now researchers are learning something new: *becoming* the right person is even more important. On-paper compatibles can do badly if they don't manage change effectively. And on-paper incompatibles who cope effectively with change can do very well indeed.

In fact, love actually *begins* in change. Although we like to believe 'that loving feeling' just happens, we create love through *changes that we make* as we get to know our partner. We try to anticipate their needs, are generous with affection and admiration and tell ourselves that attractive 'others' aren't all that attractive. Above all we make time – time for talk, time for fun and time for sex. When 'that loving feeling' withers one common reason is that we stop *making the changes* that helped create the experience of being in love. Agony Aunts who say passion can be rekindled by scheduling daily chats or going to bed together at the same time at night, are talking a kind of sense: they are encouraging us to make the kinds of changes we made to create love in the beginning.

This doesn't mean that, to keep love alive, you have to struggle to keep things the same. Keeping things the same is every bit as difficult as handling change. Nor, even if it were achievable, would it guarantee success: one of the sad things about human love is that people who *don't change* are more likely to end up unloved than those who *do*. They go on being themselves (being the way they were, doing the things they always did) while, silently, at their side, their partners are losing interest. It's not that their attracting qualities have become a turn-off (this is not *fatal attrac-tion*), simply that these have lost their impact. Researchers call this *rein-forcement erosion,* meaning that the gloss of an attracting quality is worn away (eroded) by nothing other than the fact that it is experienced a lot.

Reinforcement erosion doesn't happen with everything, of course. You may continue to get a kick out of your partner's beauty or strength or gentleness or sense of humour (you may even feel secure as you listen to the same old jokes) but this is far from guaranteed. Familiarity is enhanced by novelty. Where love is concerned, people need things to change even when they don't want them to. Yet here's the snag: as things change incompatibilities may be revealed or may develop. While couples who have been together longer are much less likely to break up than those who have been together for a shorter time, some end up going their separate ways, even after many years.

Change comes to people in different forms. Most obvious are the *changes that happen to them (life event changes)*. These can be grad-ual (like one partner slowly coming to hate their job) or sudden (like moving house). Some *Life-Event Changes* are expected (retirement), others unexpected (winning the lottery; the death of a child). Although love is supposed to conquer all, the hard truth is that these *changes* can make or break a relationship. Couples turning up in counselling report more major life events in the year leading up to their treatment (and almost twice as many in the three years before) than couples who don't seek counselling. Many an elderly couple, posing proudly with children and grandchildren for their golden wedding photographs, are unaware that, had Fate dumped on them even half the life stresses she dumped on their unfortunate neighbours, they'd by now be living in different cities.

PAINTING BY NUMBERS

THE LONGER WE ARE TOGETHER, THE LESS LIKELY WE ARE TO SPLIT UP

- almost half of all divorces occur by the eighth year of marriage
- by year 16, three-quarters of those who will divorce have done so
- the first marriages of 11% of women will end after they are 40
- for every year couples have been together before the age of 40, they are 9% less likely to split up
- break-ups late in life often affect both partners very badly – finan-cially, psychologically and physically

A SUPPORTIVE PARTNER PROVIDES...

● emotional support – s/he shows love, understanding and concern
● esteem support – s/he clearly respects your personal qualities, believes in your abilities, and regards what you think, feel or say as legitimate
● information support – s/he thinks about what you're involved in, and provides input and feedback when you are open to it (s/he doesn't insist on giving it when you aren't – that's being *un*supportive)
● tangible assistance – s/he give you practical help with the job in hand (or with other things), leaving you free to focus on your main task

Just as, when your relationship begins, you can be tricked by circumstance into thinking you are better suited or more in love than you actually are, so you can be tricked by the negative spin-off from life events into thinking your relationship is on the skids, when it isn't. This is because life events (both good and bad) generate stress, and when you are under stress your behaviour towards your partner (or theirs to you) alters. We then start seeing *that behaviour* (and, by extension, our partner) as 'the problem'. People under stress may fail to fulfil their 'roles' as expected, become touchy or argumentative or 'switch off'. They almost always cut back on warmth and supportiveness, and may even treat their partner with hostility. In a nutshell, stress increases your need for support from your mate; and reduces your ability to provide it.

supportiveness

Although it is during life crises that partners most obviously need support, it doesn't work to wait for a near-death experience before producing the goods. There has to be a general *climate* of supportiveness, and when this is present it is an absolutely top predictor of lasting love. This is partly because partner support is much, much more than a 'nice thing to do'. Partner supportiveness helps you achieve peak emotional 'fitness'. It raises your self-esteem, helps you feel positive about our life roles (as parent, worker, lover) and encourages you to believe that if you take action *it will be effective*. A supportive love relationship even protects you against physical and mental illness: it strengthens your immune system, motivates you to take care of yourself and avoid taking risks, means you are less likely to become depressed, and makes relapse after psychiatric illness less likely.

Supportiveness also ranks as a major *expectation* in close relationships. This means people believe it is something their partner owes them, so if it isn't forthcoming they feel let down: couples who break up often say that the chief reason was lack of support from their partner. The main way you can judge whether or not your partner is supportive is how *responsive* s/he is to you: that is, how accurately s/he seems to 'see' and 'hear' you. Their responsiveness helps you feel safe (it signals that they'll notice when you need support, and will be able to supply support of the right kind) and stops you feeling vulnerable and lonely. A major reason life events cause so many problems is that they absorb your attention, and so diminish your capacity to be *responsive* to your partner.

Interestingly, responsiveness is not only at the heart of good loving, it's also at the heart of good parenting: the best parents are those who don't impose on their children but respond sensitively to their needs and wishes, talents and limitations. Indeed, psychologists believe that children's actual sense of *existence* depends in large measure on how responsive their caretakers are. It now seems that, in sexual love, something similar is going on. Your partner's responsiveness goes a long way to helping you feel valued and real. Their unresponsiveness makes you feel you are a 'nobody'. You are then hurt and sad, and as a defence against these painful feelings, often become angry. Among established couples, the strongest predictor that the relationship is in trouble (stronger, even, than 'destructive fighting' which is covered later in this chapter) is the *absence* of supportive behaviour by the partners towards each other.

However, being supportive doesn't mean constantly putting your partner's needs before your own, trying not to say or do anything they will find offensive, being understanding and lovable at all times, a good listener into the early hours of the morning and working at the relationship day in, day out. Love calls for adjustment and compromise, but it should not be hard labour. In fact, if you run around trying to make your partner happy, you can make them depressed. For when a person comes to believe that their happiness will be manufactured or delivered by someone else, this makes them passive and sluggish – two states that often lead to depression.

Until recently, many experts advised couples to think of their relationship as if it were a bank account. They were to make 'deposits' (supportive words and actions) in order to balance 'withdrawals' (unsupportive words and actions). It was claimed that as long as couples stuck to the famous 5:1 ratio (five positives to every one negative) and kept their relationship bank account in 'credit', they'd be OK. In fact, while the 5:1 ratio does matter, and pleasantness can be very important (agreeable people often have long, happy relationships, just as those who are disagreeable are likely to have short or long and miserable partnerships), there are big problems with the bank account approach.

THE LOVE QUIZ
TEST 24:
HOW SUPPORTIVE ARE YOU?

If you want to know how supportive you are, ask your *partner* to reply to the questions below. S/he may also want to see how supportive you rate them. There are boxes for the scores on page 189.

6	5	4	3	2	1
Often		Sometimes			Never

1 My partner shows interest in how I think and feel
2 My partner shows interest in what I do
3 My partner is openly affectionate
4 When I am worried or upset, my partner notices
5 When I am worried or upset, my partner shows concern
6 I feel that my partner takes care of me
7 My partner is openly appreciative of what I do for them
8 My partner tries to see things from my point of view
9 I don't feel I have to put on a 'front' for my partner
10 When things are going well for my partner, I know about it

THE LOVE QUIZ

TEST 25:
LIFE EVENTS

Check the list below. Score one point for every statement that applies to your situation, or has applied to it over the past two years. Turn to page 189.

1 One of us is/has been out of work or seriously underemployed

2 One of us has had other troubles at work

3 We've faced financial difficulties/have come into a lot of money

4 One of us has had an affair

5 Someone close to one of us has been very ill, or has died

6 Someone close to one of us has been in trouble with the law

7 There's a lot of violence in our neighbourhood

8 We have young children/our first child has become a teenager

9 We've had problems with a family member

10 We have too much to do and not enough time to do it

While (as pointed out in Chapter 1) both partners need to feel they're getting a fair deal, trying consciously to do good deeds for each other doesn't seem to increase satisfaction, although negative tit-for-tatting is related to *dis*satisfaction. Indeed, couples who consciously focus on balancing the books ('I did this so you should do that') are *not* likely to see their golden wedding. Even one serious 'withdrawal' (a contemptuous look or word, a hostile personal criticism, an infidelity) can wipe out any number of 'deposits' and leave a scar that changes the nature of the relationship for ever. What's more, since partners can spot phoniness in each other with laser-like vision, it's no good dutifully 'doing' supportiveness. Pleasantries need to have the ring of truth; if they are insincere they're felt to be suspect, and what was intended as a positive becomes a serious negative. Advising you to 'be excellent to each other' can be useful if you really do believe your partner is wonderful and have just been forgetting to tell them, or you are learning to ask for change or express your feelings in a tactful, non-hostile way. But if you never really rated your partner, or have grown to mistrust or dislike them, then forcing out supportive remarks won't get you far.

problem-solving

Another reason stressful life events can cause relationships to lose their way, is that they affect your ability to solve problems. Solving problems, big and small, is something you must do successfully with your partner, year in, year out. Problem-solving is badly affected by stress because stress stops you thinking clearly, and makes you feel tired, negative, even depressed. In a negative frame of mind, you say negative things and *look* negative, both of which make your partner less than keen to work with you.

When you are flooded with anxious feelings (which can even happen when your heart rate is just eight beats per minute faster than usual) effective problem-solving goes out the window. This is partly because, when you're 'het up', you are particularly prone to reading your partner's feelings and intentions inaccurately, and to interpreting their attitude as more negative than it is. And since you tend to reciprocate the emotion you *think* your partner is feeling (and then see them as reciprocating what *you have* been feeling) it's easy to see how upsetting exchanges can develop, even when there was no serious ill-will to start with (let alone when there was). After this has happened a few times, the prospect of the simplest conversation can cause stress. Studies have shown that when unhappy couples sit down for a chat about the events of the day, their hearts start racing before either opens their mouth. This agitation can be measured, and used to predict which couples will stay together, and which won't: the greater the agitation, the less likely long-term happiness.

STRESSFUL LIFE CHANGES CAN DESTROY LOVE WHEN PARTNERS:

- blame each other for what's happening
- associate the distress triggered by the event with each other
- are too preoccupied to attend to each other's needs
- are disappointed by the sympathy or understanding their partner offers
- become depressed because of what's happened

The self-focus that's part of anxiety, negativity and depression also makes effective problem-solving less likely: it gets in the way of your understanding and appreciating your partner's point of view. And in a horrible snowball effect, your partner's problem-solving skills can take a dive when lack of recognition and support from you makes *them* depressed. Depression is contagious, too: researchers have found that college students assigned to live with mildly depressed room-mates become increasingly depressed themselves; that 50% of couples who come for counselling contain at least one depressed partner; that half of all depressed women have at-home partner problems; and that unhappy couples are 25 times more likely than the rest of the population to fall prey to depression.

Once people feel unsupported *and* are no longer successfully solving problems together, they can no longer see themselves as a good team. The costs of living together begin to appear high; the rewards, low; and one partner (feeling irritated or angry or increasingly detached) will start questioning the relationship. If detachment continues for any length of time, either person may begin trying out new (often uncharacteristic) behaviour in an area of life separate from their mate, such as work, travel, education, an affair. As separateness and secrecy increase and differences develop, a fundamentally compatible couple can begin to seem incompatible. In acknowledgement of the fact that this has been a *process,* what is often said is, 'we have *become* strangers'.

A common response to major life events is for relationships to polarize, becoming either much worse or much better. Many studies have found that when a family member is seriously ill or dies, some couples grow closer and communicate more effectively. Not only does this make both partners feel supported, but their effective communication helps problem-solving. As problems are successfully dealt with, the couple come to regard themselves as a good team, and are encouraged to tackle other difficulties. This propels their relationship into an upward spiral. Such couples can come to believe that they are exceptionally compatible. In fact, what they really are, are good team players.

After the birth of a baby, 68% of couples see no change in their relationship (or a moderate decline); 13% see it as on the way out; and 19% see it as closer and better. A study of parents whose child had died found that, 4–7 years afterwards, 50% saw no significant change in their relationship, 21% saw it as weakened and 29% saw it as improved. The key to the worsening partnerships was that one or both partners had withdrawn emotionally, whereas in the relationships that had improved, the partners took turns to be miserable. The person who was momentarily the

---

THE LOVE QUIZ

TEST 26:
HAVING A BABY

Will your relationship survive? Rate each statement below. Get your partner to do the same. Turn to page 189-90.

6	5	4	3	2	1
True			**Neutral**		**Not true**

1 We have both made it our business to find out about what can be expected of babies at different stages of development

2 We understand that baby-care skills are learned, not innate, and no one can get it right first time

3 Our goals and concerns have changed a lot since our baby was born

4 We make a conscious effort to work as a team

5 We each manage time alone with our child

6 We each give the other time off from our baby

7 We are doing as well as possible in respect of the work/child-care balance in our family

8 In our family, when the mother says 'we' she means herself and her partner, not herself and the baby

9 As partners we connect regularly in a way that nurtures our relationship

10 When we have fights, we stop before we say or do anything really hurtful

most devastated received comfort from the other, who knew that when their own emotions became overwhelming, their partner would offer comfort in return.

worry support

Not only are couples in satisfying relationships hit less hard by negative life events *at the time*, they are also less likely to fall ill afterwards. People in dissatisfying relationships more often get sick after a period of stress, which can push them further down. A terrible life event can affect some people's relationship for ever. A really sad finding from US research on the Great Depression of the 1930s, was that couples who'd had a hard time were often showing 'diminished' marriages and 'brittle personalities' 15 years on, well after their finances had recovered.

Like major life events, day-to-day stresses affect relationships by subtly altering the way people behave towards each other. For example, a stressful working day tends to make you angry and impatient with your family, and research has shown that arguments at work are often followed by arguments at home. Even one person starting on night shifts increases the number of rows at home, while workers who, after a day-shift, walk in the door still feeling stressed are reported by their partners as acting 'bored and uninterested' later in the evening. Dealing effectively with a partner's stress is no easy matter. One famous study found that some air traffic controllers who'd had a stressful shift or been bullied by their boss recovered their mood if their partners allowed them 'withdrawal time' when they came home. That might have been nice for them, but was probably not so nice for their mates. Other studies have shown that if work-stressed people regularly withdraw into themselves, their *partners* start getting stressed.

MYTH BUSTERS
MEN AND INTIMACY

Men are no less 'good at intimacy' than women. They just apply higher standards of 'feeling safe' before they'll reveal themselves. Research has found that 'where men and women feel safe from conflict early in their relationship, their communication in terms of intimacy tends to be equivalent'.

Researchers have noticed that stress is more likely to make men fed-up with their love-relationships than women. Why? Are men emotionally more fragile? No. Men often suffer more when their partner's responsiveness goes missing because they have no other source of emotional support: 74% of men aged 50 and over talk mainly to their partners when they're upset; only 48% of women do so. Women as often take their problems to professional experts, friends or wider family. Men are reluctant to do that, not because they 'can't' (as the Mars/Venus school of thought maintains) but because men often feel that talking to outsiders means they are being *disloyal to their partner.* Recently, women have been using Internet chat-rooms as support networks (something the experts once believed only men would do) and if you go to these sites (many are parenting sites) another reason why women get things off their chests more easily than men becomes clear: the women's chat-rooms are full of women complaining how awful men are.

For men to sound off about women publicly in such a way would be unacceptable, and this is partly because, where complaining couples are concerned, people operate a double standard for men and women. Both partners are not seen as being equally responsible for their actions. The female partner is seen as the weaker and the more dependent, with outside influences (other people, social forces, insecurity about the relationship) driving her behaviour. Her supposed 'dependent' status makes complaint by her seem justified. For a man, it's different. Partly because the 'big world' is mainly run by men, and partly because the definition of masculinity rests on the notion that a 'real man' is in control of his destiny, the actions of her male partner are viewed as being *his choice* (even when, in fact, he has had no control over events at all). Within a couple people focus on the *impact* of the man's behaviour (asking only, was it *harmful* or *not harmful?*) and attack a complaining man as a whinger. When men (as is often the case) do not express their dissatisfactions (to their partner or to anyone else) this may be because they do not feel *entitled to complain*. Perhaps sexist comments are sometimes a warped stab at complaint.

Men's lack of outside worry support shows up in a big way when their partner is pregnant. Research has found that they hesitate to burden her with their fears at this time, feeling she has enough to cope with. This may be true, given that many of their worries will be about her: a man may not be sure he wants the relationship (three out of ten men who move in with a partner, only do so to 'stand by her' because she's 'fallen' pregnant); or he may not feel ready to become a father (about one in three fathers-to-be hadn't expected to become one). As a result, the men who are most doubt-

WHY PARTNERS DON'T TAKE STRESS TO EACH OTHER

- 'I don't want to bother him' (women)
- 'He wouldn't understand' (women)
- 'She *couldn't* understand' (men – meaning, it's outside her sphere, probably a 'work' worry)
- 'I want to separate home from work' (men)

ful or confused will also usually be the most isolated – a recipe for disaster. Similarly, when their partner works full-time, men who would have brought their worries to a mate at home tend to keep quiet, with the result that, while full-time working mothers of pre-schoolers aren't more depressed than at-home or part-time working mothers, their *partners* are. Certainly, the men aren't experiencing more 'role strain' than the women, nor are they more exhausted. What they have lost is the opportunity, so crucial to them in the absence of other intimate support, to express their worries.

How do successful couples manage the problem of men's worry support? Recognizing it as an issue is the main thing, followed by small changes in behaviour: allowing a bit more time for chats at home, or drafting in family or friends or professionals (or Internet sites) to fill the gap. A real double-bind here can be that when men perceive they are being offered support, this can make them feel more depressed *because it makes them feel incompetent*. A reason why men can be better cheered up by a good 'kick around of a ball' rather than by a serious conversation about what's worrying them, is that they get to feel (temporarily) more competent when they kick the ball around, although serious underlying worries won't be dealt with this way.

Designing worry support for men that increases their sense of competence is really important, and might help to bring down the divorce rate.

MEN AND EMPATHY

Many people believe that men are not as empathic (sympathetic and compassionate) as women. In fact, research shows that men are as capable of demonstrating empathy as women *when they are motivated to do so*.

This approach isn't necessarily the best when offering women support (although it probably is in an area where women are supposed to be competent, such as parenting). At home, women prefer to be understood. Women whose partners *think they are wonderful* don't feel as supported as women who believe their partners *understand them*.

who changes?

The longer you live with someone, the more likely you are to want to change their behaviour. Yet bringing about changes in people's behaviour against their will or their natural tendencies is very difficult. If you are starting a relationship in the belief that everything will be fine as soon as your partner changes in some fundamental way, you should pack your bags right now: the future isn't bright. Until recently, even the experts didn't realize how hard it was to change partners' behaviour, and much couple counselling involved teaching new behaviour strategies. It all sounded fine until they tracked the couples over a couple of years, to see how many of the changes had stuck. Not many. By the end of two years, two-thirds of the couples who'd been working on behaviour change *alone* had divorced. In fact, one leading researcher has concluded that counselling of any kind only leads to happier-together couples in 11–18% of cases. (This doesn't mean that, even at this stage, counselling is a waste of time: it may be very useful in helping couples to part well.)

A major reason couple counselling so often fails is that partners get to it too late – on average, *six years* after they've first noticed *major*

LOVE BUGS

CHANGE VIA COUNSELLING IS UNLIKELY WHEN:
● a man makes hostile, derogatory and destructive comments to his partner
● a woman has difficulty contributing to solutions
● the couple are very distressed
● they feel they have reached 'the end of the road'
● they're 'hostile detached' (one – or both – ignores or avoids conflict)
● they are having little or no sex
● within their home, they operate clearly distinct man/woman roles

LOVE NOTES

CHANGE

Change is unlikely in:
- internal areas (which can't be consciously controlled) – thoughts, feelings, sensitivities, beliefs, perspectives and natural tendencies
- external areas (where change would 'cost' a lot) – wishes, independence, habits, hobbies, pastimes and friendships

Change can be hoped for in practical areas, including:
- what each partner does in the relationship
- what they do together as a couple

problems at home. When people use couple counselling like an emergency dash to A&E instead of (as, hopefully, future generations will use it) like a routine trip to the family doctor to check out worrying symptoms, they can't expect much. Emergency treatments of any kind often fail, and the key to a healthy love (as to a healthy life) is to pick up the early niggles before they turn into chronic problems. Hanging on to grand promises ('in sickness and in health', 'for richer and poorer', 'till death do us part') doesn't seem to be much help. A more useful vow might be: 'I promise to pay attention to our relationship every day, and when I sense something is starting to go wrong *not to ignore it*, but to join with my partner in taking all necessary steps to put it right.'

In small ways, couples regularly achieve change without pain. Maybe one person's family tradition is to exchange presents on Chistmas Eve, while the other's leaves the scrum until after Christmas Day lunch. If *both* change happily (agree to a year-on-year compromise) or *one* changes (either feeling 'neutral' about their partner's way of doing things, or relishing the novelty) then clearly change without pain has been achieved. One sign that a partnership is likely to be happy is that the couple quickly put together a shared vision of how they want to spend their life – a vision different from the ways in which either was raised. It should be pointed out that developing such a joint vision is very different from one partner coming on strong with opinions and the other going along with them in order to keep the peace or because they're trying to please.

Change is only an issue when one partner (or both) must go against a strongly preferred way of thinking or behaving for the good of the relationship or to make their partner happy. Then there's a price to be paid: in stress, resentment, even depression. This, of course, is the main reason why highly compatible couples start ahead of the game. For there's surprisingly little likelihood that couples will grow together as far as values, attitudes and beliefs are concerned. Certainly, as we age, some of these may change a lot, but there's no evidence to suggest that we'll change to become more like our partner. Research has shown that most older couples who think alike didn't develop a similar world view; they thought pretty much alike from the beginning. However, one (1950s) study did find that *happy* couples' attitudes and perceptions grew more similar over time, while those of *unhappy* couples became more different. This happened because, in the happier couples, the women gradually adapted their views to their partner's. Among the unhappy couples, it was the men who changed – away from their female partners.

man-changing

Despite the self-evident truth that change is at the heart of couple relationships, many people are deeply uncomfortable with the idea of one partner changing to accommodate the other. Even to hint at (let alone demand or expect) change is seen as a violation of a person's self-hood, particularly when the person asking for change is a woman and the person being asked to adjust is a man.

There are big gender issues here. A male who makes quite small, practical changes to help life as a couple go smoothly (for example, resisting invitations to go out with the boys) will quickly be dubbed hen-pecked or pussy-whipped. Women can change much more, and much more quickly, without losing face. In fact, a woman has to change a lot (and clearly against her own best interests) before she'll be called a doormat. This means that, for heterosexual couples, the stage is set for conflict. Since women are usually relationship-monitors and home-managers (and it's in these areas that partners have most to do with each other *as a couple*) women are much more likely than men to be in the position of asking their partner to change. This is probably a major reason for women's reputations as nags.

Recent research has found that one feature of happy couples is the *man's* willingness to accept influence from his mate. That doesn't mean that women's accepting of influence is of no importance: it is.

LOVE TALK ...

Q: What three things does a bride think of during the wedding service?
A: Aisle, altar, hymn.
                        ANONYMOUS

WHO CHANGES?

● one woman in three feels comfortable raising change issues with her partner

● one man in five usually makes an effort to change

● 25% of men aged under 36 usually change, compared with only 14% of older males

● 77% of men who usually change are very satisfied with their relationships (compared with 55% who rarely or never change)

In good relationships both partners accommodate each other, and to much the same degree. But because men's gender training makes them more likely to be resistant to influence, it's the *man's* willingness to accommodate that shows up in the research as the more important.

Interestingly, a man's giving in to his partner's wishes and changing his behaviour a great deal to please her *when they first get together*, doesn't bode well for the future, although at this point a woman can safely change to please quite a lot. It's only if her willingness to change continues that it points to problems, and this is most likely if her reason for changing is to avoid an argument. In fact, a woman doing the very opposite (standing up for herself and openly expressing *anger* early on) can be quite a good gauge of future happiness: open, straightforward anger (not whining or blaming) may show she feels safe with her partner, and is committed to him. However, where she is openly angry *and* her partner is struggling with challenging life events, her anger (though she may feel good about it) can make him depressed. The experts are divided about anger. Some see it as useful, others feel it's not routinely helpful and should be encouraged only with caution. A useful middle way could be to *confess* feelings of anger *after the event*, and then explore them when you are in a fit state to deal with the issues arising.

For a man to accept influence doesn't mean buckling under at the first word of command. All it means is that he takes his partner's requests for change seriously, and responds constructively. One early sign that a relationship is *not* going to last, is a man joking around when his partner asks for change (jokiness can be a way of being defensive, of rejecting influence). However, when a woman calls *all* the shots a relationship will not usually be happy, although it may be long-lasting. Interestingly, while in-charge women may appear powerful in their relationships, the opposite is mostly the case: they are often power*less*, in that they are unable to influence their mate. Women who call the shots usually only get to do so because their partners have withdrawn. A man's running the show doesn't imply that his partner has backed away: it indicates that he has real power and influence within the partnership.

Where does all this leave heterosexual couples trying to negotiate this gender minefield, which often becomes particularly acute after they've had a baby? One new father we interviewed said his name had recently changed from 'Andrew' to 'Andrew-would-you' as his partner, who previously hadn't been much of a home-manager, settled into her maternity leave and started issuing 'a stream of commands'.

Because, as pointed out earlier, we tend to see men as totally in charge of their own behaviour, a new father is seen as being either willing or unwilling to adapt and change (and is praised or blamed accordingly). In fact, his willingness is only one element, and is often much less important than people think. Research has shown, for example, that the new fathers who do lots with their babies aren't necessarily those who had planned to. The most highly involved fathers are often those whose partners aren't very competent or who have had Caesarians (women who have Caesarians often can't lift the baby for quite a while, so the fathers

---

THE LOVE QUIZ

TEST 27:
IS THIS RELATIONSHIP
GOOD FOR YOU?

Answer the questions below (or ask a close friend to answer them on your behalf: an outsider's view can give an interesting perspective)

6	5	4	3	2	1
True		Neutral		Not true	

1　Both partners have a secure belief in their own value

2　Both partners are improved by the relationship: they seem better, stronger, more attractive, more accomplished, more at ease etc.

3　Both partners maintain serious interests outside their relationship

4　Both partners maintain serious friendships outside their relationship

5　Their relationship is not a 'place apart': it's integrated into daily life

6　Neither partner is jealous of, or tries to restrict, the other's growth and expansion of interests

7　The lovers are also friends: they would seek each other out if they ceased being primary partners

ELEMENTS OF
CHANGE INCLUDE:

● motivation – your own interest, or self-interest, in changing
● opportunity – the extent to which your environment makes change possible
● skills and self-confidence – how competent you become (this helps your motivation grow and makes you push for opportunities)
● institutional practices – the extent to which the world about you (social rules, legislation, workplace attitudes) supports the change

tend to). Fathers of premature babies tend also to be more involved than the average, as do fathers who were given baby-care training in the hospital. What is common to all these men is that they develop skills, either because someone shows them, or because they are really needed. And the better they get at caring for the baby, the more confident they feel, the more rewarding they find it, and the more of it they do ...

in conflict

When one partner is looking for change and it doesn't occur spontaneously, conflict is inevitable. Researchers have learned to make a distinction between constructive and destructive conflict. In constructive conflict, serious cruelty, tension and unpleasantness are kept to a minimum; and when the argument is over, both partners regard the outcome as satisfying. Destructive conflict, by contrast, is deeply upsetting to at least one partner and, when it happens, tends to happen *a lot*. Since partners are not satisfied with the outcome, the same troublesome topic soon pops up again, and there they are – in the middle of another fight.

A great deal of conflict *of any kind* early on in a relationship bodes badly especially if the arguments are to do with sex, partying, companionship and maintenance behaviours (that is, activities designed to keep the relationship afloat, such as sharing tasks, building a network of friends and being nice to each other). But although the prognosis for stormy courtships is so poor, at this stage the fighting doesn't seem to make the couple feel unhappy. The more in love these couples are, the more likely they are to tell themselves that the conflict doesn't matter.

Among gay couples, fights about power (one person being overly critical) and intimacy (how close the partners should be) cause the most distress, but only fights about power predict a marked drop in satisfaction 12 months on. Among heterosexuals in the planning marriage stage, when women disagree with their partners an average of 2.8% of the time the couple will usually go on to be happy. However, where the disagreement level rises to 4.9% they'll often end up unhappy. It's amazing that such a tiny shift can make such a huge difference.

Interestingly, very *little* conflict also points to trouble ahead, and this is because a certain amount of conflict is absolutely essential: without it, beneficial change will never be achieved. Couples who *almost never argue* early on, often split up within three years (or, by then, are in a serious downward spiral). Similarly, couples who appear tranquil immediately after they've had a baby (she's in charge of the child, he doesn't interfere and thinks she's a great mother) are often heading for trouble. After 18 months they are likely to be fighting more (and more destructively) than couples who, in the early weeks and months, were arguing over how to do things and getting angry with each other.

This is probably because the couples who argued early on were working as a team (even if a stressed-out one) and were negotiating change. Indeed, love guru Professor John Gottman has gone so far as to say that the most important advice he can give to men who want their relationships to work is not to avoid conflict. However, following the Golden Rule of Moderation (that, in couple relationships, extremes of anything are bad) it is worth noting that while unhappy couples have arguments about once a day, happy couples argue much less frequently: on average, around once a week. Research has found that the most worrying indicator for any couple is frequent disagreement *combined with* frequent avoiding of disagreement: that is, side-stepping topics for fear they will cause a row.

IN DESTRUCTIVE CONFLICT, COUPLES:

- try to prove themselves right, and their partner wrong
- go over and over the same ground
- summarize and re-state *their* own position
- express disagreement in their words *and* in their bodies
- insult each other in personal terms
- engage in long chains of attack and counter-attack

IN CONSTRUCTIVE CONFLICT, COUPLES:

- periodically offer concession or compromise
- summarize and clarify *each other's* position
- 'read' their partner's distress signals (distress in men includes whining, getting defensive and trying to leave the room, and distress in women includes sadness and fear)
- back off before they hurt each other deeply
- have a deep love and liking for each other
- show this in their body language, even in a fierce fight

boomerangs

One reason conflict has been much written about is because it's easy for researchers to study. They arrange for partners who haven't seen each other for a few hours to meet up in front of a video camera in a research unit (or Love Lab) and discuss a problem topic in their relationship. One partner will almost always be trying to get the other to change in some way. From their Love Lab observations, the intrigued researchers have listed out change strategies that work and change strategies that don't work. They've also tracked the couples over time, to see which break up and which don't. And they've found there's a link between the kinds of change strategies the couples use and the likelihood of their relationship ending.

The unsuccessful change strategies can be called *boomerangs* because they bounce back on the sender by aggravating the situation and making change less, not more, likely. *Boomerangs* point to trouble ahead for couples at all stages of their relationship: those who have been together for a long time and those who are just starting out.

The first of the boomerangs is *criticism*. *Criticism* has a positive intent: to jolt your partner into changing, by pointing out how badly they have behaved. When you criticize, you don't simply express the opinion that your partner's action (or non-action) has hurt or inconvenienced you ('I needed you to get the bread in time for lunch'); you attack their motives or character, seeing these as the cause of their behaviour ('You let me down again – you were too lazy to lift your bum off that sofa'). The person who has been criticized then tends either to withdraw (because they feel hurt) or to go on the defensive by rejecting the criticism self-righteously or go on the offensive by hurling criticism, contempt and blame at their critic.

The second of the boomerangs is *contempt*. *Contempt* differs from *criticism* in that it doesn't even have a positive intent: its overriding purpose is to hurt. Contempt is fairly easy to recognize. It's often accompanied by a feeling of righteous indignation, and is expressed through hostile humour and mockery, or insults and name-calling (bastard, jerk, fat, stupid, ugly). People often express contempt in their bodies: they sneer, roll their eyes, curl their upper lip in disgust, or look as if they are about to be sick. Contempt points to total lack of respect and is most destructive when displayed by women, who are often signalling that, for them, the relationship is at the end of the road.

Along with *criticism, contempt* sets the stage for the third of the Love Lab boomerangs: *innocent victim*. When we 'do' *innocent victim*, we find a whole lot of ways of blaming our partner for what's been going on. Like

THE LOVE QUIZ

TEST 28:
ARE YOU A CRITIC?

Think of a recent argument with your partner or create your own Love Lab: run a tape-recorder or a video camera while you discuss a problem topic. Then rate each of the statements below as it reflects how you *felt*. Get your partner to do the same. Enter your scores on page 190.

6	5	4	3	2	1
True		**Neutral**		**Not true**	

1 I tried to make my partner see patterns in their behaviour

2 I analyzed my partner's personality/guessed their motives, as well as complaining about what they'd done (or hadn't done)

3 I didn't complain until I felt very hurt

4 I tried to make a general point, not just complain about this one thing

5 I felt ready to explode

6 Basically, I know I'm right

7 My partner has to accept *some* of the blame!

8 I used phrases like 'you always ...', 'you never ...'

9 Why am I always the one who has to raise these issues?

10 I didn't state my complaints in a neutral manner

TEST 29:
DO YOU PLAY
INNOCENT VICTIM?

Think of a recent argument with your partner or create your own
Love Lab and stage one: run a tape-recorder or a video camera while
you discuss a problem topic. Then rate each of the statements below
as it reflects how you *felt*. Get your partner to do the same. Enter your
scores on page 190.

6	5	4	3	2	1
True		Neutral		Not true	

1 My partner picks on me unfairly when we argue
2 My partner doesn't understand me
3 I do lots of good things around here – my partner doesn't notice
4 Actually, it wasn't really my fault
5 I had to explain what *really* happened
6 My partner went right over the top: s/he would try the patience
   of a saint
7 When my partner went on it me I though – hey, wait a minute, I
   haven't done anything
8 My partner only sees things from one point of view: their own
9 I thought – what you are saying bounces right off me
10 There were so many things I *could* have said

criticism and *contempt*, *innocent victim* is a defensive manoeuvre, in
that its purpose is self-defence. It can be considered a boomerang
because, like criticism and contempt, it raises the emotional temperature
which means that conflict will not be resolved. Like *contempt*, *innocent
victim* is often signalled physically: we give a false smile (the corner of
our mouth rises, but our eyes don't change); we shift our body from side
to side (as if avoiding a punch); we fold our arms across our chests; or
perhaps fiddle with our collar or neck-line.

The fourth of the boomerangs is *withdrawal*. Sometimes *withdrawal* is
active: you disapprove of something your partner says or does and want
them to change their behaviour; but instead of telling them so, you *withdraw* (sulking, closing down, turning away). More often *withdrawal* is reac-
tive: your partner is demanding change and you blank their demand, by
clamming up, seeming to misunderstand what they have said, changing

LOVE NOTES

STRAIGHT MEN MAY *WITHDRAW* MOST OFTEN BECAUSE:

● they are usually the ones being asked to change

● even if they are pushing for change it may be in a home area where their partner usually takes the lead (so they may easily feel wrong-footed)

● they may feel verbally outclassed – lost for words – by more fluent female partners

● they may be particularly scared of getting angry in case they lose control and damage their (physically weaker) partners

the subject or leaving the room. *Withdrawal* is most likely when the partner who is asking for change speaks angrily or aggressively ('you always ...', 'I can't trust you to ...'). An escalating *demand/withdrawal* 'dance' often follows, building to an ugly climax (violence is often preceded by such exchanges). Interestingly, *withdrawers* often have no idea that their behaviour is contributing to the heat of the situation. They believe that, by withdrawing, they're being neutral and reasonable.

In the Love Labs, men have been seen to withdraw more than women, which has lead some researchers to claim that *withdrawal* is a man thing. However, more recent research has shown the *demand/withdrawal* pattern in lesbian and gay male couples, too: whichever partner is being asked to change (and doesn't want to) tends to withdraw, whether they are male or female. When the *demand/withdraw* pattern happens a lot, it's a sure sign that a relationship is in big trouble. This holds true as much in gay as in straight partnerships – with one exception: among heterosexuals, a woman withdrawing during an argument can be a positive, as long as she doesn't do it very often. Perhaps this is because the average heterosexual woman withdraws so rarely that her partner sees it as a serious ultimatum, and is motivated to change. Or perhaps her withdrawal cools the emotional temperature, and gives him space to think. However, a woman withdrawing a great deal is as dangerous as a man constantly withdrawing: it stops couples resolving their differences.

irreconcilable differences

You don't necessarily need to panic if you recognize the presence of boomerangs in your repertoire. Even happy, established couples *criticize* each other, display the odd flash of *contempt*, and play *innocent victim* and *demand/withdrawal* from time to time. It's when boomerangs appear suddenly, or begin to occur more regularly than ever before, that you should take note (and action). Then boomerangs act as a useful early-warning system.

Lots of boomerangs in newly together partners should be taken very seriously. They may signal deep and troubling incompatibilities, or they may demonstrate that partners won't be good at managing change. Or they may show that one partner is uncomfortable in the relationship and wants out. However, you should not regard *absence* of boomerangs as any guarantee that your relationship is going to be a winner. The boomerangs may appear later, when the relationship has soured.

The research carried out in the Love Labs has also revealed how the journey from togetherness to having irreconcilable differences is made. Here the main culprits are three further boomerangs: *coercion, polarization* and *specialization*. These, too, may not be present early on but may develop later.

When you *coerce* our partner to change, you push them hard in a

LOVE BUGS

STEPS ON THE ROAD TO BREAK-UP INCLUDE:

- ● frequent conflict *plus* frequent avoiding of conflict
- ● frequent withdrawal
- ● demand/withdrawal
- ● criticism of a partner's personal characteristics
- ● defining difference as deficiency
- ● counter-complaining – meeting a complaint with a complaint
- ● acting the innocent victim and saying it's not your fault
- ● being contemptuous (insulting, name-calling, showing hostile humour and sneering)
- ● being physically violent (particularly men)

negative way: you demand, threaten, nag, criticize, complain, induce guilt – even attack them physically. Or else you withdraw (silence can also be a form of coercion). After you have made this huge fuss, your partner may do what you want, and this encourages you to give a repeat performance when next you want them to do something: you now believe that *coercion* works. But it doesn't work for long, because when someone gives in to you against their will, this causes them to become deeply angry, both with you and with themselves (for being weak). Although they have done what was asked, underneath they are becoming increasingly stubborn. Next time they are pushed, you'll have to apply more pressure to get the same result. Meanwhile, their resentment leaks out. They may *counter-coerce* around other issues (pushing for sex, for instance, when they know the other person doesn't want it) or may switch off, developing the famous low sexual desire mentioned in Chapter 3 or becoming generally unhelpful. Men who are unhelpful with childrearing are often *counter-coercing*, silently protesting about another area of the relationship where they feel wronged, but which they don't feel able to mention. Like the other boomerangs, coercion undermines a loving atmosphere and positive feelings, and it comes as no surprise to learn that 47% of dissatisfied

THE LOVE QUIZ

TEST 30: COERCION

Ask your partner to rate how coercive you seem by answering the questions set out below, and entering the results on page 190. They may be willing to let you do the same for them. Do not use the results to beat each other with: think carefully about your partner's perception

6	5	4	3	2	1
Often		Sometimes			Never

1 When we argue, I feel my partner threatens me
2 When we argue, I feel my partner lectures me
3 When we argue, I feel my partner is trying to make me feel guilty
4 I feel frustrated when my partner and I argue, because s/he dissolves into tears (or otherwise indicates 'it's all too much for me')
5 I feel bullied by the fact that my partner forces the argument on with calm, rational logic
6 When we argue, I feel cold-shouldered: my partner acts as if I'm stupid to be concerned

LOVE BUGS

A RELATIONSHIP IS NOT LIKELY TO LAST IF:

● *she* asks for change in a brusque way – 'harsh start-up'

● *he* rejects her influence

● *she* fails to cheer him up when he expresses strong, negative feelings such as contempt

● *he* fails to cheer her up when she expresses low-intensity negative feelings such as sadness

● *she* fails to soothe him (or *he* fails to soothe himself) when he gets het up while they're in discussion

couples regularly use coercion. Coercion is only found among 2% of satisfied couples, mainly because when one partner shows resistance, these couples back off or face facts, working on (and dealing with) the underlying problem. The most serious type of coercion is physical violence: we'll come to that in the next chapter.

The second of the boomerangs that relentlessly drive us apart is called *polarization*. Here both partners change – away from each other. This is how it works: when you feel under attack you either withdraw (flight) or defend your position (fight). To defend, you keep stating and re-stating your own argument, and this causes you to stop listening to your partner. The less you listen to their argument, and the more you listen to your own, the more convinced you are that you are right, and the more extreme your views become. Where once you could have admitted that your partner had a point, this now seems impossible. Your positions have *polarized*.

Polarization's sister process is called *specialization*. Partner A may want Partner B to spend more time with their baby. Partner B doesn't do so. This means that Partner A spends even more time with the child. Now Partner A becomes *much* better at childcare than Partner B who, feeling inadequate, pulls back even further. And so on. It is through *coercion, polarization* and *specialization* that the journey to irreconcilable difference is made. Partners who deep down are actually compatible can *become* incompatible, purely through using non-productive strategies as they struggle to manage differences and negotiate change.

acceptance

Attempting to create change (in your partner or in yourself) isn't the only possibility when you are faced with an incompatibility. You can *accept* the situation and make no attempt to change it, even putting up with quite negative behaviour from your partner because you recognize it as part of the package of who *you* are and who *they* are. When on-paper incompatibles make it to their golden wedding, it's often because they are big on *acceptance*. You hear them say, usually with resignation (but sometimes with fond amusement), 'he's like that' or 'she always...'. In its highest form *acceptance* allows you to see beyond your partner's negative actions to the good intentions from which those actions spring, and even to the positive consequences they sometimes have.

Acceptance is not the same as *submission*. *Acceptance* (the experts state) comes from a position of strength: you could cope without your partner, so you aren't obliged to accept whatever they're dumping on you, but you do so because you know they're not going to change, and you feel their bad qualities are outweighed by the good. *Submission*, by contrast, comes from a position of weakness: you put up with seriously damaging behaviour because you have, or think you have, no alternative. Distinguishing between the two sounds easy enough until you're in the middle of it: any halfway decent relationship is difficult to leave, because both partners have invested a lot in it and are seriously inter-dependent. 'Is this Relationship Good for You?', the Love Quiz, Test 27 quiz (see page 164), gives a fair idea of whether you are *accepting* healthily or *submitting* unhealthily.

One of the great things about *acceptance* is that it works in the opposite way from a boomerang: it *de*-escalates hostilities and makes agreement more likely. How? When a person feels *accepted,* they don't feel the need to defend themselves, so they are less likely to *withdraw* or play *innocent victim* or hit back with *criticism* and *contempt*. They are also less likely to take up an extreme position, so *polarization* is avoided. And because they're not being *coerced*, there's no build-up of resentment. Now they are able to look around and may see the effect their behaviour

LOVE TALK ...

Grant me the serenity to accept the things I cannot change, change the things I can, and the wisdom to know the difference

THE SERENITY PRAYER (ALCOHOLICS ANONYMOUS)

TEST 31: ACCEPTANCE

Think carefully about the following questions. List your responses on page 191. Perhaps your partner would like to do the same.

1 Which of your partner's characteristics have you, over time, come to accept?

2 Which of your partner's characteristics could you be more accepting of?

3 Which are some of your characteristics that your partner has come to accept?

4 Which of your characteristics would you like your partner to be more accepting of?

5 Which of your partner's characteristics are you *submitting* to, although they affect you very badly?

is having. This not only improves the way the relationship functions, but can also cause them to *want to change* which as anyone from Alcoholics Anonymous will tell you, is the only way lasting change is ever achieved.

The finding that *acceptance* is actually the major route to *change* has caused a lot of surprise and excitement. In fact, the experts now go so far as to say that that *no one changes without feeling accepted first.* In light of this, the absolute stupidity of using criticism, contempt, coercion and so on, becomes dazzlingly clear, since all they do is cause your partner to *resist* change. However, it's no use practising *acceptance* in order to get your partner to change: it doesn't work like that. *Acceptance* has to be absolutely whole-hearted and sincere and to have no hidden agenda. And very often it doesn't lead to change. *Acceptance* is the new buzz-word among couple counsellors, although a cynic might ask whether this is because their attempts to bring about behaviour change in their clients have failed so spectacularly to date.

conflict style 1: validating

Although all happy couples find ways of handling their incompatibilities, they don't all do it in the same way. This has come as a big surprise to researchers, who had long believed that there was only one way for couples to deal with difference, which was to work, in an orderly fashion, through the three stages of conflict resolution. (In *stage 1* you hear each other's point of view; in *stage 2* you try to persuade your partner; in *stage 3* you resolve your differences.) Now they know this isn't so. Thousands of hours spent videoing couples in Love Labs have taught researchers many things, among them the important fact that there is more than one pathway to relationship heaven. They now know that there are *five* common 'conflict styles' (ways of negotiating incompatibility and change) and that no fewer than *three* of these regularly lead to bliss. Yet only one of the three positive conflict styles is the type that conventional couple counsellors would recognize as 'good'. Rich in communication, compromise and sweet reason, this is called the *Validating Style*, because even in the midst of argument each partner *validates* the other by helping them feel that their position is reasonable.

While couples who operate the *Validating Style* often argue, they rarely fight. But that's not what makes their approach unique. The special thing about *validators* is that they don't let sleeping dogs lie. They pursue their differences *until they get to the heart of the matter*, which is generally to some kind of unacknowledged fear. Obediently following the three stages of conflict resolution, they listen to each other's point of view (Stage 1), try pleasantly to influence their partner (stage 2), and then head for a solution (stage 3).

If one *validator* wants mostly to hang out at home while the other prefers to party, they'll neither fight viciously about it nor sulk. Nor will they agree to differ and encourage one to go out a lot while the other stays behind. Instead they'll keep talking until they discover, perhaps, that the stay-at-home is scared that *any* agreement to party will be taken as a green light for nonstop socializing. Once this fear is expressed and reassurance given, they'll compromise: they'll go out sometimes; they'll stay home sometimes; and they'll do much of it *together*.

It may come as something of a relief to learn that even goody-two-shoes *Validators* don't communicate and compromise the whole time. Like everyone else, they can be petty, sulky, mean and unfair. Nor are their relationships disaster-proof. Too much reasoned communication can sap passion; and compromise isn't always possible. Researchers investigating the issues couples fight over regularly, have found that 69% of these *cannot* be resolved through give-and-take: only 31% of the time is compromise even an option. In fact, many of the hottest couple topics seem to be insoluble: most of the things couples fight over during the first year they live together are the very same things they'll be fighting over,

20 or 30 years on. The top five conflict issues for older couples are communication, recreation, money, children *and sex*! Nevertheless, the fact that *validators* can work patiently and thoroughly through delicate issues, while at the same time helping each other feel good about themselves, gives the *Validating Style* its staying power. Researchers have found loads of *validators* among elderly couples, who often touch each other affectionately, and look lovingly at each other while they are being interviewed – even when one partner has gone blind.

The *Validating Style* is very appealing *as an idea* in the twenty-first century because, in Western culture, togetherness is supposed to be all-important, and this squeaky-clean process of communication and compromise is what many people think love is all about. Many couple-counselling

THE LOVE QUIZ

TEST 32:
THE VALIDATING STYLE

Do you operate a Validating Conflict Style? Rate each statement below. Enter the total in the box on page 191. Now get your partner to do the same. If you can't answer some of the questions easily, create your own Love Lab: run a video camera while you discuss a problem topic, then watch how you and your partner behave

6	5	4	3	2	1
True		**Neutral**		**Not true**	

1 When we disagree our arguments often turn into discussions
2 My partner usually understands where I am 'coming from' even when we hold very different views
3 We don't seem to disagree very much
4 We cultivate a sense of 'we-ness' in our relationship
5 My partner encourages me to say how I think and feel
6 My partner listens carefully when I have my say and sometimes nods or smiles or makes friendly sounds
7 Sometimes, when I am worried or upset, I catch the same expressions on my partner's face
8 One of us occasionally paraphrases what the other has said, to show we understand
9 I do not feel my partner often tries to persuade me to change my mind
10 We compromise a lot of the time

ELDERLY VALIDATORS
- express *high levels of relationship satisfaction*
- communicate openly and perceptively
- when describing past events tell the same story as their partner
- treat each other with respect and dignity
- often finish each other's sentences
- openly (and accurately) read each other's minds

programmes and most books on how to save your marriage have been recommending validation-style behaviour to distressed couples. One of their most widely practised (and now discredited) ideas was *active listening*. Here, you had to paraphrase back to your partner what they'd just said – and have them agree that you'd heard (understood) them correctly – before you were allowed to say anything yourself. When, eventually, you got to utter a few words, your partner had to paraphrase them back to you, and so on. Negotiations over a cup of coffee could last a week.

Another weird recommendation, designed (reasonably enough) to counter the fact that stressed people are usually too agitated to problem-solve effectively, was to get couples to stop in the middle of a row and *take their own pulse*. If they found their heart was hammering, they had to go out for a walk and cool down before they were allowed to continue the discussion. Great idea, but if you have the self-control to stop and take your pulse under such circumstances, you probably don't have a problem. The difficulty with any of these techniques is that they only work for real communication virtuosos, that is, natural *validators* – and they comprise less than half the population.

THE VALIDATING STYLE
- is not suitable for over-emotional people
- is not suitable for people who need a lot of personal space
- needs both partners to be interested in motivations and feelings
- needs at least one *secure* partner
- needs *either* a good match in values and preferences *or* at least one very easy-going partner
- needs excellent communication skills

conflict style 2: semi-detached

To people who (unlike *validators*) are not brilliant at conflict resolution, it comes as something of a relief to learn that 'communication and compromise' isn't the only way forward. There are two other highly effective conflict styles, and they require very little of either. The first of these is the *Semi-detached Conflict Style*, so-called because the couples who follow it don't communicate much at all. Emotionally, they jog along in parallel. They do have some qualities in common with *validators*: they have little taste for conflict; they're big on *acceptance*; they're highly committed and caring; they treat each other with respect and politeness; and they score between medium and high in relationship satisfaction. But there the similarities end. *Semi-detached couples* don't explore issues in any depth; they focus more on 'I' than on 'we'; they spend a lot of time apart, each doing their own thing and, when asked about the past, can have quite different views of what really happened. Overall, they have negotiated comfortable levels of what one expert calls 'distant intimacy'.

The way semi-detached couples handle the three stages of conflict resolution would horrify the average couple counsellor. Certainly semi-detached couples spend time in stage 1 (they hear each other's point of view) but they virtually skip stage 2 (trying to persuade your partner) and leave out stage 3 (resolving your differences) altogether. And yet both partners walk away happy. How? By agreeing to differ and deciding that their current problem topic isn't important after all. Although each person goes their own way, they keep a sense of togetherness by remembering everything they do agree on and value – and there they are, 50 years on, taking turns on the Stennah stair lift and helping each other in and out of the walk-in bath.

Like the *Validating Style*, the *Semi-detached Style* has its dangers. Couples who operate this way don't get much practice in negotiation (so when this is really needed they can flounder); too much distant intimacy can mean not keeping in touch with how each other's likes and dislikes are changing; and if too many feelings are left unresolved, one or both partners can end up angry or lonely. The stress of bottling up their feelings can even make them ill: *semi-detached couples* are said to suffer more illness than other couples, and illness is one of those life events that can torpedo love. However, on the plus side, couples who operate the *Semi-detached Style* don't need to be as well suited as

TEST 33:
THE SEMI-DETACHED
CONFLICT STYLE

Is this your conflict style? Rate each statement below. Enter the total in the box on page 191. Now get your partner to do the same

6	5	4	3	2	1
True		**Neutral**		**Not true**	

1 We lead a fairly calm and pleasant life

2 There are quite a lot of things we don't see eye to eye on

3 We like to do different things and often spend time apart

4 I often hide my feelings so I don't hurt my partner

5 Getting angry doesn't solve anything

6 Trying to force your partner to see things your way is a waste of time

7 Things usually sort themselves out, if you leave them long enough

8 We often agree to disagree

9 Our relationship is strong: we don't need to agree on everything

10 Chewing over people's behaviour and motivation is a waste of time

validators. What's more, by just letting their relationship be without constantly putting it to the test, they keep strain at bay and allow love to flourish quietly.

conflict style 3:
volatile

The third highly effective conflict style is called the *Volatile Style*. Although most of us are aware that people shout more in some cultures than in others (and everyone has known warring couples who nevertheless stay together) the widespread success of the *Volatile Conflict Style* has caught the experts by surprise. For *volatile* couples do very odd things with the three stages of conflict resolution. They skip stage 1 (hearing each other's point of view) and jump with both feet into stage 2 (they try to persuade their partner) where they hang around for ages, spitting out *criticism* and *contempt* and playing *innocent victim* with great gusto.

They make little or no attempt to understand and empathize, and show zero interest in compromise. Winning is what they're about, and if they can score points on the way, so much the better.

Why do so many *volatiles* make it through? Their success comes because after their noisy trading of insults (during which they somehow manage never to hit too far below the belt, although to onlookers it may sound like it) they move to stage 3 of conflict resolution (they resolve their differences). Without warning, a compromise is suggested and agreed to, or one partner gives in, and – hey presto! – the problem is resolved. Like the other highly effective conflict styles, the *Volatile Style* has its dangers: the quarrelling and bickering can overwhelm the happy times; the teasing and relentless honesty can leave serious scars. The *Volatile Style*, more than either of the other two, requires a careful balancing act; but provided *volatiles* stay within sane limits, they can experience many good years.

The key to success for all the conflict styles is the de-escalation of conflict before it gets out of hand, accompanied by a good balance of

THE LOVE QUIZ

TEST 34:
THE VOLATILE
CONFLICT STYLE

Rate each statement below. Enter the total in the box on page 191. Now get your partner to do the same. If you can't answer some of the questions easily, create your own Love Lab: run a video camera while you discuss a problem topic, then watch how you and your partner behave

6	5	4	3	2	1
True		**Neutral**		**Not true**	

1 When we're talking, my partner often interrupts me with questions
2 We respect each other's privacy
3 It's good to let your partner know how you feel, even if it hurts them
4 We tease each other quite a bit
5 I don't hide my thoughts and feelings from my partner
6 A good argument can be exhilarating
7 I enjoy trying to persuade my partner to see things my way
8 Argue at least three times a week – that's my motto
9 A lot of the time we feel very close
10 Jealousy can be quite an issue with us

ELDERLY COUPLES

- ● tend to be more affectionate than middle-aged or younger couples
- ● tend to be less attacking than middle-aged or younger couples
- ● tend to be less negative than middle-aged or younger couples
- ● elderly men, in particular, often become gentle and tender
- ● elderly women may dislike this, declaring that the men have become clingy

positivity to negativity – the 5:1 ratio mentioned earlier. While happy *volatiles* experience lots of negatives, they balance these by at least five times as many positives: warmth, laughter, undivided attention, hugs, kisses, smiles and praise. *Semi-detached* couples don't have to deal with many negatives (their partners almost never say horrible things to them) but they probably won't experience many positives, either (they may actually interact with their partners very little). Again, as long as the positive/negative ratio is 5:1, they'll be OK. It is interesting that while researchers have found *volatiles* staying happy and together over many years, they haven't found many *volatile* couples among older people. This is very probably because (if they haven't split up) they've mellowed.

asking nicely

If you found it difficult to answer the conflict style quizzes above, or found that one partner answered one way and the other another, this points to incompatibility in conflict styles. Incompatibility in conflict styles can be a serious problem, because it can lead a couple who are actually well-suited to the false conclusion that they're totally incompatible *as people*. Grasping that it's the medium (the conflict style) not the message (who you are) that's the issue, can be transforming. And once you understand how the different conflict styles work, it can be possible to make adjustments. One partner may learn to operate in the other's style, or the couple may create a mixed style, borrowing a bit from here and bit from there. Many couples spontaneously switch conflict styles from time to time. It's not uncommon, for instance, for a pair of *validators* to switch into *semi-detached* mode when faced with an issue on which they really can't reach a compromise.

Along with finding the best conflict style for *you as a couple*, you need to retrain in the way you ask your partner to change, so that you avoid the *boomerangs – criticism, contempt, innocent victim, withdrawal, coercion* and so on. Researchers have been able to track the terrible impact of these on sexual partnerships because they've found them present *before* relationships begin to sour. This doesn't mean they're the only cause, but it is clear they have a major part to play. There is also compelling evidence that if you want your partner to change, approaching them *without* criticizing, demanding, withdrawing (and so on) can achieve spectacular results. In fact asking nicely can be so effective in terms of getting you what we want that it can make you feel that you are being manipulative.

The experts warn, that just because one partner is being sweetly reasonable doesn't mean the other will respond in kind. Even a mild request can be heard as an attack and the response may be hostile. In fact, research shows that men often interpret *any* comment from women about women and men as an attack. The trick, then, according to the 'save your marriage' gurus is to *stop the fight in its tracks*. We are to turn the other cheek, and make some loving, appreciative comment: 'I know you've been stressed lately, so going out has been the last thing on your mind. I really admire the way you've been coping with it all.' There's clear evidence that though this won't create an instant solution, it will change the *tone* of events so that, over time, conflict may become less heated and less frequent.

But often conflict doesn't become less heated and less frequent. Extraordinary and quite unjustifiable claims are made for the 'asking nicely' techniques. Virtually every divorce-busting book majors in them, implying (and often actually stating) that any relationship that isn't seriously physically or emotionally abusive can be saved by giving up on blame, contempt, criticism and so on.

Yet here's the rub: for 5 out of 6 couples changing conflict behaviour from negative to

LOVE NOTES ...

The idea that we should always be 'honest and spontaneous' with our partner is a nonsense. We cannot expect to be loved when we take our frustrations in the world out on people at home; when we treat perfect strangers more politely than our nearest and dearest. Attacks generate counter-attacks. Love and positive regard are reciprocal and conditional. If you want a happy love-life, try politeness, willingness, tact and good humour.

LAZARUS (1985)

THE LOVE QUIZ

TEST 35:
THE BLAME GAME

When you are next in conflict with your partner, note how many times you do any of the following. Give yourself one point for each instance and then fill in your score on page 192. Get your partner to do the same.

1 I denied responsibility ('it wasn't my fault')

2 I blamed my partner ('if you'd only ...')

3 I made excuses ('I couldn't help ...')

4 I mind-read, i.e. speculated on my partner's motives ('you said that because you wanted ...')

5 I yes-butted: found a reason why something couldn't be done or wouldn't work ('we could try, but ...')

6 I interpreted my partner's behaviour as due to a personal defect ('because you're selfish/lazy/don't care')

7 I cross-complained: when they complained about me, I made a complaint about them

positive *over a sustained period* proves impossible. There are several reasons for this. First, leaping on to the defensive and chucking boomerangs around is deeply ingrained behaviour, and very difficult to shift. We're trained in these techniques from our earliest years, since blame, criticism, contempt and physical coercion (smacks) feature in the average parent's daily repertoire: ('if you weren't so messy, you'd be able to find it', 'now look what you've done, stupid!'). Parents also respond far more quickly and intensely to negative behaviour from their children than to positive (children's good behaviour often passes without comment because it doesn't get in the way). Hostile parents often get results by frightening their offspring into submission, sometimes temporarily, sometimes for life and, in the process, modelling conflict strategies which their children grow up to use on their children, and on their partners.

Parenting courses now teach parents to major on the positive, noticing and praising good behaviour, paying little or no attention to bad and setting limits in a positive way: 'he's such a good boy, he never touches those dangerous plugs'. Research is finding that this works wonderfully well: even so-called difficult children can become cooperative and happy. What's more, having absorbed this constructive blueprint the chances are that they will use it automatically as adults. Now *that* could do a lot to bring down the divorce rate. Sadly, few of us have had such a training and few are teaching it to our own children. When we are hurt or frightened, we spring into action, waving our boomerangs around our heads. It can take almost superhuman effort to stop.

Another reason that the boomerangs are so easy to reach for and so difficult to give up, is that they are soothing. Blame, contempt, criticism, etc. are some of the mechanisms by which we export upsetting feelings out of our selves and dump them into our partner. When we are denied such outlets, we can become edgy and distressed, as our upsetting feelings fester inside our bodies. However, when we become a whiz at asking nicely we do eventually get to release these feelings. The relief comes because we are able to express how we feel, although not in a negative

TEST 36: ASKING NICELY

The next few times you want your partner to change their behaviour, try asking nicely. Notice how often you manage to do any of the following. Repeat the process whenever an argument rises, and keep tabs on whether their responses gradually become more positive. Give yourself one point for each instance and then fill in your score on page 192. Get your partner to do the same.

1 I spoke without blaming my partner ('we don't go out as much as I'd like to', *not* 'you never take me anywhere')

2 I said how *I* felt or what *I* hoped for or wanted, without whining or attacking) ('I felt really low when you rang to say you wouldn't be home in time to go out', *not* 'you let me down again – promises mean nothing to you, do they!')

3 I was direct and specific about a practical change I wanted ('I would like us to go out together this weekend', *not* 'Why can't you put more time into this relationship?')

4 When my partner came back at me, I said something pleasant, which showed I understood the pressures s/he was under

5 I didn't criticize my partner's personality, or insult or tease them

6 I didn't kitchen-sink: I stuck to one issue

7 I didn't mind read (make assumptions about my partner's thoughts, feelings or motives)

8 I didn't threaten my partner

9 I didn't frighten my partner

10 I didn't hurt my partner physically

and hostile way ('*I felt really low when you rang to say you wouldn't be home in time to go out*'). This means we do get things off our chest although without ratcheting up the tension. But learning to do this takes time. It also requires huge willingness, commitment, patience and, very often, professional help.

But the major reason why learning 'positive behaviour' only works for relatively few couples is that by the time they start working on them it's too late. The criticism, the contempt, the withdrawal, the blame now express what they deeply feel. The boomerangs are now more than the *cause* of a couple's difficulties; they are symptoms of enormous distress, the tip of a massive iceberg of anger, alienation and despair. To try to teach people in this kind of emotional state to ask nicely is a bit like offering a cancer sufferer a plaster. Asking nicely can't solve massive money problems or stop alcoholics drinking or drug addicts using or seriously violent people hitting out; it won't bring back a loved one or make a sick soul well; and it cannot revive a love that has really died. To suggest that to save our relationships all most of us need to do is learn to be excellent to each other is seriously misleading, even irresponsible. If things aren't going well and we want love to last, we must dig deeper.

love busters

Use these lists differently, depending on whether your relationship is still in the early stages or is deeply entwined (e.g. you have had a child together)

● **Early stages** If five or more of the negative statements below apply to you, think carefully: you will already have some sense of the relationship not being right, and these may help you understand why continuing with it may be a mistake. However, if there are also many positive reasons for being together (see Love boosters) then the negative(s) may be cancelled out.

● **Deeply entwined** No single negative indicator (or even a cluster of negatives) should be taken as a cue to give up on your relationship. Understood in the context of this chapter, they may help you grasp some of your dissatisfactions and prompt you to work at these areas, in order to create a more satisfying partnership.

Your relationship has a below-average chance when you ...
● experience lots of conflict early on
● almost never disagree or argue early on

● feel flashes of strong dislike or contempt early on
● are looking to your partner to change, so the relationship can work
● change to please a lot early on (men particularly)
● must try hard to be interested in your partner's leisure-activities
● don't change much over the years
● take little notice of your partner's requests for change (men particularly)
● joke around when your partner raises change issues (men particularly)
● ask for change in a brusque way (women particularly)
● have to hassle your partner whenever you want change
● have been struggling with infertility
● experience many stressful life events
● live in a violent neighbourhood where you feel constantly under threat
● when stressed, often become touchy and argumentative, or switch off
● are stressed a lot
● are depressed
● behave in a domineering way
● run around trying to make your partner happy
● run around trying to anticipate their every need
● constantly put your partner's needs before your own
● try to be understanding and lovable at all times
● don't feel sincere when you behave in a friendly or loving way
● feel anxious when you have to talk to or be with your partner
● experience a great deal of negative conflict, in which you:
    ● try to prove yourself right and your partner wrong
    ● keep returning to the same topics
    ● regularly blame, criticize and display contempt for your partner
● regularly cut arguments short: refuse to discuss matters any further
● one partner regularly demands, the other withdraws
● find it hard to see your partner's point or view when disagreeing
● often disagree *and* often take steps to avoid a row
● accept seriously abusive behaviour from your partner
● don't have anyone other than your partner to confide in (men particularly)
● start living together because of a pregnancy
● are not keen on the idea of the pregnancy (men)
● have a child within the first year or two
● do not go for help after noticing a serious, ongoing problem in your relationship
● take steps to restrict your partner's development

love boosters

Your relationship has an above-average chance when you ...

● are flexible and adaptable

● often meet each other halfway when change is required

● take conscious steps to manage life changes together

● create a general climate of supportiveness where you regularly and openly:

    ● show love, understanding and concern for your partner

    ● show respect and admiration for your partner

    ● do practical things to support your partner on a daily basis

● show that you understand your partner (men)

● how that you admire your partner (women)

● notice how your partner is feeling

● know about what's going on in your partner's life

● contribute, on average, five positives (smiles, friendly sounds, touches and words, etc.) to every one negative (frowns, negative sounds, touches and words, etc.)

● regularly solve day-to-day problems *together*

● when coping with a serious life event, keep channels of communication open

● develop a joint world-view/life-plan different from your own families' early on

● express straightforward anger early on (women)

● are both improved by your relationship in the eyes of outsiders

● maintain interests/friendships outside your relationship

● can be cheered up by your partner when you are sad or mildly anxious (women)

● can be cheered/soothed by our partner when you are very angry or upset (men)

● are accepting of your partner's foibles and failings

● usually treat your partner with consideration and respect

● when you have arguments are able to:

    ● communicate thoroughly about your difficulties, and compromise; or

    ● hardly fight, then allow one partner to get their way, without resenting this; or

    ● have a good fight then reach a solution that feels OK to both partners

● stop tit-for-tat arguments escalating nastily

● when you fight, don't hit below the belt

TEST RESULTS

TEST 23:
MANAGING CHANGE
Your total: ▢ Your partner's total: ▢
A medium-to-low score (less than 28) here should be a serious matter
for concern. This is one of the most important quizzes in the book and
a low score indicates that if your relationship is to continue you will
need a massive change of attitude or professional help.

TEST 24:
HOW SUPPORTIVE ARE YOU?
Your total: ▢ Your partner's total: ▢
Your total (as scored by your partner): ▢
Your partner's total (as scored by you): ▢
A low score (of less than 30) is bad news, particularly in relationships
that have already lasted some time. But take heart: you can learn to be
supportive, if you believe it is important. If you try behaviour change,
you'll need to check in with your partner with this test every couple
of weeks, until the habit is more deeply ingrained

TEST 25:
LIFE EVENTS
Your total: ▢
If you are having problems in your relationship, and you score even one
point, do not assume that you are incompatible. You may have grown
apart through stress. If you are gentle with each other and regularly
spend time together, your relationship may mend of its own accord. Or
you could try a relationship self-help book or couple-counselling (see
Resources, page 251). Even one good session may help put your relationship back on track.

TEST 26:
HAVING A BABY
1. Your score: ▢ Your partner's score: ▢
2. Your score: ▢ Your partner's score: ▢
3. Your score: ▢ Your partner's score: ▢
4. Your score: ▢ Your partner's score: ▢

5.	Your score: [ ]	Your partner's score:	[ ]
6.	Your score: [ ]	Your partner's score:	[ ]
7.	Your score: [ ]	Your partner's score:	[ ]
8.	Your score: [ ]	Your partner's score:	[ ]
9.	Your score: [ ]	Your partner's score:	[ ]
10.	Your score: [ ]	Your partner's score:	[ ]

Take the lower score to represent the state of play. A score of less than 30 indicates problems, and a low score on any individual question should prompt reflection and behaviour change.

TEST 27:
IS THIS RELATIONSHIP GOOD FOR YOU?
Your score: [ ]

A 28+ score means that you are in a healthy relationship. A lower score means you need to reconsider.

TEST 28:
ARE YOU A CRITIC?
Your score: [ ]   Your partner's score: [ ]

A 30+ score means that the way you are handling conflict is making matters worse and could even be a major cause of your difficulties. You can work on behaviour change with a professional counsellor, or through books recommended in Resources, page 251.

TEST 29:
DO YOU PLAY THE INNOCENT VICTIM?
Your score: [ ]   Your partner's score: [ ]

A 30+ score means that the way you are handling conflict is making matters worse and could even be a major cause of your difficulties. You can work on behaviour change with a professional counsellor, or through books recommended in Resources, page 251.

TEST 30: COERCION
Your score: [ ]   Your partner's score: [ ]

An 18+ score means that the way you are handling conflict is making matters worse and could even be a major cause of your difficulties. You can work on behaviour change with a professional counsellor, or through books recommended in Resources, page 251.

TEST 31:
ACCEPTANCE

Answer each question below, or use a separate sheet of paper if you need more space.

1.
2.
3.
4.
5.

Your partner:

1.
2.
3.
4.
5.

Compare and contrast your responses. Now set an 'acceptance' goal for the next month.

Your acceptance goal:

Your partner's acceptance goal:

TEST 32:
THE VALIDATING STYLE

Your score: Your partner's score:

A 40+ score suggests that your overall conflict style is validating. A big difference between your scores on any question should provide a topic for discussion. If this is not your conflict style, try the next quiz.

TEST 33:
THE SEMI-DETACHED STYLE

Your score: Your partner's score:

A 40+ score suggests that your overall conflict style is semi-detached. A big difference between your scores on any question should provide a topic for discussion. If this is not your conflict style, try the next quiz.

TEST 34:
THE VOLATILE STYLE

Your score: Your partner's score:

A 40+ score suggests that your overall conflict style is volatile. A big difference between your scores on any question should provide a topic for discussion. If neither this nor the other two conflict styles apply to you, or if you and your partner don't agree on a style, read on in the main text.

TEST 35:
THE BLAME GAME

Your score: ⬜ Your partner's score: ⬜

Any single score, let alone more than one, suggests you are refusing to look at how you are contributing to the distress in your relationship. This means that change will not be possible, because the only changes you have the power to make, are in your own behaviour.

TEST 36:
ASKING NICELY

Your score: ⬜ Your partner's score: ⬜

Even a single score here deserves applause. All this can be incredibly hard to do, if you're in the habit of doing something different. Your partner will probably not respond positively – yet. Repeat the process whenever an argument arises, and keep tabs on whether their responses gradually become more positive.

5
lying

love lies

talk shows

I think, therefore you are

making promises

breaking promises

mate guarding

doing what comes naturally?

kill or cure

forgiveness

closeness

divorce-prone people

love busters

love boosters

love lies

People approach love, as they do any experience that is much talked about, with strong expectations and beliefs. In Chapter 3, we saw what happens when sexual expectations are not met: sexual satisfaction becomes impossible. Disappointed expectations in other areas can be just as damaging: in fact, one researcher claims that the extent to which a couple's expectations of their relationship are not fulfilled is the most powerful single predictor of divorce. A major reason why young love often falters is thought to be the split between expectation and reality: expectations are high, but the young have neither the cash nor skills to create real-life love to match their hopes and dreams.

Some false expectations of love (love lies) are unreasonable at any age. One leading US counsellor sees couples with good relationships who believe them to be on the rocks, simply because they fail to match an unattainable ideal. Many love lies are hangovers from the way society used to be organized. For example, researchers have learned that the idea of love as an uncontrollable, life-shattering force is often found in cultures

THE LOVE QUIZ

TEST 37: PERFECT LOVE

Be ruthlessly honest: which of these statements rings a bell with you, even if you'd say they were absurd. Score each of them individually, and enter the scores on page 237. Your partner may like to do the same.

6	5	4	3	2	1
True		Maybe		False	

1 Love can make you happy
2 Miscommunication and misunderstanding mean things aren't right
3 Some lucky people have perfect relationships
4 When love is real, loving and being-loved come easy
5 True love lasts for ever
6 Intimacy means being able to read each other's minds
7 Intimacy you work to achieve isn't as good as natural intimacy
8 Only lovers who know everything about each other, can be close
9 Only lovers who agree on most things can be close
10 Feeling close makes all couples happy

● sex differences in relationships are profound: people should recognize and honour them
● sex differences cause most of the problems in heterosexual relationships
● monogamy is for women
● competition between partners adds sparkle
● very few people have happy relationships
● if your partner wants to leave, hang on and fight
● dead love can sometimes be rekindled

where there are strict mating rules. Love has to be seen as virtually heaven-sent to justify stepping out of line. Currently in the West there's a decline in high romanticism, and this makes sense: when we can have sex with (and marry) just about anyone we like, love doesn't have to be presented as near-mystical.

Behaving in accordance with false beliefs can seriously damage love. Take the love lie that partners should do everything together. The truth is that the constant physical nearness of a live-in partner, plus the burdens and responsibilities of a shared life, are so stressful that wise lovers take deliberate steps to preserve some separateness. When men used to hang out in garden sheds in the 1950s, this probably kept quite a few couples together.

False beliefs about men's and women's supposed real natures are rife. Western society has long believed in the idea that men and women are very different. This is because, until about a hundred years ago, biology was destiny: women spent much of their adult lives pregnant or breastfeeding and were often dead before their last child reached 20; men's rough, tough qualities were cultivated – they were needed for hard physical labour and for going into battle at a moment's notice. Now that the organization of life is entirely different (men are more likely to work in offices than down mines, and childbearing takes up a minuscule part of women's lives) Western society has been through a phase of believing there are no sex differences. Now society is in the middle of a backlash. Sex differences are again being emphasized, with most relationship problems put down to men's and women's different places of birth: men on Mars and women on Venus.

Academic research (including many of the studies quoted in this book) contributes, by setting up studies to ask the question 'how are men and women *different*?' When it finds even tiny sex differences (most sex

MORE LOVE LIES

- lovers should do everything together
- lovers should tell each other everything
- lovers should be able to read each other's minds
- love means never having to say you're sorry
- if you feel guilty, confess
- always say what you feel

differences show up in the research as very small) these grab the headlines. While it can sometimes be useful to understand sex-based *tendencies* (whether caused by biology or upbringing) overemphasizing these and closing your eyes to the many similarities between women and men, and many differences between people of the same sex, is seriously damaging. Not only does it imply that change is not possible (and so discourages you from working towards it), but it prevents you from seeing your partner as an individual and can easily cause you to attribute their behaviour to the wrong cause.

For example, if a woman believes that her (male) partner's unwillingness to talk things over is because men simply don't talk, she can miss the fact that his silence expresses deep anger and resentment, which need to be tackled. And if a man puts his (female) partner's babycare skills down to her innate talents as a woman rather than to the practice she's getting at childcare while he's at work (which in fact will be the real reason – women do *not* have innate babycare talents that men lack) he can pull back from the magic circle of mother and child, so that a split develops in the household, and in their relationship.

talk shows

Many of the most potent love lies have to do with communication. Take the popular idea that lovers should tell each other everything. Certainly, self-disclosure is strongly linked to lasting love, probably because it takes the guesswork out of communication. When you don't *know* what your partner wants, you mind-read and can easily get it wrong. Even though women are supposed to communicate well, in sexual partnerships they often don't disclose what they want and feel which, in the long term, can be destructive. A woman who is prepared to self-disclose is a good bet as a long-term partner. Among men a willingness to self-disclose also bodes well, but in a different way: young men who are open to warm, close and communicative interaction with other people show up as having above-average emotional health in middle age.

Mind-reading isn't *always* a disaster. It's common (and often *not* damaging) among older, well-established couples. And although men tend to appreciate self-disclosure by their partners (even when they're not up for it themselves), couples mostly do best when they enjoy a similar level of self-disclosure. Even more importantly, if what someone discloses is hurtful and negative, then always saying what you think and feel does more harm than good. The research shows that the happiest couples *limit* how much (and what) they tell their partner. Although they don't hesitate to raise difficult issues, much of what they disclose is pleasant and positive. By contrast, some of the most unhappy couples let it all hang out: they disclose a great deal (about unimportant as well as important things) usually in a negative way.

Although men are supposed to be less interested in communicating than women, research shows that both men and women see good communication as a top priority in love relationships. (Maybe communication in general is meant here, rather than communication about problem areas: as has been seen, men can be more likely than women to avoid painful communication). However, talking a lot isn't the same as communicating well. Effective communication tends to result in shorter conversations: when we talk a lot it may be because we're communicating *badly.* Courting couples who have long conversations the male partner finds unsatisfactory are often found, after a few years, to be communicating poorly.

Does good communication lead to a satisfying relationship, or does a satisfying relationship lead to good communication? Although this can be a two-way street, the research suggests that satisfaction leads to good

MORE AND MORE LOVE LIES

- having a child will improve a bad relationship
- only through very hard work can a relationship succeed
- love should be a 50:50 partnership
- a good relationship will make you happy
- love can make your dreams come true
- an affair always destroys love
- without total trust, no relationship can succeed

communication more often than good communication leads to satisfaction. It's important to know this because it means that when things start going wrong, you do better trying to be kind to each other than honing your communication skills. Communication is often presented as a panacea. In fact it's a double-edges sword, effective communication may reveal incompatibilities and make you dissatisfied. And the more skilled you are at putting words together and predicting how they will affect your partner, the more effective you can be at causing them pain. If your motive for communicating is to hurt, then the better your communication skills, the more unhappy your partner will be.

Couples heading for break-up usually name communication problems as their biggest stumbling block; and even partners who are rumbling along fairly happily together tell researchers that communication difficulties cause them the most grief. For a long time, researchers took this at face value, assuming that when couples didn't communicate it was because they couldn't, that their communication skills were poor. They now know this needn't be so. Most non-communicating couples communicate perfectly well when communicating *with other people*. It's communicating *with each other* they find difficult. Researchers have now concluded that when many couples say they 'can't communicate' what they mean is that one or other is *refusing* to communicate. Perhaps they've learned that communication with their partner is painful, or they may wish to keep their distance (maybe they've fallen for someone else).

Sometimes poor communication skills really are the problem. In violent relationships both partners often have poor communication skills. Violence may be an aggressor's only 'tool' for expressing how they feel

COMMUNICATION AND SATISFACTION

● early in relationships, women who feel they communicate well with their partners also tend to feel highly satisfied with the relationship

● as time passes, this changes: many women can still feel satisfied with their relationship, even when they recognize that communication is not so good

● this is not the case for men, for whom the link between satisfaction and communication becomes ever stronger over time: maybe men are only prepared to continue communicating when they like their partner, and therefore feel safe

LOVE NOTES

THE BUILDING BLOCKS OF COMMUNICATION INCLUDE:

● sending skills — encoding your message so that the hearer easily understands

● receiving skills — decoding correctly (and remembering) their communication

● crystal-balling — predicting how your message will be received

● people-reading — working out what people are thinking and feeling, and why

and/or trying to get their partner to change. When the violence is stopped they can literally be 'struck dumb'. They have no other communication/ change strategies at their disposal. Researchers investigating the daily lives of violent couples have been intrigued to discover that many of them *only come together in violence.* The rest of the time, they are living in isolation in the same house, rarely doing the ordinary things that allow for everyday communication, such as eating together or renting a video or going for a walk.

Difficult topics make communication difficult, even when you are very much in love. The research shows clearly that both high- and low-satis-faction couples have problems discussing upsetting things. As pointed out in the last chapter, feeling upset can cause miscommunication, by making you hear your partner's communication as more negative than they intended it to be. There's a double-trouble syndrome here: unhappy part-ners are both *less likely* to interpret their partner's communication correctly and *more likely* to believe they've got it right.

Some couples who say they can't communicate mean they're into a vicious cycle of contempt, criticism, withdrawal, blame and so on (although these are less communications than attempts to get a partner to change). When some people (often women) self-righteously complain that their partner won't talk, what they really mean is that he's refusing to stand and listen to blame and criticism. Other couples who complain about non-communication may mean that intimacy has disappeared. A drop in intimacy is usually noticed when there's a drop in the amount of tenderness *being expressed.* Never hearing words of affection can lead not only women *but men too* to question whether their partner really cares. One of the best ways of keeping a sense of open communication is to pay attention to ways of expressing tenderness. While tenderness and affection can be expressed through sex, expressing them *only* during sex tends to be interpreted as 'I love having sex with you' rather than as 'I love you'. Love actually means never stopping saying 'I love you'.

Partners' communication *styles* also need to be similar, particularly where people-reading is concerned. Couples often grow increasingly dissatisfied if only one partner has a deep interest in human motives and behaviour. This mismatch is likely to be most troubling where a woman isn't interested in people-reading but her partner is. Men who don't go in for people-reading don't get as irritated when their partner likes to dig deep into emotional topics. Maybe they think women are like that or maybe, because people-readers are often good at providing worry support, they put up with the people-reading in order to get the support.

Very often when communication seems faulty (there's either no communication or one partner gets angry) it's because someone is deeply hurt. Anger is an automatic response when self-esteem is knocked. Underlying the simplest daily events (a partner's failing to hear what you say; or forgetting to get something you asked them to get; or not feeling like sex) are massive themes: love, respect, caring, status, influence. An apparently trivial daily rejection can represent the tip of an enormous iceberg, made up of one or more of those themes.

When you feel the familiar surge of anger, you have two choices: you can focus on the external world (direct anger at your partner); or you can

LOVE NOTES

DECODING AND ENCODING

● when a man feels negative towards his partner, he often misreads her *emotional* state

● women's feelings of negativity towards their partner don't cause them to misread how their partner is *feeling* to the same extent

● the longer a couple are together, the better both partners get at decoding each other's *non-verbal* communications (mind-reading)

● both sexes decode positive messages less accurately than neutral or negative messages. This means that both men and women are less likely to recognize when their partner is feeling loving towards them, than when they are feeling hostile or angry

● women often decode their (male) partner's positive messages very poorly, possibly because the men encode less effectively (e.g. they smile less)

TEST 38:
DIGGING DEEP

When your partner is behaving in a way that you find upsetting or annoying, ask yourself the following questions. Turn to page 238.

1 What important reasons does my partner have for behaving in this way?

2 What fears, values, expectations or beliefs underlie their behaviour?

3 How does their behaviour make me feel (threatened, irritated or indifferent)?

4 When have I experienced this kind of reaction before?

5 What fears, values, expectations or beliefs lie behind my response?

6 How does my anger, irritation or indifference affect my partner?

7 How does my partner respond?

8 What part do I play in this problem?

9 If there is a clash of wills or interests involved, why is it so important for me to get my way, or be right?

think about your hurt. The first route brings the short-term gain (you get to deflect psychological pain) but makes further attack by your partner more likely. *Thinking about* your hurt causes discomfort (even pain) in the short-term but makes further attack by your partner less likely. So here you have the paradox: the behaviour that most effectively protects your self-esteem *in the short term*, is the least effective in making an intimate connection with your partner – and so strengthening your self-esteem *in the long run*.

Communication-blocking distress often has its roots in the past. Everyone has *vulnerabilities* – emotional hot-spots which, like a physical weakness (a proneness to headaches, back-ache or diarrhoea) can flare up when you are under stress. If being ignored by your lover reminds you of being ignored as a child, you may get angry when they are going through a busy patch. If you have never felt good enough then their disapproval can make you feel really awful. Understanding the origin of your vulnerabilities can go a long way to helping you handle them, which is important: since vulnerabilities are deeply embedded and are unlikely to disappear. In fact, how well they are managed is an important predictor of lasting love. The future is bright when the couple can name the vulnerabilities and work on modifying their own and accepting their partner's.

LOVE BUGS

COMMON EMOTIONAL VULNERABILITIES

- *vulnerability* to abandonment or rejection: 'don't ever leave me'
- *vulnerability* to being overwhelmed: 'help, I'm trapped!'
- *vulnerability* to not being good enough: 'tell me I'm OK'
- *vulnerability* to being ignored: 'please pay attention to me!'
- *vulnerability* to being out of control: 'I've got to do everything'

The outlook is poor when either denies their own vulnerabilities, or criticizes their partner for theirs, insisting that the vulnerability *should not be there* – that their partner is overreacting.

Vulnerabilities raise issues connected with love lies, because when a vulnerability is activated, you switch from responding to your partner *as they are*, and start responding to them *as if they were someone else* – usually someone from your past (very often a parent) who hurt or frightened you, even though you may have no conscious memory of this. Without realizing what you are doing, you *attribute* to your partner the old persecutor's motives, or what you believe their motives to have been.

I think, therefore you are

In order to make sense of the world, you are constantly *attributing* causes and motives to the things that you do, that are done to you, and that happen around you. You create these causes and motives (researchers call them *attributions*) from a mix of things, both imagined and real. For example, you reach the conclusion that your mate is reliable (or unreliable) partly through your real-life experience of them. But, spookily, you can also create that behaviour in them through your *attributions*: that is, through what you imagine the reasons for their behaviour to be. If you make a *positive attribution* (you believe your partner is doing the best they can, under difficult circumstances) then that can *cause* them to do the best they can: people who feel valued and admired are likely to behave well. If you make a *negative attribution* then this, too, can be a self-fulfilling prophecy: a partner who is viewed as selfish can start to behave selfishly. Researchers have found that attributions often precede behaviour: *negative attributions* (sad love lies) can send relationships downhill; *positive attributions* (happy love lies) can make them improve.

Sad love lies (*negative attributions*) are one of the main ways unhappy couples become more unhappy. As already established, all couples notice negative behaviour in their partner more than they notice positive; and unhappy couples are particularly likely to do this. Having noticed such behaviour, the unhappy couples *attribute* the worst possible reasons to it. They see it as *blameworthy* ('it's their fault') and this stops them examining their own behaviour. They see it as *stable* ('it's not going to change') and this means they make no attempt to improve matters. And they see it as *intentional* ('s/he wanted to upset me'), which means they see it as *personally relevant*.

Researchers have learned that when people see something as *personally relevant* their brain processes the information very fully; and that when they feel *emotional* about it, they tend to remember it later. This means that in the brains of unhappy partners, negativity looms large; so large, that it can even cause them to rewrite the history of their love affair. They may be unable to remember why they ever loved their partner, or put it down to something short-term ('I fancied them'). (When a man starts to do this it is a particularly powerful indicator that a love-affair is on the rocks.) They will now tell you that the scales have fallen from their eyes and that they see their partner as they really are. While this can of course be true, very often it's only partly true, or may not be true at all. What the unhappy person is seeing is an elaborate, negative caricature – a kind of *Spitting Image* puppet, which they are mentally superimposing on their partner.

MEMORY BIAS

Memory tested a week after keeping a diary of day-to-day events in their relationship:

● *unhappy couples* recall *more* bad times and *less* good times than they had originally written down

● *happy couples accurately* recall bad times but significantly *overestimate* the number of good times recorded

One reason that the false beliefs about love mentioned earlier can be so destructive is that they stimulate people to make *negative attributions.* When you aren't aware that your expectations of love are unrealistic, you have to keep coming up with reasons why you are constantly disappointed. Your tendency, then, is to *attribute* your disappointment to your mate's deficiencies. If you recognize that you are prone to attribution you need to be on your guard that your active imagination isn't making things worse. Self-disclosure can be a great antidote: voicing your attributions can allow them to be corrected, provided you do this without attacking your partner for the things you *imagine* s/he is doing, feeling or being.

Although happy love lies (*positive attributions*) can also have their downside (some people use them to blank out information they really need – such as that their partner is having an affair) it is through them that people keep love alive. Like falling out of love with someone, continuing to love someone is built to a surprisingly great extent on fantasy. It used to be thought that only in the first flush of sexual enthusiasm would you see your partner through rose-tinted spectacles but researchers now understand that happy couples view each other through rose-tinted spectacles *for life.* As already stated, where love is concerned, the *imagined* can be as vital as the *real* (couples who *believe* they are similar will often do as well as partners who *really are* similar). A key objective for long-term love is *sustaining the illusion*, and telling yourself that happy love lies is an important way you do this. Once you have taken those rose-tinted spectacles off, it is incredibly difficult to put them on again.

Understanding how *positive* and *negative attributions* work has helped researchers grasp why 'in love' couples are more likely to stay happy than satisficing couples (couples who got together for reasons such as 'it's time to settle down' or 'my partner makes a good living'). Because the in-love couples start off thinking highly of each other, they attribute negative behaviour by their partner to benevolent causes and/or see it as temporary. This motivates them to *accept* their partner's behaviour and *change* when change is required. As incompatibilities become clear, they often meet each other halfway. As life circumstances change, they develop joint strategies to cope. The spontaneous changes they make enable them to become the right people for their relationship. Also, expecting that things are likely to improve or to work out well wards off

THE LOVE QUIZ
TEST 39: STRENGTHS

If you feel your relationship is slipping, work through the following. Turn to page 238.

1 What characteristics in your partner drew you to them?
2 What are the positive aspects of each of those characteristics?
3 What are the negative aspects of each of those characteristics?
4 Think of a situation where you have negotiated a negative aspect successfully. What did you do?
5 What strengths are now working to keep you together as a couple?
6 Think of an area of conflict between you which you manage effectively. What is it that you do?
7 Can you apply those same strategies to another area where you're less successful in resolving conflict?
8 Name an area in which you function well as a couple. How do you behave?
9 Is any of this behaviour transferable to a more difficult area?
10 Name an area where you often feel that your partner is *deliberately* trying to hurt or upset you. What could be another explanation?

LASTING LOVE TIPS
'ACTING HAPPY'

● *when a problem seems insoluble,* schedule couple time to deal with it. During this time, agree to act as if you are very happy together (even if you aren't).

● *when partners act happy* they say more positive things and display more positive body-language, *and then seem to* problem-solve more effectively

depression; and depression, as has been seen, can be a serious destroyer of love.

Although some satisficers do this, the *attributions* they reach for when their partner's behaviour displeases them tend to be *negative*. Starting from a position of low faith in their relationship, satisficers interpret differences as proof of incompatibility, and so see little point in trying to resolve them. While the in-love couples make the changes that will bring them closer together, the satisficers, making few such changes, grow further apart. By the time couples have been living together for two years, a majority of the in-love couples are experiencing relatively little conflict and only occasionally have deep doubts about their partnership. This is much less likely to be the case among satisficers.

making promises

How important is 'making promises' (particularly marriage promises) in helping love last for tomorrow? Some people see their partner's willingness to marry as meaning a great deal and put enormous pressure on them to do so; and, on the face of it, this makes sense. Smug marrieds are much less likely to split up than couples who only cohabit (or 'live in sin' as it used to be called). However, much of this is due to something researchers call *the selection effect*: the main reason cohabitation is, statistically, more risky, is due to the kinds of people who *select* it. The average cohabitor comes to the relationship younger, with more baggage, and from a poorer and more troubled background, than someone who marries. Perhaps most importantly, over half of all cohabitations start because the woman is pregnant, which makes their likely outcome similar to that of the shot-gun weddings of the 1950s and 1960s: not good.

Does living together first bode well or badly? The divorce rate of those who cohabited first used to be much higher but that was largely because unconventional types did it (and at any point in history unconventional people are more prone to divorce). But now that so many young people live together before marrying, the pattern is changing: the marriages of couples who have lived together first tend to be more prone to break-up within the first five years (some probably marry to try to shore up flaky relationships) but after this period it's the relationships of the couples who *didn't* live together first that are more likely to end. One recent study showed that married men who had *not* lived with their partners first (or

LOVE NOTES

COHABITORS ARE:

- more likely to be poorer and less well educated
- more likely to have remarried parents
- more likely to have bad relationships with their parents
- more likely to live away from home (no social supports)
- more likely to abuse alcohol and drugs
- more likely to be violent (men)
- more likely to be unemployed (men)
- more likely to be financially independent (women)

had only done so for a very short time) became unhappy much more quickly than men who'd lived longer with their partners before marriage.

Recent research is finding that cohabitation, instead of being mainly a fore-runner to marriage, is being seen by many couples as a long-term arrangement very much like it. With more than two out of five babies now born to unmarried parents, most of whom are living together, the quiet revolution on the streets of suburbia, as in the inner cities, is the *ignoring* of marriage. If you are worrying whether just living together bodes worse for your future than marrying, you are asking the wrong question: it's the risk factors in your background and current circumstance (see the next two boxes) that should absorb your attention.

For some people the M word resonates negatively with old ideas of possession and of doing time in miserable partnerships. If your reason for cohabiting, rather than marrying, is that you don't like *the institution of marriage* (older people and people who've already been married often feel like this) then not marrying is neither here nor there.

When women, in particular, are reluctant to marry, this may *not* mean they don't love their partner. They may see the relationship as being for life; they just don't want to give up their on-paper independence. This is less likely when the person refusing to marry is a man. If one or other person is refusing to marry because they have doubts about their partner then this certainly points to trouble ahead; and research shows that men who say they're against marriage are often not properly in love and are shying away from investing in marriage with that particular partner. (Men who say they don't want children are also often speaking in code. What they may mean is they don't want children *with that partner*).

When both partners sincerely feel that making a public commitment (or a commitment in the sight of God) gives them extra strength, actually

LOVE NOTES

COHABITORS:

- are more likely than people getting married to be on the rebound
- are less likely to consider their partner the 'love of my life'
- often (10%) consider the relationship entirely temporary
- are 27% more likely to have children from a previous relationship
- frequently (55% women, 33% men) begin cohabitation because of pregnancy

Note: Marriages *after a period of cohabitation* also often begin with pregnancy, but this is not such a risk factor because the couple already have an established relationship.

to marry may help them. Many claim that it does, although the main glue may be their community, which makes it difficult for them to leave their marriage. However, this is not an unmixed blessing: for example, communities that punish and shame adulterers also tend to advise battered wives to stay put and pray that their husbands will stop hitting them.

Nor is there evidence that renewing wedding vows every year ('like a dog licence' as the much-married Mr Rod Stewart has suggested we should) would reduce the nation's (or Mr Stewart's) divorce rates. Even people who marry *and* are committed to marriage as an institution are only slightly less likely to end up divorced than the average. And that's mainly because they tend to be conventional types, who don't like to step out of line on anything. While making promises can keep a couple legally bound, it cannot keep them *emotionally* united. There are plenty of people who are committed to the institution of marriage but who aren't committed to the person they're married to.

This doesn't mean that getting married (or renewing vows) is of no value. The latest research suggests that a relationship benefits when both partners know it has a future. A joint sense of *intention*, there on both sides and *known* to be there on both sides, delivers a sense of security. This feeling of being safe for the foreseeable future (although not necessarily 'until death us do part' which was probably more relevant when death came so much earlier)

LOVE TALK ...

Formal promises to love are promises no one can keep, for love is not an act of will; and legal bonds have no power to keep love alive when it is dying.

MORTON HUNT

helps partners behave constructively towards each other: they are more accepting, more forgiving and less likely to attack or blame. These processes then make their relationship more likely to last. Clearly, when getting married expresses this sense of permanence, it can be of enormous benefit. The trouble is that saying 'I do' in a church or anywhere else does not necessarily deliver this, and everyone knows it. At many weddings you'll hear the guests speculating as to whether 'this one will last', and a recent US study of highly educated first-time marrieds with sensibly aged brides (whose relationships would be expected to last longer than most) found that one in three had separated within four years.

The tradition of marriage can even be counter-productive, in that such enormous expectations are built in to it that some couples may not feel able to take them seriously and so end up taking nothing seriously. Traditions also involve making assumptions, and as has been seen making assumptions about your partner is always risky, particularly when you don't yet know them through and through. People have all kinds of reasons for getting married, which may have little or nothing to do with a sense of permanence. Pre-wedding nerves may be a clue that the real reasons for marrying haven't been aired; and while mild nerves are nothing to worry about, the experts believe that intense or persistent nagging doubts should never be ignored. And that is especially when they're underpinned by any of the thoughts set out below.

For any promise to deliver the necessary sense of security, both partners need to know that *they are promising the same thing* and that *they both sincerely mean it.* Some experts suggest that whenever a relationship moves into a new stage of closeness people need to find ways of discussing, in a formal way, what their expectations are – not only when they are getting married but on moving in together, or buying property jointly, or thinking about having children. Many people marry for the

STUPID CUPID

I'M GETTING MARRIED BECAUSE:
- my partner is keen we should
- my family is keen on it
- it seems like the next thing to do
- not to get married now would seem impolite
- I couldn't cope without my partner at the moment
- our relationship's not going well and marriage might sort things out

practical benefits: inheritance tax in the UK, for example, seriously favours married people (death-bed marriages are often about property); and one elderly man we interviewed explained that he and his long-term partner had married because 'wives can jump the queue for membership of the golf club!' Provided such reasons for marrying build on an agreement that the relationship is already permanent, and provided the idea of marriage isn't distasteful or scary to either partner, these need not be bad reasons, because they represent increased *investment* in the partnership.

> **LOVE TALK ...**
>
> Cohabitation is acting as a screening process (as, in the 1960s and 70s, people hoped it would) weeding out a high proportion of the incompatible and the uncommitted, so that those who do go on to marry have a (relatively) high chance of success. Without widespread cohabitation, the divorce rate would rocket.
>
> **BUMPASS & SWEET (1989)**

However, politicians and family-values enthusiasts, who hope to 'save marriage' by bribing couples, via tax breaks and so on, to tie the knot, are barking up the wrong tree. That would send the divorce rate *up* because more potentially unstable couples would marry, and because they'd marry for reasons *external* to the relationship. As has been seen, reasons *internal* to a relationship ('I really love my partner') are the ones most likely to help it last. In fact, getting people to focus on the *external* reasons for being together actually tends to make them *less* pleased with their relationship.

breaking promises

But while *making* a promise doesn't seem to do much to help love last, *breaking* a promise can go a long way to ensuring that it won't. Since almost everyone (except some gay men and a minuscule number of swingers) believes that when you are in a committed relationship, outside sex is totally wrong, virtually every infidelity (whether a one-night stand or an ongoing affair) means that a promise has been broken, whether that promise was explicitly made or not.

Some people try to explain away outside sex by seeing it as always following on from misery in the at-home partnership, but research shows this isn't so. People are actually less likely to fall out of love (and decide

SEX FACTS

INFIDELITY

● affairs often follow personal crises and losses (e.g. abortion, miscarriage, infertility, a sick child)

● 56% of men and 33% of women who have outside sex say they are very happy with their at-home relationship

● 44% of married men who have outside sex, are not emotionally involved in the affair

● by the time of divorce, 73% of the extramarital relationships are over

● men's affairs (20%) are less likely to continue than women's (33%)

to have an affair) than to fall into an affair (and decide they must have fallen out of love). People in high quality relationships have affairs, and affairs are common in relationships which are no different from faithful partnerships: the couple do quite a lot together and are averagely happy; they argue an average amount and have an average number of problems. In fact, affairs which lead to break-up are more likely to happen in these 'good-enough' relationships, than in seriously unhappy partnerships.

Despite the fact that many unfaithful men *and* women say they love their main partner the whole time and do not want to jeopardize that relationship, there can be no doubt that infidelity is a serious love buster. Some would say it is the biggest love buster of all, and they may well be right. Infidelity is the most commonly given cause of separation and divorce. It is a factor in 90% of first-marriage divorces (although it often goes unadmitted *right through the divorce process*) and even when there has been no actual sex, much falling out of love is fuelled by intensely romantic flirtation and budding intimacy.

One important reason why is that it offers an *alternative*. As was pointed out in Chapter 3, a major stimulus to commitment is *lack* of alternatives. The alternative partner threat is one that successful couples take seriously at all times, however secure and happy they may feel. They gently discourage their partner from growing close to attractive others and restrict themselves in the same way. They also take steps to head off potential poachers. One of the love lies everyone is brought up with is that perfect love is based on perfect trust. In fact, certainty of your partner's fidelity and devotion isn't a good thing. It can easily stop you treating them well, and breed a subtle lack of respect. Perfect love, far from being based on perfect trust, is based on a tinge of insecurity.

THE LOVE QUIZ

TEST 40:
WHAT DO YOU KNOW?

Think about each statement below. Do you agree or disagree? Turn to page 238 for the answers

1 Everybody has affairs

2 Affairs are good for a relationship

3 Affairs prove love has gone

4 Someone with whom you are having an affair is sexier than the at-home partner

5 The affair is the fault of the at-home partner

6 After an affair, break-up is inevitable

In Chapter 4, it was found that couples can be put under great strain when the men rely exclusively on their partners for emotional support. The plus side may be that this keeps them away from alternative partners. Researchers have been intrigued to discover that many men do not distinguish greatly between loving and liking: when they like a woman, they also tend to fancy her. This is not so marked among women, who quite often fancy men they don't like, and like men they don't fancy. This doesn't mean that for a woman an opposite-sex friend is never a potential alternative partner, only that the existence of such a friendship isn't *quite* such a risk. However, once it has developed into a sexual affair, it tends to pose a greater threat to the at-home relationship than a man's affair.

Same-sex couples face serious problems here, in that same-sex friends can easily become alternative partners. This may be an important reason for high partner-turnover among gay people, particularly gay activists and

LOVE NOTES
POSITIVE MATE GUARDING
- making yourself physically attractive
- behaving in a loving and thoughtful way
- agreeing with your partner
- decorating your lover with signs of possession (e.g. a ring)
- holding your lover's hand or arm in public (to indicate possession)
- providing material goods
- providing sexual favours

gay ghetto-dwellers, who are the most likely to come across lots of alternative partners, and the most likely to have them (though, again, this is a bit more of a risk for gay men than for gay women). One explanation for the rather surprising finding that while regular churchgoers have lower divorce rates than other people they aren't less likely to have outside sex, may be that while their close community can put brakes on divorce, it also provides a rich hunting-ground for alternative partners.

mate guarding

Behaviour designed to keep your mate away from alternative partners is called *mate guarding*. *Mate guarding* is a big sign of commitment: people who aren't serious about a lover make little attempt to guard them; and an unguarded lover gradually becomes less committed themselves: your own commitment is *strongly* influenced by how committed you believe your mate to be. Yet *mate guarding* has to be subtle. If you guard too obviously you imply that your partner's mate value is higher than your own, which can cause them to look for a better deal.

Researchers have listed 104 mate guarding acts, some designed to increase a partner's satisfaction (so high standards are set and alternatives are less attractive), others to keep your mate away from alternative partners, or alternative partners away from your mate. Both sexes mate-guard about as much as each other, and mainly in the same ways, although women spend more time and money on their appearance and men spend more money on their mates. Interestingly, men more often report using *sex* to keep their partners committed to them (the researchers had thought women would do more of this). Another research surprise has been that men are more likely than women to report 'going along with everything she says' and 'acting against my will to please' as strategies for keeping their mate. Both sexes resent negative mate guarding.

How many people have sex outside their main relationship? Studies that come up with the kinds of high percentages that hit the headlines (75% for married men; 50% for married women) in fact survey *un*typical populations, such as people who complete questionnaires in magazines like *Playgirl* or *Cosmopolitan*. Truly random samples (where researchers telephone or 'door-step' ordinary people) yield the most reliable results, and their figures are much lower. In the early 1980s in the US such an investigation found that just over 1 in 4 married men and 1 in 5 married women had had extra-marital sex.

LOVE NOTES

NEGATIVE MATE GUARDING

- making your partner feel guilty ('I can't live without you')
- making them feel incompetent ('no-one else would want you')
- threatening/hurting them physically ('you behave or else ...')
- 'running down' potential poachers (so they seem less attractive)
- flirting with other people to make them jealous
- not letting them out of our sight
- keeping them at home
- constantly checking up on them

A 1994 study came up with even lower rates: just *under* 1 in 4 for married men; and 1 in 6 for married women. *Married* infidelity is likely to keep on dropping, not because people are being faithful but because they are not *marrying*. The baby-boom generation has done most of its marrying and divorcing and, since the birth rate has fallen a lot since then, there are currently far fewer young people reaching mating age. They're also delaying marriage. Infidelity is *strongly* age-related: young people are much the most likely to be unfaithful, and though they are setting up their first household at much the same age as young couples did in the 1950s and 1960s (late teens/early twenties) they usually just live together at this point. Marriage (if it comes at all) comes later, at an age when infidelity is already less likely.

In Chapter 3 you read about how a sense of fairness (of feeling fairly treated, or feeling over- or under-benefited) impacted on your sex life. This can also affect fidelity. Studies have shown that people who feel under-benefited (they think they give more than they get) are more likely to play away (and will also have their first affair earlier) than people who feel

SEX FACTS

WHO HAS OUTSIDE SEX?

- 21% (wives)
- 26% (husbands)
- 30% female cohabitors (in this study they tend to be young)
- 33% male cohabitors (in this study they tend to be young)
- 28% (lesbians)
- 82% (gay men)

THE LOVE QUIZ
TEST 41:
HOW COMMITTED ARE YOU

Rate each statement below as it applies to you. Enter the total in the box on page 239. Now get your partner to do the same.

6	5	4	3	2	1
True		Neutral			False

1 When I think of myself and my partner I feel a strong sense of 'we'
2 I can see lots of future rewards in this partnership
3 I'm willing to put a lot of effort into this relationship
4 I'd lose a great deal if I left this relationship
5 I'm not likely to want to live alone again
6 The thought of building a new relationship doesn't excite me
7 My partner would be very upset if I had an affair
8 If my partner had an affair, I'd be very upset
9 I expect to be with my current partner for the rest of my life
10 I am in this relationship *because I want to be*

over-benefited or who feel fairly treated. Among both sexes, the partner who loves least is most likely to have the affair. Recent research has broken this down by gender, with interesting results: women who feel under-benefited *and* women who feel over-benefited too, are prone to be unfaithful. Men's desire for outside sex is not linked with how fair, or unfair, they perceive the relationship to be.

Two relationship qualities make infidelity much less likely. The first is *companionateness*. Only 7% of (married) men (5% women) who live as very close couples, will have affairs. Among the moderately companionate the figures are 14% for men and 9% for women. But where a couple live very separate lives, 44% of the men (22% of women) will be unfaithful. The other infidelity buster is *commitment to the relationship* (meaning substantial investment in it, and a strong belief that it has a future): only 9% of highly committed husbands (6% of wives) will have outside sex, compared with 26% of less committed husbands (21% of wives). For cohabitors and lesbians, infidelity rates are higher, but are still linked with commitment. Among gay men, the presence or absence of outside sex is not linked with commitment.

doing what comes naturally?

Just because affairs involve sex doesn't mean they're about sex, and having one affair does *not* mean you have started on a career of infidelity. Heterosexuals who have outside sex do not have less at-home sex than the sexually faithful and are just as pleased with their sex lives. Interestingly, the overall sexual pleasure experienced in an affair tends to be lower than the overall sexual pleasure experienced at home. Many affairs involve a little bad sex and a lot of time on the telephone.

However, research has shown that outside sex can be a revelation for some people, usually women (who, in the past, more often came to marriage sexually inexperienced). But this doesn't mean they'll leave their at-home partner. One in four women in the US breaks off her affair because of guilt – and the greater her passion, the greater her guilt. For men, guilt is often cancelled out by pride (not surprisingly, since one definition of successful masculinity involves notches on bedposts). Researchers say that even highly religious men, who usually *claim* guilt, actually sound most regretful about getting caught. Although the percentage of men and women who have outside sex isn't hugely different, 2 out of 5 unfaithful heterosexual women (and half of all unfaithful lesbian women) are only unfaithful with one other person. Unfaithful men are much more likely to have more than one outside sexual partner.

SEX FACTS

MULTIPLE INFIDELITY

Of the 21% of wives who are unfaithful:
- 43% have had only one outside partner
- 40% have had 2 to 5
- 14% have had 6 to 20
- 3% more than 20

Of the 26% of husbands who are unfaithful:
- 29% have had only one outside partner
- 42% have had 2 to 5
- 22% have had 6 to 20
- 7% more than 20

MULTIPLE INFIDELITY

Of the 28% of gay females who are unfaithful:

● 44% have had 1 outside partner
● 41% have had 2 to 5
● 14% have had 6 to 20
● 1.5% more than 20

Of the 82% of gay males who are unfaithful:

● 7% have had 1 outside partner
● 20% have had 2 to 5
● 30% have had 6 to 20
● 43% have had more than 20

Does monogamy come naturally to women but not men? Many have claimed so. In support of this belief they point to the wild promiscuity of many gay males, and compare the zillions of sperm men produce per ejaculation with the single ovum produced monthly by the average woman. Even the finding that lesbians have more outside sex than wives and are more prone to casual flings than husbands hasn't dented belief in female moderation, largely because no one knows about it. Most people are under the (false) impression that lesbians almost never have affairs, and have really long-lasting relationships. A good case for attitude being more important than gender in predicting sexual behaviour can be made from the fact that both male *and* female cohabitors (who tend to take a much softer line on infidelity than married people) are more likely to have outside sex than either husbands or wives. Lesbians, too, tend to be relatively unconventional people, which may partly explain their tendency to be unfaithful.

Recently biologists have suggested that monogamy isn't natural for either sex. The new view is that men have to produce their zillions of sperm in order to beat off competing sperm in their partner's vagina (from her other recent matings) and that this would be the case 'in the wild' for humans, just as it is for most other mammals. Certainly, among other species, multiple sexual partners are the norm, and there are good evolutionary reasons for this. Multiple partners ensure diversity in the gene pool; and a new partner means a lot more sex (and more likely conception).

Given the probability, when you look at the wider picture, that humans were not designed for monogamy, the amount of human monogamy (or near monogamy) in the world is startling. As is the fact that very well-established couples are much less likely to have outside sex than people who have recently partnered. Among heterosexual couples who've been together more than ten years, just 1 in 10 (of both sexes) has had a meaningful affair; and only another 1 in 10 (again, of both sexes) has had non-meaningful outside sex. It's the more newly established couples who are the most tempted by infidelity: 23% of married men (22% of married women). Research on non-meaningful sex again reinforces the notion that ideas have a bigger impact on behaviour than does biology: both male and female cohabitors are more likely to have non-meaningful outside sex than all the other groups – except for gay males.

Another interesting finding, given humans' possible programming for having multiple partners, is that it's not usually the best-adjusted human beings who seek out multiple partners but the worst. Few people will be surprised to learn that female 'serial shaggers' often have personality disorders, and/or have been sexually abused. (They also tend to have had promiscuous fathers, and have often given up all romantic and idealistic expectations of men and marriage.) However, men who become serial shaggers (or Don Juans as they are sometimes called) also tend to have serious problems.

There are two main reasons why men become multiply unfaithful. The first is because they're disgusted by their own sexuality, and this has led to low sexual desire in their at-home partnership – only the thrill of the chase and a new body can arouse them enough to overcome their self-disgust. Not surprisingly, given society's distaste at gay sex, disgust at your own sexuality is especially common among gay people. Some gay women cope by shutting down sexually, but to do this would make many

MALE SERIAL SHAGGERS
These tend to:
- be consciously stereotypically 'masculine'
- be highly competitive with other men
- be afraid of being controlled by a partner
- have had a father who was also a serial shagger or who did not help the boy feel like a man
- have a weak sense of gender identity, and look to women to define them as 'men'
- have a highly feminine partner if in a relationship
- aim to degrade their casual partners
- see women and men as different species

TEST 42:
WILL S/HE CHEAT

Rate each statement below as it applies to you. Enter the total in the box on page 239. Now get your partner to do the same.

6	5	4	3	2	1
True		Neutral		Not true	

1 My partner is very romantic
2 My partner likes to be the centre of attention
3 My partner gets bored easily
4 Sex is very important to my partner
5 My partner can think of quite a lot of situations in which infidelity would be understandable
6 My partner's work-pattern would make infidelity easy
7 My partner knows a lot of people who have had affairs
8 My partner's father/mother was unfaithful
9 I don't feel my partner pulls their weight in our relationship
10 My partner is workaholic

gay men feel bad ('real' men are supposed to want sex all the time) so that seeking new partners may be their preferred option. Research supports this idea: when asked why they go after loads of new partners, promiscuous gay men are more likely to say it's to deal with low-arousal problems than because their sexuality is uncontainable. Some gay men also seem to demand a right to promiscuity as a kind of pay-back for the enormous price they have to pay for being gay.

The second main reason that people (gay, straight, men, women) become serial shaggers is that they have big problems with intimacy. Being close to someone physically *and* emotionally is too much for them. When they're emotionally *detached*, they can become sexually aroused; but when they're emotionally *connected*, their sexuality cuts out. Some manage to stay with one lover for quite a long time by periodically having rows, breaking up and then reconciling (sometimes over other partners, sometimes not) so they have a series of short-term sexual relationships with the same person. Women like Hillary Clinton and Mary Archer may well tolerate their partner's infidelities because they have grasped this psychology: Hillary Clinton has certainly indicated so.

kill or cure

Some researchers believe that almost all infidelity occurs in the wind-down to break-up. A 1994 US study found that in the previous year only about 2% of married women (6% of married men) had had extramarital sex. And since 3–4% of marriages break down every year (and infidelity in the previous 12 months is a big predictor of a couple separating) the mathematics do suggest that infidelity *other than* when a relationship is on the way out is surprisingly un-common. That doesn't mean that relationships don't ever survive infidelity: almost 50% do, and where the infidelity is a one-off the survival rate is even higher. Both sexes see a partner's infidelity as being a much greater problem than their own.

In the heat of the affair it's tempting to think the issue is love, and that whoever is loved most (the person having the affair or the at-home partner) will 'win'. In fact love is often a side-issue. Outside sex doesn't result from uncontrollable passion; it's a course of action you *choose*, and which has a definite purpose. All people and all relationships (being naturally imperfect) contain problems: love, hate, anger, joy, dependency, admiration, fear, guilt, disgust, frustration and pity. An infidelity (even a one-night stand) is always an attempt to solve a problem: either a problem in the relationship or a problem of self. *What* the problem is, *how big* it is, *where* infidelity as a problem-solving strategy was learned, *what* it means to *both* partners and *how* the affair is conducted, can all be more relevant to the way things turn out, than the in-love feelings between any couple in the triangle.

Like a sudden reduction in the amount of sex you're having, infidelity (or thoughts of infidelity) can be thought of as a useful relationship barometer. Both point to something awry, and should never be passed over lightly. When a couple survive an affair it's either because the partners set themselves the task of rebuilding their relationship, or because the infidelity remained secret. If the issue that caused the infidelity was minor and specific to the unfaithful partner (for example, they were sexually inexperienced and wanted to try another body; they're ageing and want to feel momentarily young again; they were away from home and felt lonely) then the main relationship can be unaffected. In such cases, and particularly if the infidelity was a one-night stand or a near one-night stand, then it probably shouldn't be confessed. In a sense, it has nothing to do with the at-home partner, and confessing it to them implies that their behaviour has contributed to the situation. Nevertheless, if they suspect an affair and ask you, you should never confuse them further by

THE LOVE QUIZ

TEST 43: INFIDELITY – WOULD YOU SURVIVE?

Rate each statement below. Enter the total in the box on page 239. Now get your partner to do the same.

6	5	4	3	2	1
Not true		**Neutral**			**True**

1 I believe that we both value monogamy
2 I believe I can trust my partner
3 My partner is always honest with me
4 I believe we're committed to each other
5 I'm safe in this relationship
6 Once trust is broken, no relationship can really recover
7 I learned when I was young that you can't trust many people
8 I wouldn't say I'm a very confident person
9 I wouldn't say I'm physically attractive
10 In my family, I didn't feel especially loved or talented

denying it. That *will* put a nail through your relationship, for lies of commission are far more series than lies of omission.

Of course even a minor infidelity is dangerous: there's always the chance that the at-home partner will discover it and reject you, or that the mere existence of a new partner will destabilize your main relationship. It's been said that one of the biggest pieces of luck that can befall a couple is that, when their partnership is going through a rough patch, neither person bumps up against a viable, alternative mate.

However, where the affair results from a problem in the relationship (the couple are growing apart; desire for sex is at different levels; there's unspoken resentment) or from a serious difficulty being faced by one person (impotence; redundancy; sickness; depression) then the decision to tell or not to tell can be more difficult. There can be no doubt that some affairs enable the at-home partnership to continue (researchers refer to these as 'marital aides'). A rule of thumb (if you have had the affair) is that any direct question from your partner *must* receive an honest answer. And if you suspect your partner of having an affair, then the best strategy is to challenge them right away. Because of the way secrecy works, hanging on and hoping it will stop is the worst thing you can do. The sneaking around,

LOVE BUSTERS

IS YOUR PARTNER LYING?

Never rely on one clue: look for a number of the following:

● slight asymmetry: the emotion may be *displayed slightly* more strongly on one side of the face than on the other

● micro-expressions: contradictory, fleeting facial expressions (less than a quarter of a second)

● the emotions *you* feel when your partner is talking: the unease and sadness in you may actually be a reflection of the feelings s/he is hiding

● timing: expressions lasting five seconds or more are likely to be false

● dilated pupils

● hidden sadness: corners of lips pulled downwards *without* moving chin muscles

if it continues, can create a strong bond between the two people concerned, with the at-home partner cast as the enemy or, at the very least, as an outsider. Picking up on this, they may start to behave negatively which, to the 'wandering' partner (who no longer sees them through rose-tinted-spectacles but through eyes stained with guilt), can loom large. And since illicit love is time-consuming and requires dishonesty and betrayal (and withdrawal from the world), the partner having the affair is likely to become less and less available at home. Communication and support dry up, and daily problems don't get solved. This is often the process by which an affair that started just as a bit on the side ends up destroying house and home.

forgiveness

Does the at-home partner always know? Some may find their partner's affair a bit of a relief, in that it stops them asking for sex or pushing for emotional closeness. Others close their eyes to clues because they feel they'd have to end the relationship if they acknowledged what was going on. But all that can operate on an unconscious level. It isn't the same thing as 'knowing', and the research shows that many betrayed partners had absolutely no idea, especially when the affair was discreet, and there was still a loving relationship at home (which there often is).

Whether a relationship will survive even a minor infidelity also depends on the extent to which the betrayed partner is able to forgive. This isn't always easy to gauge, for though it will depend on the depth of the trauma (the deeper the trauma, the less likely forgiveness) trauma can be caused by a number of things. The first is how the affair is *discovered*: one researcher found that, for men, confessing was more likely to lead to forgiveness than being rumbled. The *extent* of the deception also increases the trauma. To keep their partner in the dark, the liar has to make deliberate efforts to disorient them. If the at-home partner's suspicious are met with repeated denials, the growing confusion and pain will make recovery difficult, even when discovery itself comes as a relief. The agony is often prolonged when the straying partner stays in (or comes back to) the relationship for the sake of the children. This stated act should be taken as a wish to end the relationship; it continues to label the children's mother the outsider, signals a return to the affair and makes forgiveness impossible.

A person's background can also contribute to the depth of their trauma, and make forgiveness more (or less) likely. Some betrayed partners behave like survivors of serious abuse, showing symptoms of post-traumatic stress disorder: accusatory suffering, flashbacks, obsessive and repetitive thoughts, hypervigilance, digging for details. People who get PSTD (whether betrayed lovers or war veterans) often had seriously unhappy childhoods. One study found that morbidly jealous men had often, as children, witnessed their mother's affairs; and women whose philandering fathers left their childhood home may also fall into the can't-forgive category. Some of the children of divorce who side heavily with mother against father are, without realizing it, carrying their mother's pain and grief at her two betrayals.

Other personal issues can make forgiveness less likely. People who don't think highly of themselves, or who believe they are unattractive, or who as children felt much less gifted or beautiful or successful than a sibling, are often among those who prove unable to move on. Others keep up the pain and suffering because they think that if they don't, their partner will have got away with it. And just as the after-shocks of an earthquake can

LOVE TALK ...

In my work with torture survivors and with people who have lost a child, I have seen the face of anguish. The only other people in whom I've seen anything even approaching that anguish are people who have been cheated on by their life-partner.

HAMBURG

THE LOVE QUIZ

TEST 44:
INFIDELITY –
WILL YOUR PARTNER
GIVE UP THEIR LOVER?

Rate each statement below as it applies to your partner if s/he has been having an affair. Enter the total in the relevant box on page 239.

6	5	4	3	2	1
True		Neutral		Not true	

1 My partner won't talk things over with me
2 One of us often criticizes or contradicts the other
3 We've been shown how to communicate better but my partner won't try
4 I've tried to change but s/he doesn't seem to notice
5 S/he won't talk about the affair
6 S/he still thinks very highly of her/his lover
7 I don't really feel my partner cares about me
8 When I check up on my partner s/he gets really angry
9 My partner says our relationship was totally to blame for their affair *or* My partner says the affair had nothing at all to do with our relationship
10 My partner's lover is really to blame for their affair

be more devastating to survivors than the first blast, so the trauma will be deeper if the unfaithful partner continues to have *any* kind of relationship with the illicit lover.

closeness

A common problem that an affair is designed to solve is closeness (intimacy). Most often the issue is *not enough intimacy*: the unfaithful partner is lonely. A serious predictor that a relationship will fall apart (more serious even than lots of negative conflict) is a *sense of loneliness*. Many people who have affairs are actually looking for a friend, and the relationship tips over into something different. Sometimes the revelation of such an affair can be hugely positive, if it comes early enough, before the unfaithful partner has learned to depend on their new friend. The revelation of the affair can get a couple talking deeply, and since intimacy is developed through confessions, explanations and soul-searchings, they may (after much pain) end up closer and more committed to each other than before. However, infidelity to get the partner's attention is to be avoided, if possible: it's a high-risk strategy. A happy outcome (for the at-home relationship) is if the betrayed person is emotionally secure, and is also the partner who loves most.

An affair can also be an attempt to solve the problem of *too much closeness*. Intimacy is one of the biggest issues for sexual love because, although it is universally longed for, it is also, very often, greatly feared. In Chapter 1, the idea of *attachment* (intense emotional dependence) was introduced as an important part of love. Researchers call people's ways of handling intimacy their *attachment styles*. *Attachment styles*, like *conflict styles* (to which they can be closely related) come mainly in three types. The first, the *Connecting Attachment Style*, is found in about 60% of the adult population in the West. *Connectors* are good at intimacy: they are comfortable depending on others and having others depend on them *at the same time*, and they are not prone to infidelity.

The rest of the population aren't so comfortable with closeness, and they come in two types: '*avoiders*' (around 17% of all people) and '*clingers*' (also around 17%). Both *avoiders* and *clingers* believe they'll be abandoned, but they handle this fear differently. The *avoiders* avoid closeness while the *clingers* seek it out. Being two different faces of the same problem, an *avoider* can become a *clinger* when in a relationship with an *avoider* (or with someone who is acting in an *avoiding* way, possibly because they are pulling out of the relationship). Although different

ATTACHMENT STYLES
CONNECTORS
- trust easily
- aren't much troubled by jealousy
- easily experience loving feelings
- easily experience other positive emotions (e.g. excitement and contentment)
- can remember way back to when they were small
- think and talk flexibly and thoughtfully about their childhood
- acknowledge both good and bad in the past
- recognize their influence on them as adults

attachment behaviour can be activated under different circumstances (even a happy, solid *connector* can become a *clinger* when their mate tries to ditch them), most people have a default attachment style they operate in many of their relationships. This often seems to be fixed by the age of three or four: researchers can measure attachment styles in babies, and have found 75% of young adults still in the same attachment category they were in when they were little.

Because aloof men are often seen as strong, *avoider* males can have high initial mate value (although as the years go by their partner tends to feel shut out and frustrated). *Avoider* women have the shortest relationships of all women, and *clinger* men have the shortest relationships of all men. Many of the people who never find their ideal partner are *avoiders*: their deep fear of abandonment causes them to take steps to keep love at bay. Long-running infidelities may also perform this function, keeping the *avoider* (or *avoiders* – often all three members of the 'triangle' are *avoiders*) at a safe distance so that fears of abandonment are not activated. When an *avoider* ends one affair, s/he often begins another ('The trouble with marrying your mistress is that you create a job vacancy,' admitted the late Sir James Goldsmith.) When in a relationship with a partner with whom s/he is truly compatible and which functions well day to day, an *avoider* may set up false barriers (for example, losing interest in sex) so that they keep part of themselves aloof. *Avoiders* of both sexes are prone to uncommitted sex as well as to infidelity, and some also use drugs or alcohol to stop partners getting too close. Others use work: many workaholics (both men and women) are *avoiders*. Their partners claim that commitment to work is ruining their relationship; in fact, without the safety valve provided by work, the *avoider* would have been off years before.

LOVE LESSONS

AVOIDERS

- may dislike sharing physical space
- often run more than one relationship simultaneously
- are often involved in long-distance love affairs
- can be quite jealous
- are often generally dissatisfied
- don't usually remember much about their childhoods
- either say their parents were wonderful or talk about them in contradictory ways
- dismiss the importance of early relationships and experiences

LOVE LESSONS

CLINGERS

● obsess about their relationships – past and present
● often feel unworthy
● often see others as stand-offish
● are greatly dependent on others for self-esteem and support
● are often emotionally confused
● can be jealous, possessive and demanding
● tend to nurse grudges (particularly against family members)
● often find thinking about their childhood upsetting

When both partners are *avoiders* or *clingers* their relationship is often miserable or stormy, as they push–pull (often unconsciously) around that issue of closeness. By contrast, a relationship between two *connectors* will usually be of very high quality, because it isn't undermined by the fear of being abandoned. However, an *avoider* or *clinger* can also do well if they are in a relationship with a *connector*. In fact, the quality of an *avoider/connector* or *clinger/connector* partnership is often as high as that between two *connectors*, and this is most likely when the *connector* is *male*. The researchers put this down to gender training: some *connector* males may be prepared to play a protective role with female partners who aren't so comfortable with closeness, but *connector* women may not be so willing to do this. In fact, because they feel comfortable letting angry feelings show, they may quickly lose patience. Where a mother is a *connector* and her male partner is an *avoider* or a *clinger*, they often have massive rows while raising their children.

Perhaps the biggest surprise of all has been that, although relationships containing at least one *connector* are almost always happier and of higher quality than relationships comprising only *avoiders* and *clingers*, they don't necessarily last longer. The reason is simple. *Connectors*, confident that finding a new connection (in the form of a new partner) won't be difficult, are more likely to leave when they judge a partnership is bad for them. *Avoiders* and *clingers* may not have such confidence, and may hang on even when their lives are being devastated. The relationships of *clinger* women, though often long-lasting (particularly with *avoider* males), tend to be very on/off.

divorce-prone people

For a long time now, researchers have been intrigued by the idea of 'divorce-prone' personalities, an idea that has been given credibility by the finding that divorced people don't do as well as widowed people when they re-partner: their new relationship is much less likely to last. Also, researchers who interviewed young men at college in the 1930s and then again 40 years on, found that men who stayed happily married had rated (when they were young) as significantly more mentally healthy than men who became unhappily married, or divorced.

Just as it is sensible to examine a lover's family history before you leap into commitment, so you can learn a lot from their love history. Fewer than one person in 20 engages in serial marriage (that is, in three or more marriages) and the more cohabitations/marriages a person has experienced in the past, the more likely it is that their current relationship will also end (these people are very often serious *avoiders* or *clingers*). Among people in their second marriages, 50% report the very same troublesome behaviours as in their first relationship. The other 50% don't: they seem to behave differently (and better) second time around. It may be that they've learned from experience (some people do) or that their earlier negative behaviour was a product of a poor match with their first partner or the life events they had to endure. Perhaps their new partner brings out the best in them: is, for example, comfortable with closeness, and can easily soothe their doubts and fears. Certainly most second marriages these days are *not* more likely to break down than first marriages, and many of the people in these relationships find real happiness.

STUPID CUPID

SECOND-TIME-AROUND BREAK-UP RISKS

- people who were poor and young at the time of their first marriage will often have a second marriage that fails
- the second marriages of all other people are *not* more likely than first marriages to end in divorce
- people aged over 40 who marry for the first time are 79% more likely to split than people aged over 40 who marry for the second time

LOVE-BUSTERS

WHY IMPULSIVE PEOPLE MAKE LOUSY PARTNERS

● they have short courtships (probably making a poor partner choice)

● they have a risk-taking lifestyle (they are attracted to dangerous activities, including infidelity)

● they have a low boredom threshold (needing constant novelty)

● they have difficulty tolerating daily routines (they are not great in the home)

● they have a low interest in maintaining close bonds with other people (they do not work at relationships)

● they don't care if other people think badly of them (they don't feel shame at loving and leaving)

People whose committed love relationships (whether marriages or long-term cohabitations) have fallen apart *more than twice* should be considered a serious love risk. One study of medical students, which followed them over a period of 20 years, found that the 19 who had divorced twice or more during that period differed significantly from the non-divorced or the once-divorced, in that they rated as more *impulsive*. They had a tendency to non-conformity, were likely to misuse alcohol or drugs, and were talkative and adventurous (including sexually). Other signs of their innate impulsiveness was that they tended to smoke a lot, miss breakfast, and fail to put their seat belts on. Another even larger study, which looked at moderately happy relationships and tried to understand why only some broke up, also found that *impulsiveness* was key. It tended to lead to outside sex and, from there, to divorce.

Another study found that five out of six of the twice-divorced actually have *personality disorders*. What does this mean? If you regard mental health as a spectrum, with people with recognized *mental illness* at the far end, *personality disorders* (including 'borderlines' – that is, on the borderline between crazy and sane) next to them, *neurotics* next to them and effective, *self-confident optimists* at the near end, then you can safely say that the relationship outcomes are likely to be different for each group. People with a recognized *mental illness* often fail to establish committed relationships, and when they do, have high rates of separation and divorce (particularly men). People with *personality disorders* more often form relationships (borderline women may be sexually adventurous and can be very alluring) but they find long-term love difficult to sustain.

Neurotics (who are within the normal range, but tend either to be impulsive or depressive and are often touchy and difficult) can do well if their partner is very stable and forgiving. Effective, *self-confident optimists* (most of them, it seems likely, being *connectors*) are much the most likely to create satisfying partnerships.

Sustained negativity is a real love buster (it's one of the Killer Habits mentioned in Chapter 2) and is sometimes called '*Eeyorishness*' (after Winnie-the-Pooh's friend Eeyore, the gloomy little donkey). *Eeyorishness* is described as 'the trait-like tendency to report distress, discomfort, and dissatisfaction over time and regardless of the situation'. Across every single long-term study of sexual partnerships ever made, *Eeyorishness* shows up consistently as *the* predictor of relationship breakdown in all groups: old, young, black, white, gay, straight, married, not married.

Eeyorish people aren't just sad and huffy from time to time; as the definition above makes clear, they consistently experience anxiety, tension and anger. This leads them to behave unproductively within a relationship. For a start, their behaviour is often *rigid*: this means that when faced with changing circumstances, they don't change. Secondly, they don't develop strategies to deal actively and effectively with upsetting situations: instead, they just moan or shout or sulk or clam up. Thirdly, they don't explore: they don't look for new activities to enjoy with their partner or to break a depressed mood. They also tend to be dissatisfied with their relationships from early on, which may be one reason their love affairs so often fall apart – as was pointed out earlier, relationships that start with a 'low' often go downhill quickly. *Eeyorishness* in a man is particularly likely to lead to relationship disaster.

Since people often choose partners whose degree of mental health is similar to their own, this translates not only into divorce-prone (and

LOVE BUSTERS
HOW TO RECOGNISE AN EEYORE

- they regularly have temper outbursts they 'can't control'
- they often feel sad
- they often feel rejected
- they often feel unworthy
- they are very self-involved
- they often feel incompetent (they may dwell on their own mistakes)
- they often bear grudges
- they often see people as unfriendly or as not liking them

DRUGS, ALCOHOL AND CHOOSING A MATE

● women whose fathers were problem drinkers are more than twice as likely as other women to marry men who are problem drinkers, *and* to abuse drugs/alcohol themselves

● women whose *mothers* drank are not more likely to *marry* a problem drinker, but are twice as likely as other women to *be* one (or to abuse drugs)

● more than 1 in 3 of the sons of alcoholic fathers will become alcoholic themselves, even if raised in a different family (e.g. adopted)

● women with problem drinking partners are twice as likely as other women to abuse drugs/alcohol

● young people who drink a lot and 'hold their drink well' are likely to develop serious problems later

divorce-resistant) individuals, but also into divorce-prone (and divorce-resistant) couples. In addition, one person's level of mental health can affect the other's: if you're not anxious and depressed before you start living with someone who is systematically unpleasant to you, you soon will be. Interestingly, the idea of co-dependent relationships, in which one partner, in order to be function well, needs the other to be anxious or depressed, is not borne out by serious research. When women suffering from anxiety disorders receive treatment and start to get better, the couples' relationships don't usually fall apart. Instead, the partners become more satisfied and the men begin functioning better, too.

There are other kinds of bad news partners. Top of the list come alcoholics and drug addicts (substance abuse was also listed in Chapter 2 as one of the Killer Habits that destroy relationships). One in three couples seeking help for their relationship name the male partner's alcohol abuse as a major problem. But men aren't the only offenders: in the US around one pregnant woman in ten has a drug/alcohol problem (mainly cocaine), with white women (not black or Hispanic women) showing the highest addiction rates. Drug/alcohol problems don't only cause relationship misery but can be caused by it, and where a relationship is unhappy, relapse after rehab is likely.

Also strongly linked with drug/alcohol abuse is physical abuse – the last of the major love destroyers. On average, 3–4% of marriages break up every year, but when violence is involved the annual figure is 38%.

SERIOUSLY VIOLENT MEN

- seem unusually helpful early on in the relationship
- are verbally abusive (name-calling may precede hitting)
- monitor their partner's time and movements
- like to accompany them everywhere
- display mood swings
- seem detached, then anxious and demanding
- become incredibly angry during arguments
- behave impulsively
- blame others when things go wrong
- don't like to accept advice

The more serious the violence, the more likely the split. Interestingly, when a heterosexual man attacks his partner, this doesn't mean he loves her less, though it certainly means that *she* loves *him* less: both men and women who are attacked by their partners report less liking and less positive feeling for them, as do women who attack their mates. Physical abuse is often linked with drugs/alcohol. The fact that substance abuse is a big problem in gay communities may be one reason partner violence is more common among lesbians and gays, than among heterosexuals.

Although the term 'battered woman' is widely used, not all violence between a couple can be called 'battering', and in some quite peaceful partnerships there may be violent incidents, just before the break-up. Serious violence is most common in young couples (13.9% of women aged under 25 report serious violence *from* their partner; and 16.7% serious violence *towards* their partner), whereas when the woman is over 24 the serious violence rate is 4.2% man-to-woman and 4.8% woman-to-man. The people *least* likely to hit their partners are heterosexual men. This comes as a surprise but actually makes sense. Lesbians and gay men may hit out more frequently because they feel physically equal with their partners; and straight women can feel OK about picking on someone larger than themselves: even if a woman is unusually strong she's almost always the smaller, weaker partner of the couple. But the average heterosexual male knows he can do serious damage, which is why when he crosses the line and raises his hand, the fact that he has done so should be taken very seriously.

Since physical violence is life-threatening, it's essential for a woman to be able to predict when a 'bit of pushing and shoving' is likely to end there, and when it's going to progress into battering (which, in just over a quarter of cases, it will). Because most men strongly resist hitting women, even the slightest push or shove from her partner should put a woman immediately on her guard, and if it's combined with a general feeling of threat or with a cluster of the warning signs in the boxes in this section, she should bail out immediately. Change is unlikely. It's interesting that many batterers say they believe that roughing up women can be justified (this attitude, in itself, helps predict battering), although some don't hold this view and may even believe quite seriously in sex equality. When this type of batterer hits out, he tends to batter very seriously, as does the type who appears to go cold in arguments. He actually does so: research shows that his heart rate slows.

When a man uses violence on a woman, it's usually a form of coercion: he's trying to change her behaviour. Women are less likely to do this (probably because it wouldn't be very effective) and are more likely to hit out in self-defence or because they're feeling highly emotional. Some battered people find it hard to leave their partners (they're not alone in this: many people, as pointed out in Chapter 1, find it difficult to leave damaging relationships) and one reason can be the honeymoon period which often follows a beating when the violent partner not only promises never to do it again, but may be unusually sweet and kind.

How can you know when a love affair is over? It's not as easy as you might think. Only 15% of relationships end by mutual consent. This means that in 5 cases out of 6, there's a 'leaver' (who is trying to extricate themselves) and a 'stayer' (who is often quite desperate for the relationship to

STUPID CUPID

SERIOUSLY VIOLENT PARTNERS OFTEN:

- had at least one violent parent
- had a problematic birth *and* were rejected by their parents
- have drug and/or alcohol problems
- have poor communication skills
- have a tendency to get into fights
- suffer from low self-esteem
- suffer from depression
- have strongly sexist attitudes
- have experienced a head injury
- keep weapons in the house

THE LOVE QUIZ

TEST 45:
IS YOUR RELATIONSHIP
ON THE WAY OUT?

Rate each statement below as it applies to your situation. Enter the total on page 239.

6	5	4	3	2	1
True		Neutral		Not true	

1 My partner avoids connecting with me: s/he's not home so much or, when s/he is, is busy with something

2 When my partner's in the same room, we don't interact much

3 When we do interact, there's not much eye contact

4 My partner makes declarations of wanting to retain some level of relationship ('I count you as one of my best friends')

5 My partner is rude or hostile a lot of the time: being with them isn't much fun

6 My partner has been having an affair

7 I often feel my partner is trying to pick a fight

8 My partner puts a bad interpretation on things I do and/or easily gets angry with me

9 One or both of us is preparing to live alone: saving money, looking for somewhere to live etc.

continue). A stayer can be convinced for months, even years, that a defunct relationship has a future. Wishful thinking clearly plays a part, but an important contributory factor will be the leaver's behaviour. Keen to let their partner down gently, they will often transmit mixed messages. In fact because a stayer's humiliation and distress make a leaver feel terrible, the leaver will often go to quite considerable lengths to soften the blow. Sadly, their small kindnesses and judicious lies are easily interpreted by the stayer as a desire *not* to have the relationship end.

If the leaver makes a simple statement that the relationship is over, or openly states that they feel dissatisfied with it and wishes it to be over, this should be taken seriously, *even if their other statements or behaviour would seem to contradict this*. In fact, a desire to leave doesn't have to be explicitly stated. Any or all of the points listed in the box above suggest that break-up is on the cards.

love busters

Use these lists differently, depending on whether your relationship is still in the early stages or is deeply entwined (e.g. you have had a child together).

● **Early stages** If five or more of the negative statements below apply to you, think carefully: you will already have some sense of the relationship not being right, and these may help you understand why continuing with it may be a mistake. However, if there are also many positive reasons for being together (see love boosters) then the negative(s) may be cancelled out.

● **Deeply entwined** No single negative indicator (or even a cluster of negatives) should be taken as a cue to give up on your relationship. Understood in the context of this chapter, they may help you grasp some of your dissatisfactions and prompt you to work at these areas of your love life, in order to create a more satisfying partnership.

Your relationship has a below-average chance of success when you ...
● believe a good relationship will make you happy
● believe love can make your dreams come true
● believe love is based on total trust
● believe sex differences are profound
● believe relationship problems are mostly due to sex differences
● believe lovers should do everything together
● believe lovers should tell each other everything
● believe monogamy is for women
● believe an affair always destroys love
● believe you should trust your partner implicitly
● often try to read your lover's mind
● confess whenever you feel guilty
● always say what you think or are feeling
● have a child to improve a bad relationship
● get married to improve a bad relationship
● expect love to be a 50:50 partnership
● easily believe your partner is to blame
● do not see your partner's behaviour as likely to change
● see differences as proof of incompatibility
● easily assume your partner is trying to upset you
● cannot remember what first attracted you (men particularly)
● cannot remember many very happy times (men particularly)

- let yourself be coerced into marriage
- coerce your partner into marriage
- tell your partner 'I can't live without you' (men particularly)
- flirt with other people to make your partner jealous
- have an affair
- only during sex tell your partner you love them
- are prone to uncommitted sex
- had a parent who had lots of affairs
- are highly competitive with other men (men only)
- have trouble getting sexually aroused in long relationships (men)
- have a work pattern that makes infidelity easy
- feel very lonely within your relationship
- are greatly dependent on others for your sense of who you are (men particularly)
- have had two or more separations/divorces
- marry after age 40, having never been in a stable relationship
- drink heavily or use drugs a lot
- have an eating disorder
- have been diagnosed with a personality disorder
- are intensely jealous or possessive
- are physically violent
- are self-involved, negative and moody (men particularly)
- have experienced a head injury (men particularly)
- are noticeably impulsive
- are seriously eccentric
- are a workaholic
- put a low priority on close personal relationships

love boosters

Your relationship has an above-average chance when you ...
- can create a lifestyle that matches your hopes and dreams
- have no problem saying sorry when you should
- tell your partner you love them – frequently
- can be up front about your needs and wishes
- limit negative disclosure to really important things
- are about as self-revealing as your partner
- have a similar degree of interest in human motives and behaviour
- believe long and happy love relationships are not uncommon

- recognize and name issues over which you get easily upset
- recognize and name issues over which your partner gets easily upset
- usually think the best of your partner
- value marriage, and marry within a community that also values it
- don't like the idea of living alone again
- publicly indicate possession of your mate
- would be very upset if your partner had an affair
- would feel guilty if you had an affair
- are not a good liar
- can't think of many situations when an affair would be justified
- don't know many people who have affairs
- fear your partner could have an affair if you didn't treat them well
- discourage your mate from getting close to attractive others
- are careful to keep yourself out of the way of temptation
- are emotionally secure
- are emotionally insecure, but have a secure partner (women particularly)
- had good relationships with your parents during your teenage years
- try to do things that will help your self-confidence grow
- try to help your mate's self-confidence grow

THE LOVE QUIZ

TEST RESULTS

TEST 37:
PERFECT LOVE

1.	Your score:	Your partner's score:
2.	Your score:	Your partner's score:
3.	Your score:	Your partner's score:
4.	Your score:	Your partner's score:
5.	Your score:	Your partner's score:
6.	Your score:	Your partner's score:
7.	Your score:	Your partner's score:
8.	Your score:	Your partner's score:
9.	Your score:	Your partner's score:
10.	Your score:	Your partner's score:

Not one of these statements is true. If your (or your partner's) score is high on any of them, you need to think seriously about where you got the idea, and talk it over with your partner. Three or more high scores mean that many of your problems are caused by unrealistic expectations, and by ignorance as to how love works, rather than by incompatibility.

TEST 38:
DIGGING DEEP

This is more an exercise than a test. Actually making notes on these questions can help you understand your own and your partner's special sensitivities. Talking them over with your partner, when neither of you is upset, may be good. Remember that forcing an unwilling partner to talk can be counter-productive, and can increase the tension between you.

TEST 39:
STRENGTHS

This is more an exercise than a test. If you can do all this you probably don't have a problem. Happy couples do many of these things automatically. Trying to make them a habit should be productive

TEST 40:
INFIDELITY – WHAT DO YOU KNOW?

1. Infidelity isn't normal behaviour; it's a symptom of a problem either in the relationship or in the person having the affair.
2. Although some relationships survive affairs, affairs are dangerous and can easily destroy a relationship.
3. Affairs can occur in relationships that, previous to the affair, were quite good.
4. Affairs involve sex, but sex is usually not the purpose of the affair.
5. An at-home partner can only help create the conditions in which an affair becomes more likely. The affair is always the choice of the partner doing the infidelity.
6. Relationships can become closer and better after an affair is exposed. Some survive when an affair is not revealed, particularly if it was a short-term liaison.

TEST 41:
HOW COMMITTED ARE YOU?

Your total: [ ]   Your partner's total: [ ]

A score of 40+ means a current strong level of commitment to this relationship.

TEST 42:
WILL S/HE CHEAT?

Total: [ ]

A 40+ score means the potential for infidelity is there. This does not mean that your partner has been unfaithful, but feelings of jealousy or suspicion should be taken seriously.

TEST 43:
INFIDELITY – WOULD YOU SURVIVE?

Your score: [ ]   Your partner's score: [ ]

A 40+ score means that this person would find it very hard to forgive, let alone forget, and might tend to cut loose from an unfaithful partner without considering whether the relationship could be mended.

TEST 44:
INFIDELITY – WILL S/HE GIVE UP THEIR LOVER?

Your score: [ ]   Your partner's score: [ ]

A 40+ score indicates that the affair is not over: either it is physically continuing or your partner is still emotionally tied into it.

TEST 45:
IS YOUR RELATIONSHIP ON THE WAY OUT?

The total: [ ]

A 36+ score suggests that the relationship is in a very bad way. Even then, it is worth exploring (with professional help) whether the negative feelings go very deep or whether they are the (temporary) result of pain and anger. Sometimes even relationships in this state can be turned around; however, very often this is not the case.

post-script

WE ARE PIONEERS

Not everything about love can yet be explained. There are still many gaps in knowledge and understanding. But we are getting there. In Denver, Colorado, where a major couple study is underway (couples were recruited for the project before they married, and are being regularly monitored) researchers have been able to predict with 90% accuracy, over a period of nine years, who will stay married, and who will split up. And it seems that, before long, 100% accuracy may be reached: the other 10% are couples predicted to part, who haven't yet, but who are on the wind-down to disaster.

Nor is the purpose of such love research only to predict the future and prevent incompatible couples doing silly things, like getting married or having children together. The research can also be used to bring about change. Recognizing, for example, how and why some people are divorce-prone, provides the opportunity to avoid/modify or accept the behaviour that's likely to cause stress. We won't always succeed, but through understanding and awareness we can achieve a lot. What's more, understanding the research can help us come to terms with what we really want. As we've seen, not everyone is comfortable with cheek-by-jowl togetherness.

Whatever ways we use the accumulating evidence, one thing is sure: we are pioneers – the first generation to approach love with a significant understanding of what's really going on. And though that's wonderful, it's tough as well. For believing that love 'just happens' absolves us of responsibility. It allows us to walk about with eyes wide shut. Whereas when we realize that we create and destroy love every minute of every day, not only through what we do (and don't do) but through what we expect and fear, then there is no more sitting on our hands. This knowledge puts you under an obligation to be smarter about love: to get to know ourselves; to make wise choices; to monitor, to evaluate, to nip problems in the bud; to accept; to forgive; to 'be excellent to each other'; and to raise our children kindly so that they, in their turn, will be able to create for *their* children, a love that will last tomorrow.

bibliography

Acitelli LK & Antonucci TC (1994) Gender differences in the link between marital support and satisfaction in older couples, *Journal of Personality & Social Psychology* 67: 688-698

Amato PR & Rogers SJ (1997) A longitudinal study of marital problems and subsequent divorce, *Journal of Marriage and the Family* 59: 612-624

Amato PR (2001) *A Divorce too Far?* Presentation given at One Plus One Seminar, 17 July, London

Apt C, Hurlbert DF, Sarmiento GR & Hurlbert MK (1996) The role of fellatio in marital sexuality: an examination of sexual compatibility and sexual desire, *Sexual & Marital Therapy* 11(4): 383-392

Aron A & Aron EN (1995) 'Love' in Weber Al & Harvey JH (eds) *Perspectives on Close Relationships*, Allyn & Bacon: Boston

Apter T (1999) *Mothers-in-law and Daughters-in-law: friendship at an impasse*, paper presented at the British Psychological Society Conference, 20 December, London

Baker R (1996) *Sperm Wars*, Fourth Estate: London

Barnes ML & Sternberg RJ (1997) 'A hierarchical model of love and its prediction of satisfaction in close relationships' in Sternberg RJ & Hojjat M (eds) *Satisfaction in Close Relationships*, Guildford Press: NY

Baucom DH, Epstein N & Rankin LA (1995) 'Cognitive aspects of cognitive-behavioral marital therapy' in Jacobson NS & Gurman AS (eds) *Clinical Handbook of Couple Therapy*, Guildford Press: NY

Baumeister RF & Stillwell AM (1992) 'Autobiographical accounts, situational roles and motivated biases: when stories don't match up' in Harvey JH, Orbuch RL & Weber AL (eds) *Attributions, Accounts and Close Relationships,* Springer-Verlag: New York

Beach SRH & Fincham FD (1996) Self-evaluation maintenance in marriage: towards a performance ecology of the marital relationship, *Journal of Family Psychology* 10(4): 379-396

Beach SRH & O'Leary KD (1993) Marital discord and dysphoria: for whom does the relationship predict depressive symptoms? *Journal of Social and Personal Relationships* 10:405-420

Beishom S, Modood T, Virdee S (1998) *Ethnic Minority Families*, Policy Studies Institute: London

Berscheid E & Lopes J (1997) 'A temporal model of relationship satisfaction and stability' in Sternberg RJ & Hojjat M (eds) *Satisfaction in Close Relationships*, Guildford Press: NY

Blumstein P & Schwartz P (1983) *American Couples*, William Morrow: NY

Blyth S & Straker G (1996) Intimacy, fusion and frequency of sexual contact in lesbian couples, *South African Journal of Psychology* 26(4): 253-256

Bradbury TN (ed) (1998) *The Developmental Course of Marital Dysfunction*, CUP: Cambridge

BIBLIOGRAPHY

Bradbury TN, Cohan CL & Karney BR (1998) 'Optimizing longitudinal resesarch for understanding and preventing marital dysfunction' in Bradbury TN (ed) *The Developmental Course of Marital Dysfunction*, CUP: Cambridge

Bratslavsky E, Baumeister RF & Sommer KL (1998) 'To love or be loved in vain: the trials and tribulations of unrequited love' in Spitzberg BH & Cupach WR (eds) *The Dark Side of Close Relationships*, Lawrence Erlbaum: NJ

Braver SL & O'Connell D (1998) *Divorced Dads: shattering the myths*, Tracher/Putnam: NY

Brehm SS (1992) *Intimate Relationships*, McGraw-Hill: NY

Brines J & Joyner K (1999) The ties that bind: principles of cohesion in cohabitation and marriage, *American Sociological Review* 64(3): 333-355

Brinig MF & Allen DW (2000) These boots are made for walking: why most divorce filers are women, *American Law and Economics Review* 2: 126-169

Brown L (1995) 'Therapy with same-sex couples: an introduction' in Jacobson NS & Gurman AS (eds) *Clinical Handbook of Couple Therapy*, Guildford Press: NY

Brown M & O'Connor A (1984) *Woman Talk: a woman's book of quotes*, Futura: London

Bulletin Plus 4(3) (2000) 'Evidence-Based Help for Couples', One Plus One: London

Burgess A (1997) *Fatherhood Reclaimed: the making of the modern father*, Vermilion: London

Burleson BR & Denton WH (1997) The relationship between communication skill and marital satisfaction: some moderating effects, *Journal of Marriage and the Family* 59(Nov): 884-902

Burleson BR & Denton WH (1992) A new look at similarity and attraction in marriage, *Communication Monographs* 59:268-287

Buss DM (1988) From vigilance to violence: tactics of mate-retention in American undergraduates, *Ethology and Sociobiology* 9:219-317

Buss DM (1994) *The evolution of desire: strategies of mate selection*, Basic Books: NY

Call V, Sprecher S& Schwartz P (1995) The incidence and frequency of marital sex in a national sample, *Journal of Marriage and the Family* 57: 639-652

Cameron S & Collins A (2000) *Playing the Love Market: dating, romance and the real world*, Free Association Books: London

Cate RM & Lloyd SA (1992) *Courtship*, Sage: London

Christensen A, Jacobson NS & Babcock JC (1995) 'Integrative behavioral couple therapy' in Jacobson NS & Gurman AS (eds) *Clinical Handbook of Couple Therapy*, Guildford Press: NY

Christensen A & Jacobson NS (2000) *Reconcilable Differences*, Guildford Press: NY

Christensen A & Walczynski PT (1997) 'Conflict and satisfaction in couples' in Sternberg RJ & Hojjat M (eds) *Satisfaction in Close Relationships*, Guildford Press: NY

Clapton G (2000) 'Perceptions of fatherhood: birth fathers and their adoption experiences' unpublished paper, University of Edinburgh

Clark MS & Chrisman K (1995) 'Resource allocation in intimate relationships' in Weber A & Harvey JH (eds) *Perspectives on Close Relationships*, Allyn & Bacon: Boston

Clements ML et al. (1997) 'The erosion of marital satisfaction over time and how to prevent it' in Sternberg RJ & Hojjat M (eds) *Satisfaction in Close Relationships*, Guildford Press: NY

Clulow C (ed) (2001) *Adult Attachment and Couple Psychotherapy*, Brunner-Routledge: London

Cohan CL & Bradbury TN (1997) Negative life events, marital interaction, and the longitudinal course of newlywed marriage, *Journal of Personality and Social Psychology* 73(1): 114-128

Cordova JV & Jacobson NS (1997) 'Acceptance in couple therapy and its implications for the treatment of depression' in Sternberg RJ & Hojjat M (eds) *Satisfaction in Close Relationships*, Guildford Press: NY

Cosmopolitan (UK) (2000) 'First Date Sex Survey', September, London

Counts RM & Sacks A (1991) Profiles or the divorce-prone: the self-involved narcissist, *Journal of Divorce and Re-Marriage* 15(1-2): 51-74

Cowan CP, Cowan PA, Herning G, Garrett E, Coush W, Curtis-Boles H, Boless A (1985) Transitions to parenthood his, hers and theirs, *Journal of Family Issues* 6 451-181

Cowan P & Cowan CP (2001) 'A couple perspective on the transmission of attachment patterns' in Clulow C (ed) *Adult Attachment and Couple Psychotherapy*, Brunner-Routledge: London

Cramer D (1998) *Close Relationships: the study of love and friendship*, Arnold: London

Cunningham JD & Antill JK (1995) 'Current trends in non-marital cohabitation' in Wood JT & Duck S (eds) *Understudied Relationships: off the Beaten Track*, Sage: CA

Cutrona CE (1996) *Social Support in Couples: marriage as a resource in times of stress*, Sage: CA

Cutrona CE et al. (1998) Predictors and correlates if continuing involvement with the baby's father among adolescent mothers, *Journal of Family Psychology* 12(3):369-387

Dalrymple J (1995) *Jack Dominian: lay prophet?* Chapman: London

Deal JE, Wampler KS & Halverson CF (1992) The importance of similarity in the marital relationship, *Family Process*, 31: 367-382

Demo DH (1992) The self-concept over time: research issues and directions, *Annual Review of Sociology* 1992(18): 303-26

Dickson FC (1995) 'The best is yet to be: research on long-lasting marriages' in Wood JT & Duck S (eds) *Understudied Relationships: off the beaten track*, Sage:CA

Dickson FC (1997) 'Ageing and marriage: understanding the long-term, later-life marriage' Halford WK & Markman HJ (eds) *Clinical Handbook of Marriage and Couples Interventions*, Wiley: NY

Dominian J (1996) *Marriage*, Cedar: London

Donnelly DA (1993) Sexually inactive marriages, *Journal of Sex Research* 30(2): 171-179

Dryer CD & Horowitx LM (1997) When do opposites attract? Interpersonal complementarity versus similarity, *Journal of Personality and Social Psychology* 72(3): 592-603

Duck S (1998) *Human Relationships* (3rd ed), Sage:CA

Dugatkin LA (2001) *The Imitation Factor*, Free Press: London

Eidelson RH & Epstein N (1982) Cognition and relationship maladjustment: development of a measure of dysfunctional relationship beliefs, *Journal of Consulting & Clinical Psychology* 50: 715-720

Emery RE (1999) *Marriage, Divorce & Children's Adjustment*, Sage: Thousand Oaks, CA

Erbert LA & Duck SW (1997) 'Rethinking satisfaction in personal relationships from a dialectical perspective' in Sternberg RJ & Hojjat M (eds) *Satisfaction in Close Relationships*, Guildford Press: NY

Feeney JA, Noller P & Ward C (1997) 'Marital satisfaction and spousal interaction' in Sternberg RJ & Hojjat M (eds) *Satisfaction in Close Relationships*, Guildford Press: NY

Felmlee DH (1998) 'Fatal attraction' in de Munck V (ed) *Romantic Love and Sexual Behaviour: perspectives from the social sciences*, Praeger: Westport, Connecticut

Felmlee DH, Sprecher S & Bassin E (1990) The dissolution of intimate relationships: a hazard model, *Social Psychology Quarterly* 53(1): 13-30

Fincham FD, Beach SR & Kemp-Fincham SI (1997) 'Marital quality: a new theoretical perspective' in Sternberg RJ & Hojjat M (eds) *Satisfaction in Close Relationships*, Guildford Press: NY

Freedman J (1978) *Happy people: what happiness is, who has it, and why,* Harcourt Brace: NY

Friday N (1991) *Women on Top,* Hutchinson: London

Furman W & Flanagan AS (1997) 'The influence of earlier relationships on marriage: an attachment perspective' in Halford WK & Markman HJ (eds) *Clinical Handbook of Marriage and Couples Interventions*, Wiley: NY

Giddens A (1992) *The Transformation of Intimacy*, Polity Press: London

Glass SP & Wright TL (1997) 'Reconstructing marriages after the trauma of infidelity' in Halford WK & Markman HJ (eds) *Clinical Handbook of Marriage and Couples Interventions*, Wiley: NY

Gottman JM (1994) *What Predicts Divorce: the relationship between marital processes and marital outcomes*, Lawrence Erlbaum: Hillsdale NJ

Gottman JM (1998) Presentation at 'The Chaos of Love', One Plus One Conference, London

Gottman JM (1998a) 'Towards and process model of men in marriages and families' in Booth A & Crouter AC (eds) *Men in Families: when do they get involved? what difference does it make?*, Lawrence Erlbaum: NY

Gottman JM, Coan J, Carrere S & Swanson C (1998) Predicting marital happiness and stability from newlywed interactions, *Journal of Marriage and the Family* 60: 5-22

Groskop V (2000) Interview with Anita Roddick, *Sunday Express,* 17 September, London

Grunebaum J (1997) Thinking about romantic/erotic love, *Journal of Marriage and Family Therapy* 23(3): 295-307

Haavio-Mannila E & Kontula O (1997) Correlates of increased sexual satisfaction, *Archives of Sexual Behaviour* 26(4): 399-419

Halford WK, Kelly A & Markman HJ (1997) 'The concept of a healthy marriage' in Halford WK & Markman HJ (eds) *Clinical Handbook of Marriage and Couples Interventions*, Wiley: NY

Halford WK & Markman HJ (eds) (1997) *Clinical Handbook of Marriage and Couples Interventions*, Wiley: NY

Halford WK & Bouma R (1997) 'Individual psychopathology and marital distress' in Halford WK & Markman HJ (eds) *Clinical Handbook of Marriage and Couples Interventions*, Wiley: NY

Halford WK (2000) *Australian Couples in Millennium Three*, Dept. of Family & Community Services, Canberra

Hamburg SR (2000) *Will our Love Last? a couple's road map*, Scribner: NY

Harris CC & Christenfeld N (1996) Jealousy and rational responses to infidelity across gender & culture, *Psychological Science* 7(6)

Hatfield E & Rapson R (1993) 'Love and attachment processes' in Lewis M & Haviland JM (eds) *Handbook of Emotions*, Guildford Press: NY

Hatfield E & Rapson R (1993a) *Love, Sex and Intimacy*, HarperCollins: NY

Hatfield E & Rapson R (1996) *Love and Sex*, Allyn & Bacon: Boston

Hazan C & Shaver PR (1992) 'Broken attachments: relationship loss from the perspective of attachment theory' in Orbuch TL (ed) *Close Relationship Loss: theoretical approaches*, Springer-Verlag: NY

Heiman JR, Epps PH & Ellis B (1995) 'Treating sexual desire disorders in couples' in Jacobson NS & Gurman AS (eds) *Clinical Handbook of Couple Therapy*, Guildford Press: NY

Hendrick SS & Hendrick C (1994) *Liking, Loving & Relating* (2nd ed), Brooks-Cole: CA

Hendrick SS & Hendrick C (1997) 'Love and satisfaction' in Sternberg RJ & Hojjat M (eds) *Satisfaction in Close Relationships*, Guildford Press: NY

Hill CT & Peplau LA (1998) 'Premarital predictors of relationship outcomes: a 15 year follow-up of the Boston Couples Study' in Bradbury TN (ed) *The Developmental Course of Marital Dysfunction*, CUP: Cambridge

Hinckley K & Hesse P (1997) *Plain Fat Chick Seeks Guy Who Likes Broccoli*, Gibbs Smith: Salt Lake City

Hinde RA (1997) *Relationships: a dialectical perspective*, Psychology Press: London

Hojjat M (1997) 'Philosophy of life as a model of relationship satisfaction' in Sternberg RJ & Hojjat M (eds) *Satisfaction in Close Relationships*, Guildford Press: NY

Holtzworth-Munroe A, Beatty SB & Anglin K (1995) 'The assessment and treatment of marital violence: an introduction for the marital therapist' in Jacobson NS & Gurman AS (eds) *Clinical Handbook of Couple Therapy*, Guildford Press: NY

Holtzworth-Munroe A, Smutzler N, Bates L & Sandin E (1997) 'Husband violence: basic facts

and clinical implications' in Halford WK & Markman HJ (eds) *Clinical Handbook of Marriage and Couples Interventions*, Wiley: NY

Hops H, Perry BA & Davis B (1997) 'Marital discord and depression' in Halford WK & Markman HJ (eds) *Clinical Handbook of Marriage and Couples Interventions*, Wiley: NY

Horley S (1991) *The Charm Syndrome: why charming men can make dangerous lovers*, Papermac: London

Houts RM, Robins E & Huston TL (1996) Compatibility and the development of premarital relationships, *Journal of Marriage and the Family* 58(1): 7-20

Hurlbert DF, Apt C & Rombough S (1996) The female experience of sexual desire as a function of sexual compatibility in an intimate relationship, *Canadian Journal of Human Sexuality* 5(1): 7-13

Huston TL & Houts RM (1998) 'The psychological infrastructure of courtship and marriage: the role of personality and compatibility' in Bradbury TN (ed) *The Developmental Course of Marital Dysfunction*, CUP: Cambridge

Huston M & Schwartz M (1995) 'The relationships of lesbians and of gay men' in Wood JT & Duck S (eds) *Understudied Relationships: off the Beaten Track*, Sage: CA

Hyde JS, DeLamater JD & Hewitt EC (1998) Sexuality and the Dual-Earner Couple: multiple roles and sexual functioning, *Journal of Family Psychology* 12(3): 354-368

Jackson B (1984) *Fatherhood,* Allen & Unwin: London

Jacobson NS *et al.* (1996) Psychological factors in the longitudinal course of battering: when do the couples split up? When does the abuse decrease? *Violence and Victims* 11(4): 371-391

Johnson DR & Booth A (1998) Marital quality: a product of the dyadic environment or individual factors? *Social Forces* 76(3): 883-904

Jones AC & Chao CM (1997) 'Racial, ethnic and cultural issues in couples therapy' in Halford WK & Markman HJ (eds) *Clinical Handbook of Marriage and Couples Interventions*, Wiley: NY

Jones M (1993) *Marrying an Older Man,* Piatkus: London

Julien D, Arellano C & Turgeon L (1997) 'Gender issues in heterosexual, gay and lesbian couples' in Halford WK & Markman HJ (eds) *Clinical Handbook of Marriage and Couples Interventions*, Wiley: NY

Karney BR & Bradbury TN (1996) The longitudinal course of marital quality and stability: a review of theory, method and research, *Psychological Bulletin* 118: 3-34

Karney BR & Bradbury TN (1997) Neuroticism, marital interaction and the trajectory of marital satisfaction, *Journal of Personality and Social Psychology* 72(5): 1075-1092

Kets de Vries MFR (1995) *Life and Death in the Executive Fast Lane*, Jossey-Bass: San Francisco

Kiecolt KJ & Fossett MA (1998) 'The effects of mate availability on marriage among black Americans' in Taylor RJ, Jackson JS & Chatters LM (eds) *Family Life in Black America*, Sage: CA

Klohnen EC & Mendelsohn GA (1998) Partner selection for personality characteristics: a couple centered approach, *Personality and Social Psychology Bulletin* 24(3): 268-278

Koski LR & Shaver PR (1997) 'Attachment and relationship satisfaction across the lifespan' in Sternberg RJ & Hojjat M (eds) *Satisfaction in Close Relationships*, Guildford Press: NY

Knap ML & Taylor EH (1995) 'Commitment and its communication in romantic relationships' in Weber A & Harvey JH (eds) *Perspectives on Close Relationships*, Allyn & Bacon: Boston

Kurdek LA (1991) Marital stability and change in marital quality in newlywed couples: a test of the contextual model, *Journal of Social and Personal Relationships*, 8: 27-48

Kurdek LA (1996) The deterioration of relationship quality for gay and lesbian cohabiting couples: a five-year prospective longitudinal study, *Personal Relationships* 3: 417-442

Kurdek LA (1998) 'Developmental changes in marital satisfaction: a six-year prospective longitudinal study of newlywed couples' in Bradbury TN (ed) *The Developmental Course of Marital Dysfunction*, CUP: Cambridge

Kurdek LA (1998a) Relationship outcomes and their predictors: longitudinal evidence from heterosexual married, gay cohabiting and lesbian cohabiting couples, *Journal of Marriage and the Family* 60: 553-568

Laslett (1983) *The World We Have Lost Revisited: further explored,* CUP: Cambridge

Lawson A (1990) *Adultery: an analysis of love and betrayal*, OUP: Oxford

Lazarus AA (1985) *Marital Myths*, Impact: CA

Lee JA (1973) *The Colours of Love*, New Press: Toronto

Lee JA (1998) 'Ideologies of lovestyle and sexstyle' in Munck VC (ed) *Romantic Love and Sexual Behaviour: perspectives from the social sciences*, Praeger: Connecticut

Lee M & Spears R (1995) 'Love at first Byte? Building personal relationships over computer networks' in Wood JT & Duck S (eds) *Understudied Relationships: off the beaten track*, Sage: CA

Leng GA (2001) unpublished paper, Edinburgh University Medical School

Leonard KE & Roberts LJ (1998) 'Marital aggression, quality and stability in the first year of marriage: findings from the Buffalo newlywed study' in Bradbury TN (ed) *The Developmental Course of Marital Dysfunction*, CUP: Cambridge

Lester D (1942) *The Psychological Basis of Handwriting Analysis,* Nelson-Hall: Chicago

Liker JK & Elder GH (1983) Economic hardship and marital relations in the 1930s, *American Sociological Review* 48: 343-359

Lindahl K, Clements M & Markman H (1998) 'The development of marriage: a 9-year perspective' in Bradbury TN (ed) *The Developmental Course of Marital Dysfunction*, CUP: Cambridge

Lindahl KM, Malik NM & Bradbury TN (1997) 'The developmental course of couples' relationships' in Halford WK & Markman HJ (eds) *Clinical Handbook of Marriage and Couples Interventions*, Wiley: NY

Lindahl KM, Clements M & Markman HJ (1998) 'The development of marriage: a nine-year perspective' in Bradbury TN (ed) *The Developmental Course of Marital Dysfunction*. CUP: Cambridge

Macdonald WL & DeMaris A (1005) Remarriage, stepchildren and marital conflict challenges to the incomplete institutionalisation hypothesis, *Journal of Marriage and the Family* 57(May) 387-398

Mackay J (2000) *The Penguin Atlas of Sexual Behaviour,* Penguin: London

Macneil S & Byers ES (1997) The relationships between sexual problems, communication and sexual satisfaction, *The Canadian Journal of Human Sexuality* 6(4): 277-283

McGrath H & Edwards H (2000) *Difficult Personalities: a practical guide to managing the hurtful behaviour of others*, CHOICE Books: NSW, Australia

McNulty S 'In a single-minded state' *Financial Times* (weekend section), 16/17 September 2000: London

McQuillan J & Ferree MM (1998) 'The importance of variation among men. . .' in Booth A & Crouter AC (eds) *Men in Families: when do they get involved? what difference does it make?* Lawrence Erlbaum: NJ

Masters WH, Johnson VE & Kolodny RC (1995) *Human Sexuality*, HarperCollins: NY

Matthews LS, Conger RD & Wickrama KAS (1996) Work-family conflict and marital quality: mediating processes, *Social Psychology Quarterly* 59(1): 62-67

Maticka-Tyndale E, Herold ES & Mewhinney D (1998) Casual sex on a spring break: intentions and behaviors of Canadian students, *The Journal of Sex Research* 35(3): 254-264

Metts S (1992) 'The language of disengagement: a face-management perspective' in Orbuch TL (ed) *Close Relationship Loss: theoretical approaches*, Springer-Verlag: NY

Michael RT et al (1994) *Sex in America: a definitive survey* (National Health and Social Life Survey, 1992) Little, Brown & Co: NY

Middleton C (1998) 'Bridal Paths', *Sunday Times Magazine*, 18 October: London

Moeller K & Stattin H (2001) Are close relationships in adolescence linked with partner relationship in midlife? A longitudinal, prospective study, *International Journal of Behavioral Development* 25(1): 69-77

Money J (1993) *Lovemaps,* Prometheus: NY

Mongeau PA, Carey CM & Williams MLM (1998) 'First date initiation and enactment: an expectancy violation approach' in Canary DJ & Dindia K (eds) *Sex Differences and Similarities in Communication*, Erlbaum: Mahwah, NJ

Mruk CJ (1999) *Self-esteem: Research, Theory and Practice*, Free Association Books: London

Murphy M (2000) The evolution of cohabitation in Britain, 1960-95, *Population Studies* 54: 43-56

Murray SL, Holmes JG & Griffin DW (1996) The self-fulfilling nature of positive illusions in romantic relationships: love is not blind, but prescient, *Journal of Personality and Social Psychology* 71(6): 1155-1180

Murstein BI & Tuerkheimer A (1998) Gender differences in love, sex and motivation for sex, *Psychological Reports* 82: 435-450

Niven D (2000) *The 100 Simple Secrets of Happy People*, HarperCollins: San Francisco

Noller P, Beach S & Osgarby S (1997) 'Cognitive and affective processes in marriage' in Halford WK & Markman HJ (eds) *Clinical Handbook of Marriage and Couples Interventions*, Wiley: NY

Noller P & Feeney JA (1998) 'Communication in early marriage: responses to conflict, nonverbal accuracy and conversational patterns' in Bradbury TN (ed) *The Developmental Course of Marital Dysfunction*, CUP: Cambridge

Notarius CI, Lashley SL & Sullivan DJ (1997) 'Angry at your partner? Think again' in Sternberg RJ & Hojjat M (eds) *Satisfaction in Close Relationships*, Guildford Press: NY

O'Leary KD (1998) 'The status of family violence research in Europe' in Klein RCA (ed) *Multidisciplinary Perspectives on Family Violence*, Routledge: London

O'Leary KD & Cascardi M (1998) 'Physical aggression in marriage: a developmental analysis' in Bradbury TN (ed) *The Developmental Course of Marital Dysfunction*, CUP: Cambridge UK

Pahl J (1989) *Money and Marriage*, Macmillan: London

Paris M (1990) *Falling in love and the transformation of self-concept.* Unpublished doctoral dissertation, California Graduate School of Family Psychology, San Francisco

Pierce CA (1996) Body height and romantic attraction: a meta analytic test of the male-taller norm. *Social Behaviour and Personality* 24(2): 143-150

Pinkus L & Dare C (1978) *Secrets in the Family,* Faber & Faber: London

Pittman F (1997) Just in love, *Journal of Marital and Family Therapy* 23(3): 309-312

Pittman FS & Wagers TP (1995) 'Crises of infidelity' in Jacobson NS & Gurman AS (eds) *Clinical Handbook of Couple Therapy*, Guildford Press: NY

Rampage C (1995) 'Gendered aspects of marital therapy' in Jacobson NS & Gurman AS (eds) *Clinical Handbook of Couple Therapy*, Guildford Press: NY

Renaud C, Byers ES & Pan S (1997) Sexual and relationship satisfaction in mainland China, *Journal of Sex Research* 34(4): 399-410

Repetti RL (1989) Effects of daily workload on subsequent behaviour during marital interaction: the roles of social withdrawal and spouse support, *Journal of Personality and Social Psychology* 57(4): 651-659

Rohlfing ME (1995) 'Doesn't anyone stay in one place anymore? an exploration of the understudied phenomenon of long-distance relationships' in Wood JT & Duck S (eds) *Understudied Relationships: off the Beaten Track*, Sage:CA

Rohsenow DJ (1998) 'Alcoholism' in Blechman EA & Brownell KD (eds) *Behavioral Medicine and Women: a comprehensive handbook*, Guildford Press: NY

Romkens R & Mastenbroek S (1998) 'Budding happiness: the relational dynamics of the abuse of girls and young women by their boyfriends' in Klein RCA (ed) *Multidisciplinary Perspectives on Family Violence*, Routledge: London

Root MPP (1995) 'Conceptualization and treatment of eating disorders in couples' in Jacobson NS & Gurman AS (eds) *Clinical Handbook of Couple Therapy*, Guildford Press: NY

Ross CE & Mirowsky J (1988) Childcare and emotional adjustment to wives' employment, *Journal of Health and Social Behaviour* 29: 127-138

Rudner R (1994) *Rita Rudner's Guide to Men,* Hodder & Stoughton: London

Rusbult CE, Bissonnette VL, Arriaga XB & Cox CL (1998) 'Accommodation processes during the early years of marriage' in Bradbury TN (ed) *The Developmental Course of Marital Dysfunction*, CUP: Cambridge

Ruszcynski S (1995) 'My partner, my self' in Clulow C (ed) *Women, Men and Marriage*, Sheldon: London

Russell RJH & Wells PA (1992) Social desirability and quality of marriage, *Personality and Individual Differences*, 13: 787-791

Rutter V &Schwartz P (1998) *The Love Test*, Thorsons: London

Ryff CD (1998) 'Positive mental health' in Blechman EA & Brownell KD (eds) *Behavioral Medicine and Women: a comprehensive handbook*, Guildford Press: NY

Sachs G (1998) *The Astrology File,* Orion: London

Sarsby J (1980) *Romantic Love and Society*, Penguin: London

Sanders MR, Markie-Dadds C & Nicholson JM (1997) 'Concurrent interventions for marital and children's problems' in Halford WK & Markman HJ (eds) *Clinical Handbook of Marriage and Couples Interventions*, Wiley: NY

Sanders MR, Nicholson JM & Floyd FJ (1997) 'Couples' relationships and children' in Halford WK & Markman HJ (eds) *Clinical Handbook of Marriage and Couples Interventions*, Wiley: NY

Schmaling KB & Sher TG (1997) 'Physical health and relationships' in Halford WK & Markman HJ (eds) *Clinical Handbook of Marriage and Couples Interventions*, Wiley: NY

Shackelford TK & Buss DM (1997) 'Marital satisfaction in evolutionary psychological perspective' in Sternberg RJ & Hojjat M (eds) *Satisfation in Close Relationships*, Guildford Press: NY

Shaver PR, Wu S & Schwartx JC (1991) 'Cross-cultural similarities and differences in emotion and its representation: a prototype approach', *Review of Personality and Social Psychology* 13: 175-212

Sher TG (1996) 'Courtship and marriage: choosing a primary relationship' in Vanzetti N & Duck S (eds) *A Lifetime of Relationships*, Brooks/Cole: CA

Slipp S (1995) 'Object relations marital therapy of personality disorders' in Jacobson NS & Gurman AS (eds) *Clinical Handbook of Couple Therapy*, Guildford Press: NY

Scanzoni J (1969) *Sexual Bargaining: power politics in the American marriage*, Prentice-Hall: NJ

Schafer R B, Wickrama KAS & Keith PM (1996) Self-concept disconfirmation, psychological distress, and marital happiness, *Journal of Marriage and the Family* 58: 167-177

Shackelford TK (1998) 'Divorce as a consequence of spousal infidelity' in de Munck VC (ed) *Romantic Love and Sexual Behaviour*, Praeger: Westport, Connecticut

Shackelford TK & & Buss DM (1997) Anticipation of marital dissolution as a consequence of spousal infidelity, *Journal of Social and Personal Relationships* 14(6): 793-808

Sher TS (1996) 'Courtship and marriage: choosing a primary relationship' in Vanzetti N & Duck S (eds) *A Lifetime of Relationships*, Brooks/Cole (ITP): NY

Simons J (ed) (1999) *High Divorce Rates: the state of the evidence on reasons and remedies*, Research Series 2/99 (Vol 1), Lord Chancellor's Department: London

Simons J (1998) presentation at One Plus One 'Can marriage be rescued?' working seminar, London

Smart C & Stevens P (2000) *Cohabiting parents' experience of relationships and separation* Joseph Rowntree Foundation: York

Smith, Godfrey 'Take a bloke like Kingers', *The Sunday Times*, 26 November 2000: London

Sonntag L (1998) *Finding the Love of your Life*, Piccadilly Press: London

Speed A & Gangestad SW (1997) Romantic popularity and mate preferences: a peer-nomination study, *Personality and Social Psychology Bulletin* 23(9): 928-936

Spence SH (1997) 'Sex and relationships' in Halford WK & Markman HJ (eds) *Clinical Handbook of Marriage and Couples Interventions*, Wiley: NY

Sprecher S & McKinney K (1995) 'Sexuality in close relationships' in Weber A & Harvey JH (eds) *Perspectives on Close Relationships,* Allyn & Bacon: Boston

Sternberg RJ (1996) Love stories, *Personal Relationships* 3: 59-79

Sternberg RJ (1998) *Love is a Story: a new theory of relationships*, OUP: NY

Sternberg RJ & Hojjat M (eds) (1997) *Satisfaction in Close Relationships*, Guildford Press: NY

Sweet JA & Bumpass LL (1992) 'Disruption of marital and cohabitation relationships: a social demographic perspective' in Orbuch TL (ed) *Close Relationship Loss: theoretical approaches*, Springer-Verlag: NY

Sweeting H (1998) 'Life events' in Blechman EA & Brownell KD (eds) *Behavioral Medicine and Women: a comprehensive handbook*, Guildford Press: NY

Tallman I, Burke PJ & Gecas V (1998) 'Socialization into marital roles: testing a contextual, developmental model of marital functioning' in Bradbury TN (ed) *The Developmental Course of Marital Dysfunction*, CUP: Cambridge

Taylor RJ, Jackson JS & Chatters LM (1997) *Family Life in Black America*, Sage: CA

Tennov D (1979) *Love and Limerance: the experience of being in love*, Stein & Day: NY

Thiessen D, Young RK & Delgado M (1997) Social pressures for assortative mating, *Personality and Individual Differences* 22(2): 157-164

Thompson BM (1997) 'Couples and the work-family interface' in Halford WK & Markman HJ (eds) *Clinical Handbook of Marriage and Couples Interventions*, Wiley: NY

Thornton A et al. (1992) Reciprocal Effects of Religiosity, Cohabitation and Marriage, *American Journal of Sociology* 98(3): 628-651

Trost MR & Alberts JK (1998) 'An evolutionary view of understanding sex effects in communicating attraction' in Canary DJ & Dindia K (eds) *Sex Differences and Similarities in Communication*, Lawrence Erlbaum: NJ

Tucker BM & Taylor RJ (1997) 'Gender, age and marital status as related to romantic involvement among African American singles' in Taylor RJ, Jackson JS & Chatters LM (eds) *Family Life in Black America*, Sage: CA

Vanzetti N & Duck S (1996) *A Lifetime of Relationships*, Brooks/Cole: Pacific Grove

Veroff J, Douvan E, Orbuch TL & Acitelli LK (1998) 'Happiness in stable marriages: the early years' in Bradbury TN (ed) *The Developmental Course of Marital Dysfunction*, CUP: Cambridge

Wallerstein JS & Blakeslee S (1996) *The Good Marriage,* Bantam Press: London

Wallerstein JS, Lewis J & Blakeslee S (2000) *The Unexpected Legacy of Divorce: a 25 year landmark study*, Hyperion: NY

Walsh F, Jacob L & Simons V (1995) 'Facilitating healthy divorce processes: therapy and mediation approaches' in Jacobson NS & Gurman AS (eds) *Clinical Handbook of Couple Therapy*, Guildford Press: NY

Weinraub B (1998) 'The price of love', *The Guardian*, 8 May, London

Weiss RL & Heyman RE (1997) 'A clinical-research overview of couples interactions' in Halford WK & Markman HJ (eds) *Clinical Handbook of Marriage and Couples Interventions*, Wiley: NY

Weldon F (1996) *Wicked Women*, Flamingo: London

White LK & Booth A (1991) Divorce over the life course: the role of marital happiness, *Journal of Family Issues* 12(1): 5-21

Willi J (1997) The significance of romantic love for marriage, *Family Process* 36(2): 171-182

Windle M (1996) Mate similarity, heavy substance use and family history of problem drinking among young adult women, *Journal of Studies on Alcohol* 58(6): 573-580

Winstead BA, Derlaga VJ & Rose S (1997) *Gender in Close Relationships*, Sage: CA

Wu Z & Penning MJ (1997) Marital instability after midlife, *Journal of Family Issues* 18(5): 459-478

Young L (1985) *Love Around the World*, Coronet: London

Young M, Luquis R, Denny G & Young T (1998) Correlates of sexual satisfaction in marriage, *Canadian Journal of Human Sexuality* 7(2): 115-127

Zilbergeld M (1995) *Men and Sex,* Harper Collins: London

resources

FURTHER READING

LOVE IS A STORY: a new theory of relationships by Robert J Sternberg (Oxford University Press, USA, 1998, ISBN: 0195131029)
Lists all the main 'love stories' referred to in Chapter 2, so you can identify your own

DIFFICULT PERSONALITIES: a practical guide to managing the hurtful behaviour of others by Helen McGrath & Hazel Edwards (Choice Books, Australian Consumers' Association, N.S.W., 2000, ISBN: 09472768-4)
A totally brilliant guide to personality types and how to handle them – in our partner, and in our selves

FINDING MR WRITE by Beverley East (Villard, New York, 2000, ISBN: 0-375-50370-6)
Helps you read your mate's personality from their handwriting

HOW LOVE WORKS by Steve & Shaaron Biddulph (Thorsons, London, 2000, ISBN: 0-7225-3935-5)
A friendly, supportive book for well-established couples, full of wise stories and useful exercises

WHY MARRIAGES SUCCEED OR FAIL by John Gottman (Bloomsbury, London, 1999, ISBN: 07477536031)
Ddetailed examination, with illuminating quizzes and case-studies, of your conflict styles – how they may be destroying your relationship, and what you can do to save it

TAKE BACK YOUR MARRIAGE: sticking together in a world that pulls us apart by William J Doherty (Guildford Press, New York, 2001, ISBN: 1-57230-459-6)
Contains a brilliant chapter on what to look for in a couple-counsellor

THE TRANSFORMATION OF INTIMACY: sexuality, love and eroticism in modern societies by Anthony Giddens (Stanford University Press, USA, 1993, ISBN: 0804722145)
A serious, exciting read, by one of the world's top sociologists

MARRIED LIFE: a rough guide for couples today
A well-designed magazine given free to all couples in England and Wales who give notice of their intention to marry. Ask your Registrar or Church for your copy!

Couple-support organizations – United Kingdom

KEY to Services Provided:
- ♥ Preparation for Commitment
- ☺ Improving your Relationship
- ♂☞ Counselling (heterosexual)
- ♀☞ Counselling (lesbian)
- ♂♂ Counselling (gay male)
- ⚔ Mediation (sorting out the practicalities of separating)
- ☾ Sex therapy
- ☎ Crisis telephone helpline

RELATE
National network, but Head Office is:
Herbert Gray College
Little Church Street
Rugby
Warwickshire CV21 3AP
tel: 01788 573241
web: www.relate.org.uk
Services provided:
♥ ☺ ♂☞ ♀☞ ♂♂ ⚔ ☾

Couple Counselling Scotland
40 North Castle Street
Edinburgh EH2 3BN
tel: 0131 225 5006
web: www.couplecounselling.org
Services provided:
♥ ☺ ♂☞ ♀☞ ♂♂ ⚔ ☾

WPF Counselling (Westminster Pastoral Foundation)
23 Kensington Square
London W8 5HN
tel: 020 7361 4800
web: www.wpf.org.uk
Services provided: ☺ ♂☞ ♀☞ ♂♂ ⚔

London Marriage Guidance Council
76a New Cavendish Street
London W1G 9TE
tel: 020 7580 1087
web: www.lmg.org.uk
Services provided: ♥ ☺ ♂☞ ♀☞ ♂♂ ☾

The Tavistock Marital Studies Institute (couple psychotherapy)
The Tavistock Centre
120 Belsize Lane
London NW3 5BA
tel: 020 7435 7111
web: www.tmsi.org.uk
Services provided:
♥ ☺ ♂☞ ♀☞ ♂♂ ⚔ ☾

Couple Psycotherapy Service
Studio House
Temple Wood Avenue
London NW3 7UY
(full members of the Society have qualified at the Tavistock Marital Studies Institute)
tel: 0870 902 4878
web: www.couplepsycotherapy.co.uk
Services provided:
♥ ☺ ♂☞ ♀☞ ♂♂ ⚔

British Association for Sexual & Relationship Therapy (BASMT)
PO Box 13686
London SW20 9ZH
tel: 020 8543 2707
web: www.basrt.org.uk
Services provided: ☾
(also has list of relationship therapists)

The Cog-Wheel Trust
41 High Street
Chesterton
Cambridge CB4 1NQ
tel: 01223 464385
e-mail: cwt@btclick.com
web: none
Services provided: ♥ ☺ ♂☞ ♀☞ ♂♂

London Lesbian & Gay Switchboard
PO Box 7324
London N1 9QS
tel: 020 7837 7324
web: www.llgs.org.uk
Services provided: ♥ ☺ ♀☞ ♂♂ ⚔ ☾

Derwent Rural Counselling Service
Newholme
Baslow Road
Bakewell DE45 1AD
tel: 01629 812710
email: drcs@care4free.net
Services provided:
♥ ☺ ♂☞ ♀☞ ♂♂ ⚔ ☾

Institute of Family Therapy
(London based – no regional offices)
24-32 Stephenson Way
London NW1 2HX
tel: 020 7391 9150
web: www.instituteoffamilytherapy.org.uk
Services provided:
♥ ☺ ♂☞ ♀☞ ♂♂ ⚔ ☾

National Family Mediation
9 Tavistock Place
London WC1H 9SN
tel: 020 7383 5993
   (10am - 2pm Mon - Fri)
web: www.nfm.u-net.com
Services provided: 🖋

UK College of Family Mediators
24-32 Stephenson Way
London NW1 2HX
tel: 020 7391 9162
web: www.ukcfm.co.uk
Services Provided: 🖋

SSAFA (The Welare Advisory Service for Families of Service & Ex-Service Men & Women)
19 Queen Elizabeth Street
London SE1 2LP
tel: 020 7463 9229
web: www.ssafa.org.uk
Services provided:
♥ ☺ 🖋☞ ☞☞ ♩♩ 🖋🖋 ☯

The Marriage Study Consortium
PO Box 25391
Provo, Utah
UT8 4602-5391
tel: (United States) 801 378 4359
fax: (United States) 801 378 4385

web: www.relate.byu.edu
A comprehensive, solidly-tested questionnaire available on-line at a small cost. Can be taken by single people (not in a relationship), by one partner of a couple or by two partners (well-established or not yet living together).

The Impotence Association
PO Box 10296
London SW17 9WH
tel: 020 8767 7791 (9.00-5.00 Monday –Friday)
email: theia@btinternet.com
web: www.impotence.org.uk
Services provided: information and support for men & women who find sexual arousal or functioning difficult

One Plus One Marriage & Partnership Research
The Wells
7-15 Rosebery Avenue
London EC1R 4SP
tel: 020 7841 3660
web: www.oneplusone.org.uk
Services provided: information and research on couple relationships (not a helpline)

UK couple-support organizations with specific cultural/religious base

Marriage Care Ltd (Christian)
Clitheroe House
1 Blythe Mews
Blythe Road
London W14 0NW
tel: 0845 660600
   Helpline (11am - 3pm every day)
tel: 020 7371 1341 Admin
web: www.marriagecare.org.uk
Contains comprehensive directory of Christian counsellors and support organizations
Services provided:
♥ ☺ 🖋☞ ☞☞ ♩♩ 🖋🖋 ☯

2-in-2-1 (Christian)
11 Lamborne Close
Sandhurst

Berks GU47 8JL
tel: 01344 779658
web: www.2-in-2-1.com
Christian base but wider application – excellent website with lists of counsellors, events and couples' organizations, including the Salvation Army and the Asian Family Mediation Service
Services provided: ♥ ☺ 🖋☞

Willow Counselling Service (Christian)
87 Warwick Road
Olton
Solihull
West Midlands B92 7HP
tel: 0121 707 6797
Services provided: ☺ 🖋☞ ☞☞ ♩♩

MARRIAGE RESOURCE (Christian)
24 West Street
Wimborne
Dorset BH21 1JS
tel: 01202 849000
web: www.marriageresource.org.uk
Services provided: ♥ ☺ ♪☞

Care For The Family (Christian)
PO Box 488
Cardiff CF15 7YY
tel: 02920 810800
web: www.care-for-the-family.org.uk
Services provided: ☺ ♪☞

Association For Marriage Enrichment (Christian)
Church Cottage North
Sea Lane
Kilve
Nr Bridgewater
Somerset TA5 1EG
tel: 01278 741302
web: www.amefocus.demon.co.uk
Services Provided: ☺ ♪☞

African Caribbean Family Mediation Service
2-4 St Johns Crescent
Brixton
London SW9 7LZ
tel: 020 7737 2366
Services provided: ♪☞ 🚗

Muslim Marriage Guidance Council
8 Caburn Road
Hove
Sussex BN3 6EF
tel: 01273 722438/01273 299345

mobile: 07971 861972 (m)
Services provided: ♥ ☺ ♪☞ 🚗 plus cross cultural guidance & interfaith religious/legal advice

Asian Counselling Services, Leicester
80 Burleys Way
Leicester LE1 3BD
tel: 0116 262 9636
web: www.acserve.org
Services provided:
♥ ☺ ♪☞ ☞☞ ♪♪ 🚗 ✆

Asian Family Counselling Service
76 Church Road
Hanwell
London W7 1LB
tel: 020 8567 5616
(info on www.2-in-2-1.com)
Services provided: ♥ ☺ ♪☞ 🚗

Muslim Women's Helpline
Room 7
11 Main Drive
GEC East Lane Estate
Wembley HA9 7NA
tel: 020 8908 6715/020 8904 8193
web: www.armnet.demon.co.uk
Services provided: ♥ ☺ ♪☞ ☞☞ 🚗 ✆ ☎ (and can refer on for ♪♪)

Jewish Marriage Council
23 Ravenshurst Avenue
London NW4 4EE
tel: 020 8203 6311
emergency tel: 0345 581999
e-mail: info@jmc-uk.org
Services provided:
♥ ☺ ♪☞ ☞☞ 🚗 ✆ ☎

UK organisations offering crisis support on wider, often relevant, issues

Samaritans
PO Box 9090
Stirling
FK8 2SA
tel: 08457 909090 (UK)
tel: 1850 609090 (Rep of Ireland)
web: www.samaritans.org.uk
e-mail support service:
jo@samaritas.org.uk
Services provided: ☎ (for anyone in distress)

Saneline
First Floor
Cityside House
40 Adler Street
London E1 1EE
tel: 0845 767 8000
web: www.sane.org.uk
Services provided: ☎ (for individuals/ families coping with mental illness

National Debtline
318 Summer Lane
Newtown
Birmingham B19 3RL
tel: 0808 808 4000
  (Mon & Thurs 10am - 4pm)
  (Tues & Wed 10am - 7pm)
  (Fri 10am - noon)
web: www.birminghamsettlement.org.uk
Services provided: ☎ (debt counselling
& self-help material)

Money Advice Scotland
Suite 306
Washington Street
Glasgow G3 8AZ
tel: 0141 572 0237
web: www.moneyadvicescotland.org.uk
Services provided: ☎ (debt-counselling)

Women's Aid Federation
PO Box 391
Bristol BS99 7WS
tel: 08457 023468
web: www.womensaid.org.uk
Services provided: ☎
(advice/information/refuge for women
in England threatened by mental,
emotional or physical abuse)

Welsh Women's Aid
38–48 Crwys Road
Cardiff CF24 4NN
tel: 0292 0390874

Services provided: ☎
(/advice/information/refuge for women
in Wales threatened by mental,
emotional or physical abuse)

**Northern Ireland Women's Aid
Federation**
129 University Street
Belfast BT7 1HP
tel: 02890 249041/ 02890 331818
web: www.niwaf.org
Services provided: ☎
(advice/information/refuge for women
in NI threatened by mental, emotional
or physical abuse)

Scottish Women's Aid
Norton Park
57 Albion Road
Edinburgh EH7 5QB
tel: 0131 475 2372/0800 0271234
(Scottish Domestic Abuse Helpline)
web: www.scottishwomensaid.co.uk
Services provided: ☎
(advice/information/refuge for women
in Scotland threatened by mental,
emotional or physical abuse)

Rape Crisis Federation
7 Mansfield Road
Nottingham NG1 3FB
tel: 0115 934 8474
web: www.rapecrisis.co.uk
Services provided: ☎

AUSTRALIA

Anglican Engaged Encounter (WA)
(08) 9446 1641
Services provided: ♥

Anglican Marriage Encounter (WA)
(08) 9456 2872
Services provided: ☺

Anglicare Australia
Head Office:
12 Batman St West Melbourne 3003
(03) 9328 3544
State offices (also have offices in
regional areas):
Anglicare NSW – (02) 9895 8000
Anglicare SA – (08) 8305 9200
Anglicare Central Queensland –
(07) 4927 8200

www.anglicare.asn.au
Services provided: ♥ ☺ ♫

Anglicare Palmerston
17 University Ave Palmerston 0830
(08) 8932 6048
Services provided: ♥ ☺

Anglicare Tasmania Inc
18 Watchorn St Hobart 7000
(03) 6234 3510
Services provided: ♥ ☺

Burnside
13 Blackwood Pl
North Parramatta 2150
(02) 9768 6866
www.burnside.org.au
Services provided: ☺

RESOURCES

Centacare Agencies (also have offices in regional areas)
New South Wales – Polding House
276 Pitt St Sydney 2000
(02) 9283 4899
Victoria – 383 Albert St East
Melbourne 3002
(03) 9287 5555
Queensland – 58 Morgan St Fortitude
Valley 4006
(07) 3252 4371
Western Australia – 456 Hay St Perth
(08) 9325 6644
South Australia – 33 Wakefield Street
Adelaide 5000
(08) 8210 8200
Tasmania – 23 Stoke St Hobart 7000
(03) 6278 1660
Australian Capital Territory –
42 Canberra Ave Manuka 2603
(02) 6239 7700
Northern Territory – 18 Geranium St
The Gardens Darwin 0820
(08) 8941 0022
6 Hartley St Alice Springs 0870
(08) 8953 3177
14 Giles St Katherine 0850
(08) 8971 0777
Services provided: ♥ ☺ 🚗

C.O.P.E – Centre of Personal Education Inc.
116 Hutt St Adelaide 5000
(08) 8223 2433
Services provided: ♥

Drummond Street Relationship Centre
195 Drummond St Carlton 3053
(03) 9663 6733
Services provided: ☺

Engaged Encounter (Catholic)
These week-ends are run in most states. For details contact the local Catholic church or the website –
www.engagedencounter.org.au
Services provided: ♥

Family Mediation Centre
PO Box 2131
Moorabbin Vic 3189
(03) 9555 9300
www. mediation.com.au
Services provided: 🚗

Family Relationships Institute (Relatewell)
21 Bell St
Coburg Vic 3058
(03) 9354 8854
www.relatewell.com.au
Services provided: ♥ ☺

Gay & Lesbian Counselling
Sydney (02) 9207 2800
Melbourne (03) 9816 3721
Brisbane (07) 3342 4258
Perth (08) 9420 7201
Adelaide (08) 8362 3223
Services provided: ☺ ☞☞ ♫♫

Interrelate
16 Jersey Rd
Strathfield NSW 2135
(02) 9745 1288
www.interrelate.org.au
Services provided:
♥ ☺ ♫☞ ☞☞ ♫♫ 🚗 ☺

Kinections
PO Box 10448
Brisbane QLD 4000
(07) 3839 1333
www.kinections.com.au
Services provided: ♥ ☺

Lutheran Community Care
309 Prospect Rd Blair Athol 5084
(08) 8269 5788
Services provided: ♥ ☺

LifeWorks Relationship Counselling & Education Services
Level 5, 227 Collins St Melbourne 3000
(03) 9654 7360
www.lifeworks.com.au
Services provided: ♥ ☺

Migrant Resource Centre
251 High St Preston 3072
(03) 9484 7944
Services provided: ♥ ☺ ♫☞ ☞☞ ♫♫ 🚗
Relationships Australia
National Office
15 Napier Cl Deakin 2600
(02) 6285 4466

State offices (also have offices in regional areas):
New South Wales – 5 Sera St Lane
Cove 2066
(02) 9418 8724

Victoria – 1 Princess St Kew 3101
   (03) 9205 9570
Queensland – 58 Hope St South
   Brisbane 4101
   (07) 3217 2900
Western Australia – 115 Cambridge St
   West Leederville 6007
   (08) 9489 6363
South Australia – 55 Hutt St Adelaide
   5000
   (08) 8223 4566
Tasmania – 306 Murray St Hobart 7000
   (03) 6211 4050
Australian Capital Territory –
   15 Napier Cl Deakin 2600
   (02) 6281 3600
Northern Territory – Gregory Tce
   (cnr Bath St) Alice Springs 0870
   (08) 8952 7344
   Woods St (cnr Lindsay St) Darwin
   0800
   (08) 8981 6676
www.relationships.com.au
Services provided:
♥ ☺ ☞ ☞ ♫ ♫ ♪♪ ♫ ☺

**Stepfamily Association of South
Australia**
PO Box 1162
Gawler SA 5118
(08) 8522 7007
Services provided: ♥ ☺ ♫

Stepfamily Association of Victoria
PO Box 322
Clifton Hill Vic 3068
(03) 9481 1500
Services provided: ♥ ☺ ♫

USEFUL BOOKS/RESOURCES:

Australia. Dept. of Human Services
and Health & Australia. Attorney
General's Dept. (1994) Is love
enough? Relationships kit. – Canberra
: The Departments.

Clohesy, Bernadette. (2001) Eyes wide
open. – Port Melbourne : Lothian.

Harris, Roger. (1992) Love, sex and
waterskiing : the experience of pre-
marriage education in Australia.
Adelaide : Centre for Human Resource
Studies, University of South Australia.

Simons, Michelle, Harris, Roger &
Willis, Peter. (1994) Pathways to
marriage : learning for married life in
Australia. – Underdale, SA : Centre for
Research in Education and Work,
University of South Australia.

Tuettemann, Elizabeth. (2000) Little
book of insights into couple relationships. – Boyup Brook,W.A.

notes

Page number followed by line or box bullet number
For full references, see Bibliography

INTRODUCTION: DREAMS OF LEAVING

9/7: Hatfield & Rapson (1993a)
9/11: Young et al. (1998)
9/14: Halford et al. (1997)
9/18: Kurdek (1996)
10/5: Giddens (1992)
10/7: Tallman (1998)
10/12: Giddens (1992)
11/4: Russell & Wells (1992)
11/9: Gottman (1998)
11/12: Hatfield & Rapson (1993) p. xvii
11/13: Hatfield & Rapson (1993) pp. xix–xx
11/16: Hatfield & Rapson (1993) pp. xix–xx
11/22: Lee (1998)

CHAPTER 1: MEETING

13/14: Felmlee (1998)
13/15: Hatfield & Rapson (1993)
13/28: Baker (1996)
13/37: For review see Hatfield & Rapson (1993)
13/box: Parker (1944) cited by Hatfield & Rapson (1993b)
14/box1: Hatfield & Rapson (1993)
14/box2: Hatfield & Rapson (1993)
14/box3: Sarsby (1980)
14/box4: Paris M (1990)
14/3: Studies cited by Hatfield & Rapson (1993b) p.62–3
14/14: Hendrick & Hendrick (1994) p.91
14/21: Studies cited by Cohan & Bradbury (1997)
14/22: Surra (1990) cited by Hatfield & Rapson (1993a) p.165
14/23: Willi (1997)
14/24: Lawson (1990)
14/26: Willi (1997)
15/box: Pittman (1997)
16/4: Paris (1990)

16/15: Surra (1990) cited by Hatfield & Rapson (1993) p.165
16/20: Hamburg (2000)
16/box1: Grunebaum (1997)
16/box2: Willi (1997)
16/box3: Willi (1997)
16/box4: Willi (1997)
17/2: Willi (1997)
17/11: Hendricks & Hendricks (1994)
17/13: Gershuny (1996)
18/1: Buss (1994)
18/18: Muehlenhard et al. (1986) cited by Hatfield & Rapson (1993b)
18/box: Muehlenhard et al. (1986) cited by Hatfield & Rapson (1993b)
19/11: Hill & Peplau (1998)
19/13('passion'): Cramer (1998) p.72
19/13: Contreras (1996)
19/16: Gottman (1998a)
19/20: Pittman & Wagers (1995)
19/23: Studies cited by Karney & Bradbury (1997)
19/box: Pittman & Waagers (1995)
19/25: Mills & Boon survey (2000)
19/27: Weinraub (1998)
19/29: Grunebaum (1997)
19/32: Mills & Boon (2000)
19/36: Slater & Woodside (1951) cited in Cramer (1997) p.45
20/3: Willi (1997)
20/box1: Grunebaum (1997)
20/box2: Grunebaum (1997)
20/box3: Kamin et al. (1970) cited in Cramer (1997) p45
20/box4: Grunebaum (1997)
20/13: Kurdek (1993) cited by Cramer (1998) p.33
20/16: Rutter & Schwartz (1998)
20/24: Kurdeck (1998)
22/3: Traupmann & Hatfield (1981) cited in Aron & Aron (1995)
22/21: Tennof (1979) cited in Aron & Aron (1995)

22/box1: Baumeister *et al.* (1993) cited by Hatfield & Rapson (1996)
22/box2: Baumeister *et al.* (1993) cited by Hatfield & Rapson (1996)
22/box3: Willi (1997)
22/box4: Aron & Aron (1995)
23/3: Aron & Aron (1991) cited in Aron & Aron (1995)
23/7: Hatfield & Rapson (1993)
23/17: Hendrick & Hendrick (1992)
23/23: Hendrick & Hendrick (1992)
23/box: cited in Smith (2000)
25/box1: Dion & Dion (1975) reported by Aron & Aron (1995)
25/box2: Dion & Dion (1975) reported by Aron & Aron (1995)
25/box3: Lin & Rusbult (1995) cited by Hinde (1997) p.276
25/box4: Swann, Hixon & De La Ronde (1992) cited by Schafer, Wickrama & Keith (1996)
25/box5: Klohnen & Mendelsohn (1998)
25/4: Bratslavsky *et al.* (1998)
25/14: Hinde (1997) p.126
25/16: Klohnen & Mendelsohn (1998)
25/24: Huston & Schwartz (1995)
26/4: Mruk (1999)
26/5: Demo (1992)
26/16: Lee (1998)
27/11: Sher (1996) p.249
27/17: Shackelford (1998)
28/1: Shackelford (1998)
28/6: Shackelford & Buss (1997)
28/12: Hill & Peplau (1998)
28/18: Michael *et al.* (1994) p.66
28/23: Michael *et al.* (1994) p.64
28/24: Brinig & Allen (1999)
28/box4: Shackelford (1998)
29/top box: Brown & O'Connor (1984) p.237
29/24: *The Economist*, 27 January 2001
29/bottom box1-3: Lee (1998)
29/bottom box4: Mackay (2000)
30/8: Dugatkin & Cunningham, cited by Dugatkin (2001)
30/box1: Hinde (1997) p.126
30/box2: Speed & Gangestad (1997)
30/box3: Hendrick & Hendrick (1992) p.45
30/box4: Dion (1977) cited by Hendrick & Hendrick (1992)

31/9: Blumstein & Schwartz (1983)
31/11: Derenski & Landsburg (1981) cited by Masters *et al.* (1995) p263
31/21: Hendrick & Hendrick (1992) p.45
31/25: Mackay (2000)
31/box1: Cramer (1998) p.82
31/box2: Hinde (1997) p.450
31/box3: Cramer (1998) p.82
31/box5: Hinde (1997) p.450
32/top box: Hendrick & Hendrick (1992) p.45
32/top box4: Cramer (1998) p80
32/2: Hendrick & Hendrick (1992) p.45
32/12: Blumstein & Schwartz (1983) p.251
32/15: Hill & Peplau (1998)
32/bottom box: Hinckley (1997)
33/box1: Cramer (1998) p.82
33/box2: Hendrick & Hendrick (1992)
33/box3: Cramer (1998) p.77
33/box4: Cramer (1998) p.77
33/6: Hinde (1997) p.286
33/14: Hatfield & Rapson (1993b)
33/19: Hatfield & Rapson (1993b)
34/2: Michael *et al.* (1994) p.82
34/12: Fay *et al.* (1989) cited by Hatfield & Rapson (1993) p.85
34/13: Masters *et al.* (1995) p.372
34/box: Michael *et al.* (1994)
35/box1: Sprecher et al. (1994)
35/box2: Young (1985) p.59
35/box3: Hinde (1997) p.449
35/box4: Young (1985) p.53
35/box5: Mackay (2000) p.28
35/10: Michael *et al.* (1994)
35/17: Tucker & Taylor (1997)
35/24: Cramer (1998) p.83
36/box: Cramer (1998) p.83
36/4: Speed & Gangestad (1997)
36/9: Dugatkin & Cunningham (2000)
37/top box2: Mongeau *et al.* (1998)
37/top box4: Mongeau *et al.* (1998)
37/10: Hatfield & Rapson (1993a) p.25
37/bottom box: Michael *et al.* (1994) p.95
37/bottom box4: Mackay (2000)
38/box1: *Cosmopolitan*, August 2000
38/box2: *Cosmopolitan*, August 2000
38/box3: *Cosmopolitan*, August 2000
38/box4: *Cosmopolitan*, August 2000

38/box5: Michael *et al.* (1994)

38/1: Cramer (1998) p76,77

38/13: *Cosmopolitan*, August 2000

39/box1: Mackay (2000)

39/box2: Thiessen, Young & Delgado (1997)

39/box3: Mackay (2000)

39/box4: Mackay (2000)

39/box5: Pierce (1996)

39/box6: Pierce (1996)

39/12: David Rowley 'Can you find your perfect partner?', the *Sunday Times ('Doors')*, 1 April 2001

40/16: Lee (1998)

41/box1: Cameron & Collins (2000) p.53

41/box2: Michael *et al.* (1994) p.72

41/box3-5: Michael *et al.* (1994) p.72

41/9: Michael *et al.* (1994) p.75

41/19: Hatfield & Rapson (1993b)

41/23: Various studies cited by Halford (2000) p.17

41/24: Hill & Peplau (1998)

42/bottom box: Beishon *et al.* (1998)

42/1: Benson, Larson, Wilson & Demo (1993) cited in Halford (2000) p.17

42/3: Cramer (1998) p.69

43/4: Hatfield & Rapson (1996) p.55

43/8: Cameron & Collins (2000) p.52

43/10: Cameron & Collins (2000)

43/14: Rusbult *et al.* (1998)

43/15: Michael *et al.* (1994) p.72

43/20: Michael *et al.* (1994) p.72 and Appendix A

43/23: Cameron & Collins (2000) p.53

43/24: Michael *et al.* (1994) p.72

43/box1: Cameron & Collins (2000) p.61

43/box2: Mackay (2000) p.30

43/box3: Cameron & Collins (2000) p.61

43/box4: Mackay (2000) p.30

43/box5: Cameron & Collins (2000) p.61

43/box6: Cameron & Collins (2000) p.61

43/box7: Cameron & Collins (2000) p.61

43/box8: Mackay (2000) p.37

44/4: Thornton *et al.* (1992)

44/15: Sher (1996)

44/20: Sonntag (1998)

44/bottom box1-3: Mackay (2000) p.31

44/bottom box5: Mackay (2000) p.87

44/bottom box6: David Rowley 'Can you find your perfect partner?' the *Sunday Times ('Doors')* 1 April 2001

45/box: Adapted from www.match.com

46/5: Michael *et al.* (1994) p.72

46/8: Michael *et al.* (1994) p.72

46/31: Sonntag (1998)

46/33: Lee (1998)

47/2: Sonntag (1998)

47/top box1-4: Cameron & Collins (2000) p.53

47/top box5: *Newsnight* 11 February 2000, BBC TV: London

47/top box6: Mackay (2000)

47/bottom box7: Cameron & Collins (2000), p.68

48/4: Cameron & Collins (2000)

48/13: Sonntag (1998)

48/16: Sonntag (1998)

48/31: Cameron & Collins (2000) p.74

48/36: Hatfield & Rapson (1993) p.16

49/box: Cameron & Collins (2000) p.74

49/12: Sonntag (1998)

49/26: Troupp (1994)

50/box: Adapted from www.match.com

50/13: McNulty (2000)

51/bottom box: Adapted from www.match.com

CHAPTER 2: MATCHING

57/7: Money (1993)

57/box: Money (1993)

58/box2: Pincus & Dare (1978)

58/box3: Dattilio & Bevilacqua (2000) p.111

58/24: Pincus & Dare (1978); Money (1993)

59/1: Sternberg (1998)

59/6: Sternberg (1998)

62/22: Houts *et al.* (1996)

62/27: Cunningham & Antill (1995)

62/30-63/6: *Cosmopolitan UK* April 1998; October 1999; March 2000

62/box: cited by Hatfield & Rapson (1993) p.10

63/box1-3: Sachs (1998)

63/box4: Young (1985) p.164

64/2: Sachs (1998)
68/4: Felmlee (1998)
68/12: Gottman (1997)
68/20: Tennov (1979)
68/bottom box1: Halford et al. (1997)
68/bottom box2: Horley (1991)
68/bottom box3: Felmlee (1998)
68/bottom box5: Halford et al. (1997)
68/bottom box6: Felmlee (1998)
68/bottom box7: Halford et al. (1997)
68/bottom box8: Hendrick & Hendrick (1994)
69/7: Felmlee (1998)
69/17: Cramer (1998) p.94
69/18: Cramer (1998) p.94
70/9: Cramer (1998) p.75
70/10: Hatfield & Rapson (1993) p.17
70/16: Thiessen, Young & Delgado (1997)
70/21: Paris (1990)
70/24: Hendrick & Hendrick (1994) studies cited p.41;Cramer (1998) studies cited p.77
70/box1: Thiessen, Young & Delgado (1997)
70/box2: Sprecher et al. (1994)
70/box3: Hojjat (1997)
70/box4: Klohnen & Mendelsohn (1998)
71/top box: Hamburg (2000)
71/11: Hendrick & Hendrick (1994) p.33; Cramer (1998) p.87
71/13: Kurdek (1991)
73/17: Hendrick & Hendrick (1994) p.34
74/10: Cramer (1998) p.74
75/11: Burke & Greenglass (1987) cited by Thompson (1997)
76/2: Burke & Greenglass (1987) cited by Thompson (1997)
76/8: Wharton & Erikson (1993) cited by Thompson (1997)
76/9: Kets de Vries (1995)
76/12: Cramer (1998) pp.84–7
76/25: Hojjat (1997)
76/27: Deal, Wampler & Halverson (1992)
76/35: Buss (1985) cited in Sher (1996) p.248
77/3: Hojjat (1997)
77/6: Burleson & Denton (1992)
77/top box3: Felmlee (1980)
77/top box3: Thiessen, Young & Delgado (1997)
77/top box5: Deal, Wampler & Halverson (1992)
77/bottom box1: Hatfield & Rapson (1993a)
77/bottom box4: Rushton (1989) cited by Hatfield & Rapson (1996)
78/13: Houts et al. (1996)
78/30: Felmlee, Sprecher & Bassin (1990)
78/35: Beishon, Modood & Virdee (1998)
79/box: Beishon, Modood & Virdee (1998)
80/top box: Amato & Rogers (1997)
80/bottom box: Apter (1999)
81/4: Apter (1999)
82/box: Blumstein & Schwartz (1983)
82/8: Rands (1988)cited Julien et al. (1997)
82/12: Julien et al. (1997)
83/3: Julien et al. (1997)
83/box: Julian et al. (1997)
83/5: Cramer (1998) p.78
83/10: Rusbult et al. (1998)
83/13: Houts, Robins & Huston (1996)
83/16: Huston & Houts (1998)
83/19: Huston & Houts (1998
84/1: Houts, Robins & Huston (1996)
84/6: Halford et al. (1997)
84/box1: Cramer (1998) p.78
84/box2: Cramer (1998) p.78
84/box4: Hamburg (2000)
85/10: UK Relate survey (1998) cited by Slater 'What's love got to do with it', the Sunday Times, 18 February 2001 (London)
86/3: Hamburg (2000)
86/7: Hojjat (1997)
86/14: Braver S.L. & O'Connell D. (1998) p.139
86/18: Studies cited Cramer (1998) pp.66–8
86/20: James Meek 'Quiz mission to save marriages', the Guardian, 16 August 1999 (London)
86/23: Gottman (1998)
87/11: Cramer (1998) pp.78–9
88/1: Hill & Peplau (1998)
88/7: Studies cited by Feeney, Noller & Ward (1997)
88/10: Cramer (1998) p.71

NOTES

88/14: Blumstein & Schwartz (1983)
88/19: Ross & Mirowski 1988)
89/3: Studies cited by Hyde *et al.*
(1998)
89/7: Studies cited by Hyde *et al.*
(1998)
89/9: Ross & Mirowsky (1988)
89/14: Cramer (1998) p.68; Feeney,
Noller & Ward (1997)
89/19: Brines & Joyner (1999)
89/22: Gottman (1994)
89/26: Jones (1993)
89/28: Cramer (1998) p.79
89/box: Ross & Mirowsky (1988)
90/box1: Cramer (1998) p.79
90/box2: Sweet & Bumpass (1992)
90/box3: Julian *et al.* (1997)
90/box4: Jones (1993)
90/2: Wu & Penning (1997)
90/9: Laslett (1983)
91/20: Huston & Schwartz (1995)
91/29: Hendrick & Hendrick (1994)
92/19: Julian *et al.* (1997)
92/26: Emery (1999)
92/31: Wallerstein *et al.* (2000)
92/38: Amato & Rogers (1997)
92/box: James cited by Hamburg
(2000) p.94
93/box2: Halford (2000) p.19
93/box3: Simons (1999)
93/box4: Sweet & Bumpass (1992)
93/8: Wallerstein & Blakeslee (1996)
93/15: McGue & Lykken (1992) cited
by Emery (1999)
93/21: Wallerstein *et al.* (2000)
93/23: Amato & Rogers (1997)
93/27: Moeller & Stattin (2001)
94/top box1: Sweet & Bumpass (1992)
US data. UK findings are similar:
Haskey (1996) cited by Simons
(1999) showed the figures to be
35% (for teen brides), 22% (for those
who married in their early twenties)
and 15% (for brides aged 25–30)
94/top box4: Amato & Rogers (1997)
94/5: Kurdek (1991)
94/7: US Bureau of Census (1996)
cited by Emery (1999)
94/10: Zimiles & Lee (1991) cited by
Emery (1999)
94/19: Clements *et al.* (1997)
95/5: Sweet & Bumpass (1992)
95/9: Amato & Rogers (1997)
95/10: Blumstein & Schwartz (1983)

95/11: MacDonald & Demaris (1995)
95/20: Hojjat (1997)
96/19: Taylor, Jackson & Chatters
(1997)
96/20: Sweet & Bumpass (1992)
97/15: Veroff *et al.* (1998)
97/title: Ruszcynski (1995)
98/box: Rudner (1994)
99/3 : Pinkus & Dare (1978)
100/2: Pinkus & Dare (1978)
100/box: Pinkus & Dare (1978)

CHAPTER 3: MATING
106/6: Hill & Peplau (1998)
106/9: Hatfield & Rapson (1993)
106/24: Heaton & Albrecht (1991)
cited by Hinde (1997)
106/26: White & Booth (1991)
107/4: Rusbult *et al.* (1998)
108/9: Blumstein & Schwartz (1983)
108/17: Blumstein & Schwartz (1983)
108/box5: Hamburg (2000)
108/box6: Many of these questions are
taken from Hamburg (2000), a
really excellent book
109/box1: Sweet & Bumpass (1992)
109/box2: Tallman *et al.* (1998)
109/box3: Relate statistic, reported in
Cosmopolitan (UK) April 1998
109/box4: Feeney, Noller & Ward
(1997)
109/4: Blumstein & Schwartz (1983)
109/6: Blumstein & Schwartz (1983)
109/7: Kurdek (1991)
109/11: Blumstein & Schwartz (1983)
109/12: UK Relate survey (1998)
cited by Slater 'What's love got to do
with it', the *Sunday Times,* 18
February 2001
109/13: Blumstein & Schwartz (1983)
109/16: Blumstein & Schwartz (1983)
109/19: Blumstein & Schwartz (1983)
109/23: Wallerstein & Blakeslee
(1996)
110/box title: Blumenstein & Schwartz
(1983)
110/5: Blumstein & Schwartz (1983)
110/8: Sweet & Bumpass (1992)
110/11: Tallman *et al.* (1998)
111/2: Eurobarometer (1996)
111/14: Amato (2001)
111/box1: Gottman & Porterfield
(1981) cited by Cramer (1998)
p.108

111/box2: Gottman & Porterfield
(1981) cited by Cramer (1998)
p.108

111/box3: Gottman (1998a)

111/box4: Heaton & Albrecht
(1991) cited by Cramer (1998) p.24

112/7: Karney & Bradbury (1997)

110/10: Clements et al. (1997)

113/8: Pittman & Wagers (1995)

113/30: Haavio-Mannila & Kontula
(1997)

113/box: adapted from Hamburg
(2000) p.67

114/box: adapted from Hamburg
(2000) p.70

114/22: Karney & Bradbury (1995)

114/23: Kurdek (1991) cited by
Cramer (1998) p.135

114/26: Cramer (1998) p.134

114/33: Hamburg (2000)

114/bottom box: adapted from
Hamburg (2000) p.68

114/41: Darling et al. (1991),
Asyayma (1975) cited by Hatfield
& Rapson (1996)

115/2: Hunt (1972) cited by Hatfield
& Rapson (1993a) p.88

115/8: Haavio-Mannila & Kontula
(1997)

115/box: adapted from Hamburg
(2000) p.64

115/26: Cramer (1998) p.135

115/34: Leng (2001)

115/38: Lazarus (1985)

115/39 Hamburg (2000)

116/box title: includes items from
Zilbergeld's (1978) scale cited by
Brehm (1992), Chapter 5

116/5: Zhou (1993) cited by Young
et al. (1998)

116/11: Renaud et al. (1997)

116/12: Hurlbert & Apt (1994) cited
by Apt et al. (1996)

117/7: Friday (1991)

118/1: Haavio-Mannila & Kontula
(1997)

118/14: Studies cited by Apt et al.
(1996)

118/15: Cramer (1998) p.131

118/16: Hurlbert et al. (1996);
Apt et al. (1996)

118/16: Apt et al. (1996)

118/18: Hurlbert & Apt (1994) cited
by Hurlbert et al. (1996)

119/8: Cupach & Comstock (1990)
cited by Hinde (1997)

119/9: Sprecher & McKinney (1993)
cited by Haavio-Mannila & Kontula
(1997)

119/10: Huberle (1991) cited by
Haavio-Mannila & Kontula (1997)

119/11: Haavio-Mannila & Kontula
(1997)

119/17: Hurlbert & Apt (1994)

119/20: Blumstein & Schwartz (1983)

119/box: Hendrick & Hendrick (1994);
MacNeil & Byers (1997)

120/9: Atwood & Dershowitz (1992)
cited by Spence (1997)

120/10: Studies cited by Hendrick &
Hendrick (1994) p.129

102/17: Hamburg (2000)

120/22: Hamburg (2000)

121/2: Young et al. (1998)

121/8: Blumstein & Schwartz (1983)

121/10: Greeley (1991) cited by
Sprecher & McKinney (1995) p.202

121/11: Hatfield (1988) cited by
Hatfield & Rapson (1996)

121/12: Young & Luquis (1998)

121/15: Blumstein & Schwartz (1983)

121/18: Rubin & Adams (1986) cited
by Masters et al. (1995) p.443

121/box title: Greeley (1991) cited by
Sprecher & McKinney (1995) p.202

121/box1: Masters et al. (1995)
p.443

121/box2: Masters et al. (1995) p.443

122/2: Blumstein & Schwartz (1983)

122/5: Blumstein & Schwartz (1983)

122/6: Rubin & Adams (1986) cited
by Masters et al. (1995) p.443

122/9: Blumstein & Schwartz (1983)

122/16: Masters et al. (1995)
pp.443–4

122/19: Blumstein & Schwartz (1983)

122/20: Blumstein & Schwartz (1983)

122/25: Kanin & Davidson (1972)
cited by Cramer & Howitt (1998)

122/30: Dermer & Pyszczynski (1978)
cited by Hendrick & Hendrick
(1994)

122/39: Reiss (1989) cited by
Sprecher & McKinney (1995) p.196

123/box1: Murstein & Tuerkheimer
(1998)

123/box2: Murstein & Tuerkheimer
(1998)

123/box3: Murstein & Tuerkheimer (1998)

123/box4: Vanfossen (1981) cited by Cutrona (1996)

123/box5: Vanfossen (1981, 1986) cited by Cutrona (1996)

123/9: Gottman (1994)

123/11: Yamamoto (1972) cited by Mruk (1999)

123/14: Karney & Bradbury (1995) cited by Halford, Kelly & Markman (1997)

123/20: Donnelly (1993)

123/25: Howard & Dawes (1976) cited by Brehm chapter 5

124/5: Blumstein & Schwartz (1983)

124/8: Murstein & Tuerkheimer (1998)

124/11: Waterman & Chiauzzi (198s) cited by Young et al. (1998)

124/11: Lief (1980) & Hurlbert et al. (1993) cited by Young et al. (1998)

124/11: Perlman & Abramson (1981) cited by Young et al. (1998)

124/13: Cramer (1998) p137-139; Hinde (1997) p.264

125/1: Darling et al. (1991) cited by Hatfield & Rapson (1996) p.142

125/3: Cramer (1998) p. 73; p.135

125/5: Cramer (1998) p.135

125/10: Murstein & Tuerkheimer (1998)

125/12: Edwards & Booth (1976) cited by Cramer & Howitt (1998)

125/14: Michael et al. (1994)

125/17: Michael et al. (1994)

125/21: Young et al. (1998)

125/box1: Darling et al. (1991) cited by Young et al. (1998)

125/box2: Darling et al. (1991) cited by Young et al. (1998)

125/box3: Michael et al. (1994) p.127

125/box4: 'Finland': Haavio-Mannila & Kontula (1997)

125/box4: 'us': Michael et al. (1994) p.127

125/box5: Michael et al. (1994)

126/box title: Blumstein & Schwartz (1983)

126/box4: Apt et al. (1996)

126/1: Waterman & Chiauzzi (1982) cited by Young et al. (1998)

126/4: Cramer (1998) p.137-9; Hinde (1997) p.264

126/5: Kelley & Donn Byrne (1992) cited by Sprecher & McKinney (1995) p.209

126/6: Vanfossen (1981) cited by Cutrona (1996)

126/9: Studies cited by Clark & Chrisman (1995)

126/9: Hatfield et al. (1982) cited by Donnelly (1993)

126/14: Blumstein & Schwartz (1983)

126/19: Blumstein & Schwartz (1983)

126/22: Terman (1938) cited by Cramer (1998) p.131

127/1: Studies cited by Masters et al. (1995) p.271

127/6: Lentz & Zeiss (1984) cited by Cramer & Howitt (1998)

127/8: Cramer & Howitt (1998) p.125

127/9: Hessellund (1976) cited by Cramer & Howitt (1998)

127/top box: Terman (1938) cited by Cramer (1998) p.131

127/bottom box: Terman (1938) cited by Cramer (1998) p.131

128/2: Studies cited by Haavio-Mannila & Kontula (1997)

128/9: Lentz & Zeiss (1984) cited by Cramer & Howitt (1998)

128/11: Murstein & Tuerkheimer (1998)

128/13: Lentz & Zeiss (1984) cited by Cramer & Howitt (1998)

128/15: Murstein & Tuerkheimer (1998)

128/26: Blumstein & Schwartz (1983)

128/box: Blumstein & Schwartz (1983) p.252

129/box title: Michael et al. (1994)

129/box2: Michael et al. (1994)

129/box3: Call, Sprecher & Schwartz (1995)

129/box4: Michael et al. (1994)

129/box5: Peplau, Rubin & Hill (1977) cited by Sprecher & McKinney (1995)

129/4: Hurlbert et al. (1996)

129/14: Kolodny (1983) cited by Masters et al. (1995) p.261

129/17: Blumstein & Schwartz (1983)

130/20: Studies cited by Hendrick & Hendrick (1994)

131/top box1: Rubenstein (1983) cited by Masters et al. (1995) p256

131/top box2: Blumstein & Schwartz (1983)
131/top box3: Cramer (1998) p.131
131/7: Brown (1995)
131/10: Studies cited by Donnelly (1993) p.173
131/13: Masters *et al.* (1995)
131/bottom box title: Blumstein & Schwartz (1983)
131/bottom box2: Studies cited by Sprecher & McKinney (1995) p.208
131/bottom box3: Buss (1989) cited by Sprecher & McKinney (1995) p.208
131/bottom box4: Buss (1989) cited by Sprecher & McKinney (1995) p.208
132/4: Maticka-Tyndale *et al.* (1998)
132/12: Heiman (1977) cited by Hatfield & Rapson (1993a) p.96
132/20: Blumstein & Schwartz (1983)
132/box1: Masters *et al.* (1995) pp.338–9
133/box title: Blumstein & Schwartz (1983)
133/box1&4: Blumstein & Schwartz (1983)
133/18: Masters *et al.* (1995) p338–9
134/3: James (1981) cited by Call *et al.* (1995)
134/13: Hatfield & Rapson (1996) pp.138–9
134/box title: Blumstein & Schwartz (1983)
135/13: Hill *et al.* (1976) cited by Hinde (1997) p.159
135/14: Masters *et al.* (1995) pp.338-9
135/16: Masters *et al.* (1995) pp.338-9
136/20: Call, Sprecher & Schwartz (1995)
136/24: Studies cited by Masters *et al.* (1995) p.271
136/box: Call, Sprecher & Schwartz (1995)
137/3: Zilbergeld (1995)
137/10: Pittman & Wagers (1995)
137/13: Call, Sprecher & Schwartz (1995)
137/15: Call, Sprecher & Schwartz (1995)
137/17: Studies cited by Blyth & Straker (1996)

137/bottom box1: Call, Sprecher & Schwartz (1995)
137/bottom box2: Call, Sprecher & Schwartz (1995)
138/4: Studies cited by Blyth & Straker (1996)
138/6: Donnelly (1993)
138/8: Jacobsen *et al.* (1996)
138/12: Henderson-King & Veroff (1994)
138/15: Blumstein & Schwartz (1983)
138/20: Blumstein & Schwartz (1983)
138/box: Blumstein & Schwartz (1983)
139/box title: Donnelly (1993)
139/3: Blumstein & Schwartz (1983)
139/10: Hyde *et al.* (1998)
139/17: Hyde *et al.* (1998)
139/26: Hyde *et al.* (1998)
139/28: Call, Sprecher & Schwartz (1995)
140/2: Call, Sprecher & Schwartz (1995)
140/6: Koch (1982) cited by Masters *et al.* (1995)
140/9: Blumstein & Schwartz (1983)
140/13: Blumstein & Schwartz (1983)
140/15: Donnelly (1993)
140/box: Call, Sprecher & Schwartz (1995)

CHAPTER 4: LASTING
147/12: Huston & Houts (1998)
147/box: Christensen, Jacobson & Babcock (1995)
148/box: Cited by Niven (2000)
148/7: Kurdek (1998); Kurdek (1998a)
149/24: Cutrona (1998)
149/box title: Figures for England & Wales cited by Cramer (1998) p.24
149/box3: US statistics cited by Wu & Penning (1997)
149/box4: Wu & Penning (1997)
149/box5: Wu & Penning (1997)
150/box: Cutrona (1998)
150/9: Lavee *et al.* (1987) cited by Cohan & Bradbury (1997)
150/11: Matthews *et al.* (1996)
151/4: Lindahl (1997)
152/9: Lazarus (1985)
152/13: Gottman (1994)
152/15: Gottman (1994)

152/box: Gottman (1994) p.57

154/6: Christensen & Walczynski (1997)

154/8: Studies cited by Cohan & Bradbury (1997)

154/10: Gottman (1994)

154/17: Noller, Beach & Osgarby (1997

154/21: Noller *et al.* (1997)

154/23: Levenson & Gottman studies cited by Vanzetti & Duck (1996) p.280

154/box: Gottman (1994)

155/box: Cutrona (1998)

155/3: Christensen & Walczynski (1997)

155/6: Studies cited by Cohan & Bradbury (1997)

155/12: Studies cited by Hatfield & Rapson (1993a) pp.198-201

155/24: Walsh *et al.* (1995)

156/9: Belsky & Kelly (1994)

157/3: Cutrona (1996)

157/7: Studies cited by Cutrona (1996)

157/11: Liker & Elder (1983)

157/19: Studies cited by Matthews *et al.* (1996)

157/23: Repetti (1989)

157/26: Piotrowski (1979) cited by Matthews *et al.* (1996)

157/box: Clements *et al.* (1997)

158/6: Cutrona (1996)

158/10: Masters *et al.* (1995) p.340

158/22: Orvis *et al.* (1976) cited by Hendrick & Hendrick (1992) p.180

158/27: Orvis *et al.* (1976) cited by Hendrick & Hendrick (1992) p.180

158/29: *Late Night London,* Carlton TV, 16 July 2001

158/39: Smart & Stevens (2001)

158/41: Burgess (1996)

159/top box: Weir & Harrison (1976) cited by Hendrick & Hendrick (1992)

159/5: Studies cited by Hyde *et al.* (1998)

159/bottom box: Hare-Mustin & Maracek (1990) cited by Ram (1995)

160/5: Cutrona (1998)

160/17: Gottman (1998)

160/19: *Bulletin Plus* (2000)

160/box title: Christensen, Jacobson & Babcock (1995)

160/box1: Lindahl *et al.* (1998)

160/box2: Lindahl *et al.* (1998)

160/22: Gottman (1998)

161/20: Deal, Wampler & Halverson (1992)

162/11: Hinde (1997) p.128

163/box: McQuillan & Ferree (1998)

163/2: Rusbult *et al.* (1991) cited by Hinde (1997) p.176

163/10: Gottman & Krokoff (1989), Markman (1990) cited by Vanzetti & Duck (1996)

163/16: Cohan & Bradbury (1997)

163/20: Pittman (1997)

163/23: Rusbult *et al.* (1991) cited by Hinde (1997) p.176

164/1: Gray-Little & Burks (1983) cited by Cramer (1998)

164/4: Madden & Janoff-Bulman (1981) cited by Hendrick & Hendrick (1992) p.182

164/box: Peele & Brodsky (1976) cited by Masters *et al.* (1995) p.308

165/15: McGonagle *et al.* (1993) cited by Cramer (1998)

165/20: Cate & Lloyd (1992)

165/23: Hill & Peplau (1998) cited by Bradbury (1998)

166/3: Kurdek (1994) cited by Hinde (1997) p.157

166/8: Vanzetti & Duck (1996) p.274

166/13: Gottman (1996)

166/18: Cowan *et al.* (1985)

166/23: Gottman (1994) cited by Hinde (1997)

166/27: Burgess (1981) cited by Hinde (1997) p.154

166/29: McGonagle *et al.* (1993) cited by Cramer (1998) p.120

167/box: Belsky & Kelly (1994)

168/box: Adapted from Gottman (1994) p.77

169/box: Adapted from Gottman (1994) p.91

169/8: Gottman (1994) p.89

171/box: Studies cited by Hinde (1997) p.184; Gottman (1994)

172/box: Hatfield & Rapson (1999)

173/box: *Bulletin Plus* (2000)

173/5: Raven *et al.* (1975) cited by Cramer (1998) p.124

173/21: Christensen & Walczynski (1997)

174/11: Christensen & Jacobson (2000)

174/18: Christensen & Jacobson (2000)

175/box: Adapted from Christensen & Jacobson (2000)

176/31: Gottman (1994)

176/39: Gottman (1998)

177/2: Dickson (1995, 1997)

177/8: Dickson (1995, 1997)

178/13: Gottman (1994)

179/35: Gottman (1994)

181/14: Gottman (1994)

182/box: Dickson (1997)

182/14: Gottman (1994)

182/21: Gottman (1994)

183/10: Gottman (1994)

183/17: Masters *et al.* (1995) p.340

183/box: Gottman (1994)

CHAPTER 5: LYING

194/7: Gottman & Katz (1991) cited by Hojjat (1997); Lazarus (1985)

194/14: Studies cited by Hinde (1997) p.440

195/5: Lazarus (1985)

195/9: Lazarus (1985)

195/box title: Baucom, Epstein & Rankin (1995)

195/box5: Winstead *et al.* (1997)

196/1: Studies cited in *FatherFacts: what good are dads?* Fathers Direct: London

196/16: Lazarus (1985)

196/box: Sprecher (1987) cited by Hendrick & Hendrick (1992)

196/21: Hinde (1987) p.171

196/22: Miller & Read (1981) cited by Hinde (1997)

197/4: Hendrick & Hendrick (1992) chapter 7

197/16: Lazarus (1985)

197/box: Feeney, Noller & Ward (1997)

197/19: Noller & Feeney (1998)

197/27: Burleson & Denton (1997)

198/10: Noller & Feeney (1998)

198/box: Studies cited by Burleson & Denton (1997)

198/14: Burleson & Denton (1997)

198/23: Gottman (1994)

199/8: Noller & Feeney (1998)

199/11: Noller & Venardos (1986) cited by Hendrick & Hendrick (1992) p.177

199/16: Masters *et al.* (1995) p.333

199/28: Noller & Feeney (1998)

200/box: Notarius *et al.* (1997)

200/18: Christensen & Jacobson (2000) p.93

202/3: Christensen & Jacobson (2000)

202/box: Halford & Sanders (1992) cited in Halford *et al.* (1997)

203/box1: Fincham & Bradbury (1989b) cited by Hinde (1997) p.326

203/box2: Studies cited by Hinde (1997) p.325

203/box3: Noller & Ruzzene (1991) cited in Noller *et al.* (1997)

203/box4: Gottman (1994)

203/3: Hemans (1998) cited by Hinde (1997) p.325

203/21: Noller *et al.* (1997)

204/box: Fincham & Bradbury (1989a) cited by Hinde (1997) p.328

204/6: Vanzetii, Notarius & Nee-Smith (1992) cited by Baucom *et al.* (1995)

205/bottom box: Smart & Stevens (2000)

206/1: Huston & Houts (1998)

206/12: Olson & Ryder (1970) cited by Cramer (1998) p.117

206/26: Cunningham & Antill (1995)

206/28: Cunningham & Antill (1995)

207/box: Cunningham & Antill (1995)

207/2: Kurdek (1991)

207/5: Cunningham & Antill (1995)

207/6: Office of National Statistics, England & Wales, 2000

207/16: Cunningham & Antill (1995)

208/top box1-3: Willi (1997)

208/top box4-5: Smart &Stevens (2001)

208/5: Hatfield & Rapson (1993a)

208/10: White &Booth (1991)

208/bottom box: Morton Hunt (1997) 'The Future of marriage' cited by Master *et al.* (1995) p324

209/10: Karney & Bradbury (1997)

208/21: Dominian (1996)

210/26: Bumpass & Sweet (1989)

211/box2-3: Glass & Wright (1997)

211/box 4-5: Spanier & Margolis (1983) cited by Glass & Wright (1997)

211/2: Pittman & Wagers (1995)

211/7: Amato (2001)

211/10: Masters et al. (1995) p.440

211/13: Amato & Rogers (1997)

211/16: Pittman & Wagers (1995)

212/7: Rubin (1970) cited by Hendrick & Hendrick (1994)

212/11: Blumstein & Schwartz (1983)

212/box: Buss (1988)

213/3: Blumstein & Schwartz (1983)

213/5: Blumstein & Schwartz (1983)

213/13: Nock (1995) cited by Berscheid & Lopez (1997)

213/19: Buss (1988)

213/27: Buss (1988)

213/32: Masters et al. (1995) p.438

214/box1: Buss (1988)

214/2: Studies cited by Masters & Johnson (1995) p.438

214/box2: Blumstein & Schwartz (1983)

215/box: Quiz: adapted from Taylor (1991) cited by Knap & Taylor (1995) p.159

215/1: Hatfield et al. (1982) cited by Brehm (1992)

215/2: Blumstein & Schwartz (1983)

215/6: Prins et al. (1993) cited by Hinde (1997) p346-7

215/18: Blumstein & Schwartz (1983)

216/2: Blumstein & Schwartz (1983)

216/4: Blumstein & Schwartz (1983)

216/6: Masters et al. (1995) p.440

216/13: Masters et al. (1995) p.440

216/16: Masters et al. (1995) p.440

216/21: Blumstein & Schwartz (1983)

216/box: Blumstein & Schwartz (1983)

217/box: Blumstein & Schwartz (1983)

217/7: Blumstein & Schwartz (1983)

218/5: Blumstein & Schwartz (1983)

218/10: Blumstein & Schwartz (1983)

220/3: Johnson et al. (1994) cited by Cramer (1998)

220/5: Blumstein & Schwartz (1983)

220/9: Lawson (1995)

220/10: Amato & Rogers (1997)

220/15: Lazarus (1985)

221/box: Hatfield & Rapson (1999)

223/7: Lawson (1995)

223/16: Glass & Wright (1997)

223/24: Dougherty & Ellis (1976) cited by Glass & Wright (1997)

223/26: Glass & Wright (1997)

223/box: Hamburg (2000)

225/17: attachment styles are discussed more fully in Clulow (2001); Hinde (1997) p.438; Furman & Flanagan (1997); Ochiltree (1996) and Koski & Shaver (1997)

227/15: Cowan & Cowan (2001)

227/23: Furman & Flanagan (1997)

228/4: Bentler & Newcomb (1978) cited by Cramer (1998) p.69

228/8: Vaillant cited by Cate & Lloyd (1992)

228/16: Cohan & Bradbury (1997)

228/box1: Brehm (1992) Chapter 13

228/box2: Brehm (1992) Chapter 13

228/box3: Wu & Penning (1997)

229/10: McCranie & Kahan (1986) cited by Counts & Sacks (1991)

229/13: Amato (2001)

229/15: Counts & Sacks (1991)

229/23: Halford & Bouma (1997)

231/box2: Windle (1996)

231/10: Halford & Bouma (1997)

231/15: Halford & Osgarby (1993) cited by Halford & Bouma (1997)

231/18: Windle (1996)

231/20: Halford et al. (1997)

232/box: all material in this box taken from O'Leary & Cascardi (1998) or Holtzworth-Munroe et al. (1998) unless otherwise indicated

232/1: Jacobsen et al. (1996)

232/5: Arias et al. (1987) cited by Cramer (1998) p.127

232/16: National Family Violence Survey (1985) cited by Cramer (1998) p.126

233/2: O'Leary & Cascardi (1998)

233/12: O'Leary & Cascardi (1998)

233/23: Hill et al. (1976) cited by Masters et al. (1995) p.316

233/box: All material in this box taken from O'Leary & Cascardi (1998) or Holtzworth-Munroe et al. (1998) unless otherwise stated

233/box4: Babcock et al. (1993) cited by Halford & Bouma (1993)

POSTSCRIPT

240/9: Lindahl et al. (1998)

index